Colm Ó Briain

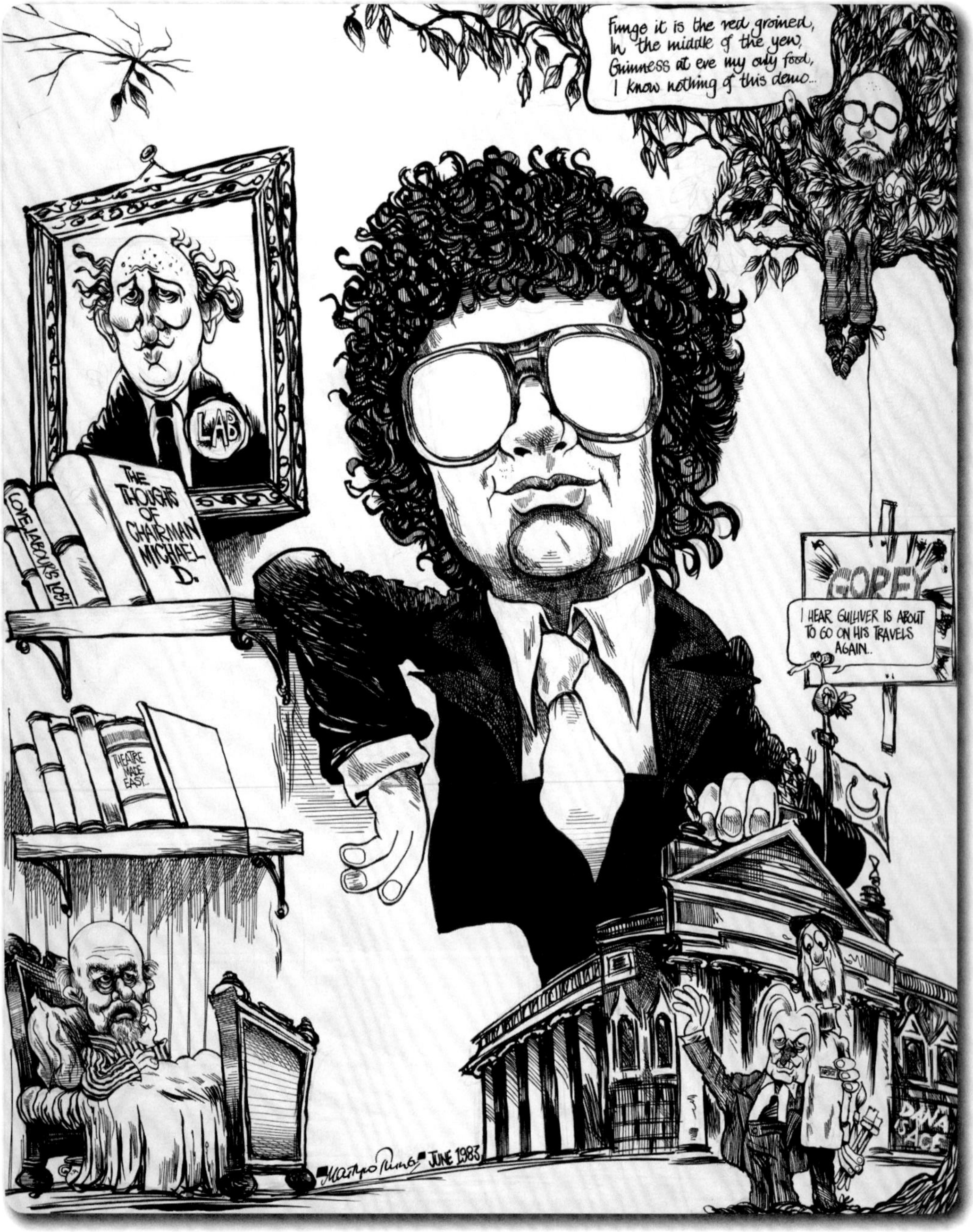

Martyn Turner cartoon presented by the staff of the Arts Council to Colm Ó Briain in 1983 on his resignation as Director. (© Martyn Turner National Gallery of Ireland)

Colm Ó Briain

A Coat of Many Colours

Compiled by
Muireann Ó Briain

MARTELLO

COLM Ó BRIAIN: A COAT OF MANY COLOURS
First published in 2023 by
Martello Publishing
Glenshesk House
10 Richview Office Park
Clonskeagh
Dublin D14 V8C4
Republic of Ireland
martellopublishing.ie

ISBN: 978-1-7396086-4-4

British Library Cataloguing in Publication Data. A CIP catalogue record for this book is available from the British Library.

Edited and managed by A. & A. Farmar
Designed, typeset and indexed by Warren Yeates
Cover photograph by Louise Roden
Printed by Dimma Print Services, Roscrea, Co. Tipperary

Contents

Preface

Having thought that the best way to show who you were and what you did with your life was to write a memoir, this publication has taught me that an even better way is by having other people write in your memory. Each person who allowed themselves to be cajoled, persuaded, bullied, even exploited, by me into writing about Colm Ó Briain has provided a gem of social history, political realities, family life, artistic courage, and the growth of the cultural community in Ireland over the last seventy years.

My thanks to all those who contributed to this book; each piece is both a wonderful piece of writing, and an expression of the writer's own personality and wisdom. A reader can dip in anywhere, and find laughter or tears, knowledge or understanding, and throughout, the recognition of a shared humanity.

On the sidelines of the writing, my thanks also to the following, who guided or helped with the practicalities of compiling a book:

Tara Doyle of Dublin City Archives; Glenn Dunne, Berni Metcalfe, James Harte and the wonderful door-stoppers at the National Library of Ireland; Fiona Eogan, Greg Sparks, Helen Carney, Cliodhna Dukes, Dara de Brí, the 'connectors' *par excellence*; Las Fallon, historian; Dennis Keeley and William Maher of the Dublin Fire Brigade Training Centre; Maureen Kennelly of the Arts Council; Sinead Kerins for the gift of the family portrait to the O'Brien Institute; Fiona McHugh for suggesting the title; David McConnell, the keeper of the important memories; David Monahan and Louise Roden, photographers; Ramona Mulcahy of ADI; Warren Yeates for design, typesetting and patient indexing; Niamh O'Brien of The National Gallery of Ireland.

For permission to reproduce illustrations thanks to:

Arts & Disability Ireland; Dublin City Library and Archive; Martyn Turner; RTÉ; The National College of Art and Design; The National Gallery of Ireland; The National Library of Ireland; The O'Brien

Institute, Marino; *Sunday Business Post*; *The Irish Times*; The Tyrone Guthrie Centre.

All other illustrations are from family and private sources. Every effort has been made to contact copyright holders.

Finally, my profound thanks to Anna Farmar for her imagination, flair and dedication, without which this book would not have been produced.

Muireann Ó Briain, Dublin, May 2023

An End and a Beginning: Eulogy at the Funeral Mass of Colm Ó Briain 12 August 2020

Art Ó Briain

Memories of my older brother Colm often go back to our early days.

I'll speak personally and focus on events that, in retrospect, I feel shaped his growth and development as a remarkable human being.

Colm Peadar Ó Briain was the eldest child of six to Peter and Brídín O'Brien. Born in 1943 he was raised in an Irish Catholic family who adhered to the norms and values of Ireland in the 1940s and 1950s. Our father became a successful businessman who provided well for his family and Brídín was a stay-at-home mother. It was a loving household; we were, to all intents and purposes, a happy family.

For Colm, being the eldest in the family of four boys—Colm, Piaras, myself and Garry and two girls—Máirín and Bairbre—meant parental expectation that he would, at all times, give good example to his brothers and sisters. The burden of being the first born was in our mother's refrain and demand that rang in his ears forever more—

'Colm! Cathfaidh tú dea shampla a thabhairt!'

'I blazed a trail for you all,' an older Colm proclaimed to us, his younger siblings, as he saw us stretch toleration limits. Compared to the strictures and constraints he had to endure as a teenager he grew to witness parental discipline ease for the rest of us as the liberal '60s progressed. We benefited from a more relaxed approach as boundaries stretched.

But he didn't. The first-born had to toe a firm line about being home early and on time, and had to seek more or less constant approval and permission for his adolescent social life.

When our parents went out of an evening he was, as a young teenager, sometimes left in charge of us. He had to make sure we behaved ourselves and that we went to bed on time. But we were an unruly bunch when free of our parents' firm control and we often exasperated poor Colm's patience.

Once when disorder and childish chaos broke out in the living room, cowboys and Indians galloping, shouting, and shooting, much jumping up and down on the couch etc. he burst into the room and in a dramatic voice declaimed:

'Blow, blow, thou winter wind
Thou art not so unkind
As man's ingratitude.'

We held our horses. Astonished. Dumbfounded.

What on earth was this? . . . befuddled, we fell into line and did what we were told, tidied up the room. And behaved ourselves. Colm had found an effective way of exercising authority.

Our family holiday location in the 1950s, and early '60s was Skerries. We loved Skerries—its sailing seas, sunny sandy beaches and freedom. It was special for Colm too in one particular way.

He relished and enjoyed the phenomenon that was a touring fit-up company which pitched its tent and caravans in an open field on the Dublin Road. Flash Parade had no roadies, or stage hands—actors/performers were required to do everything—publicise the show, erect the tent, organise front of house. A kaleidoscope of shifting identities was on display, exotic change and transformation visible for all to see before our eyes.

A typical evening performance would feature melodrama, with stock characters, heroes and villains and put-upon lovers. Also stand-up comedy, risqué *Carry On* jokes, slapstick sketches and singalong songs sending us home happy at the end.

In pre-television Ireland this was our entertainment and it fascinated Colm. He spent day after day, night after night, up there where the fit-up was pitched, taking it all in.

He came to know the master of ceremonies, a slick Clarke Gable lookalike and his elderly mother, Vic Loving, a flamboyant, larger than life lady in bright yellow dresses, who ran the show. And Colm being Colm he worked out how they did it. And if they could do it, why couldn't he?

His chosen location was the Orr family garage at the other end of Sion Hill Road, Drumcondra, where we lived at the time. It was a long cavernous space where a stage could be marked off and curtained. Piaras and David Orr were put in charge of production practicalities. A kindly and tolerant Mr Orr arranged stage lighting using car batteries. Garry and I were the gofers, running here, there and everywhere without a clue, and Colm chose members of the neighbourhood gang to play parts in sketches, sing songs, play the piano. Elizabeth Orr proudly pinned her paintings on the garage walls and Máirín sold sweets from a tray. Tickets were sold and money collected at the box office for a good cause, a cause I can't recall. The show was called 'Happy Days Are Here Again'.

This was Colm's first production based on the Flash Parade formula, and as master mind and master of ceremonies he hosted and starred in what was a great success. A truly memorable experience, not to be repeated! Except it was, in various guises, repeated in his later life.

The same Colm was chosen to play major roles in Belvedere College productions of Gilbert and Sullivan operas—*The Mikado*, *Iolanthe*, *HMS Pinafore* and *The Pirates of Penzance*. He was centre stage and star of those school shows.

As a result, at family parties later in Clontarf, Colm's party piece was:

'I am the very model of a Modern Major-General
I've information vegetable, animal, and mineral
I know the kings of England and I quote the fights historical
From Marathon to Waterloo, in order categorical;
I'm very well acquainted, too, with matters mathematical,
I understand equations, both the simple and quadratical,
About binomial theorem I'm teeming with a lot o' news
With many cheerful facts about the square on the hypotenuse.
I'm very good at integral and differential calculus;
I know the scientific names of beings animalculous,
In short, in matters vegetable, animal, and mineral,
I am the very model of a Modern Major-General.'

Colm, the Modern Major-General who produced and performed in ground-breaking productions in UCD Dramsoc.

The Modern Major-General who spearheaded Project '67, *Waiting for Godot*, *The Beaux Stratagem* in the Gate Theatre, dovetailing into the Project Arts Centre in Abbey Street.

When asked why he did not pursue his great passion for theatre and performance in 1968 but applied for and was successfully appointed a producer/director with RTÉ TV he revealed that he had had no choice; he had given personal guarantees for the theatre production loans and had huge debts to pay off. And it took him years to do so.

But pay them off he did. And at the same time he made his mark in RTÉ as an innovative and courageous and creative producer of television programmes. He was impressive.

And so I come to 'Dreams and Responsibilities'—two words that resonate when I think of Colm.

He made his dreams his own responsibility, and in due course forged a role for himself as an enabler of other people's dreams, believing that having your dream head in the clouds was alright, if your feet were on the ground.

He was both a visionary and a pragmatist, a doer and a dreamer.

At our father Peter's funeral Colm identified integrity—the quality of being honest and having strong moral principles—as our father's defining characteristic. Colm inherited that same precious quality in abundance too. He had an active and informed intellect, held strong political views, but on a personal level had a warm and generous heart. He was a good son, a good brother, a good husband, a good father, a good father-in-law and last but not least, a good Dadó. And in my book that made him a great man.

His final days were very difficult and were hard especially for Muireann, for Aisling and Seóna and for their families. His was a slow fading into silence during lockdown in Rathmines.

When Colm was admitted to Kiltipper Woods Care Home a few weeks ago, Aifric, his grand-daughter, wrote a note to his new carers.

'Dear Nurses,
Here is a list of some things my Dadó really likes, and I think
he will enjoy them if you do them.

1. He likes listening to the radio and his favourite station is Lyric FM.
2. He likes art, and so if you hang up some of the pictures myself and my sister give to him he will be able to look at them whenever he likes.
3. He loves reading, and he loves stories, but I am not sure he can still read, so maybe he would like it if someone read something to him once in a while. He also likes articles in the newspaper.
4. He likes to watch the 6.01 News on RTÉ, so if you put that on for him on a daily basis I think he would like that.

Best wishes,
Aifric.

And an angel carer in Kiltipper Woods called Hugo read the note and did precisely what Aifric had asked for her Dadó. Colm died on Thursday 30 July at 10.00 a.m.

I speak for all the family when I say we loved Colm dearly, and we miss him greatly.

Go ndéana Dia trócaire air agus suaimhneas síoraí dá anam dílis.

Something on Where Colm Got it From

Ruaidhrí Ó Briain

Even though Colm and I were first cousins, we rarely saw much of each other. One spring evening our paths happened to cross in Marlborough Street car park in Dublin. Giving each other a long, though not a hard look, we knew immediately both of us must have been attending the performance of Bach's *Saint Matthew Passion* that had just ended in the nearby Pro-Cathedral, but in the vivid afterglow of that extraordinary music neither of us felt much need to talk. With quiet goodwill and with the simple but heartfelt mutual salutation 'Good old Bach!' we continued on our respective ways.

What could we have nattered about, had we been so inclined? School-days, for one thing.

Marlborough Street held memories. Opposite the Pro-Cathedral stands a sober but elegant neoclassical building, Tyrone House, whose grounds are imposingly fronted by huge cast-iron gates and by tall ornamental railings atop a low granite wall. The Department of Education has its campus here. It includes the primary school where Colm was a pupil years ago, a decade ahead of me. That was in the middle of the twentieth century. The country had reached one of several important junctures in its affairs. To find a start for the story, we need to go back a lot further.

When in the nineteenth century Catholic Emancipation, the Land Acts, and Home Rule, were adopted by the general populace and by some of the élite as common objectives, the arts were in play. Oratory, literature, and music helped to cultivate a degree of shared feeling and purpose in Ireland and empathy in England. At the end of the nineteenth century, when Home Rule proved disappointingly elusive, creative writers drew on studies of ancient Irish poetry and heroic epics and folklore and folk tales; and, retaining in English many Irish linguistic patterns and idioms, they brought new poetry, storytelling, and drama into being out of old mythologies. Their highly artistic achievement, which blossomed into a tradition of world-class literature, offered inspiration and a collective pride in oral traditions so enduring that it had been early Irish Christian scholars who first began recording them. Their writing even came to have greater cultural and moral scope than some people were able to accept as proper for a patriotic Irish voice. Many, meanwhile, especially in Protestant parts of the North, were elaborating another patriotic self-image that envisioned the continued Union of Britain and Ireland without Home Rule.

Thus it was that diverse ideas and initiatives were about to catch the country's imagination when, in 1892 at the age of twenty, Colm's grandfather (and mine), William O'Brien, coming from a Wexford family of nine children, took his leave of their farmstead on Oulart Hill (first battle site of 1798), and set out for Dublin. By then the population of County Wexford was 45 per cent of what it had been before the Great Famine, and the total remaining population of Wexford was continuing to decline in number, as indeed was that of Ireland as a whole; the latter would not level off until the 1930s nor rise until the 1960s. Nearly as many Irish lived abroad as lived in the country of their birth.

Wexford's economy was based largely on farming. The ongoing Land Acts were gradually making farming life more secure as far as tenure was concerned. There were also some small industries in the county, where typically work was modestly paid for long hours; and Wexford had a maritime tradition. The international economy was struggling to emerge from two decades of depression. The social norm at this time was that just one son would inherit the family farm and that there would be a marriage dowry for just one daughter. These would not necessarily be the eldest.

Young people generally either stayed helping on the farm or entered the local market for work or moved to a town or abroad for employment and maybe training. Many remained single.

William had looked after horses on behalf of a local doctor, whom he was now accompanying in a move to Glasnevin in Dublin. After a couple of years, he joined the fire brigade at Chatham Row, where his skill with horses must have come in useful. He served on mobile ladder duty and also on the very first callout of the Corporation's horse-drawn ambulance service in 1899, and became personal aide to Fire Chief Purcell.

A portrait of William hangs in the O'Brien Institute in Marino, headquarters of the Dublin Fire Brigade Training services. The Institute takes its name from the family of Michael O'Brien, a Dublin draper—unrelated to William O'Brien—who died in 1829. From her

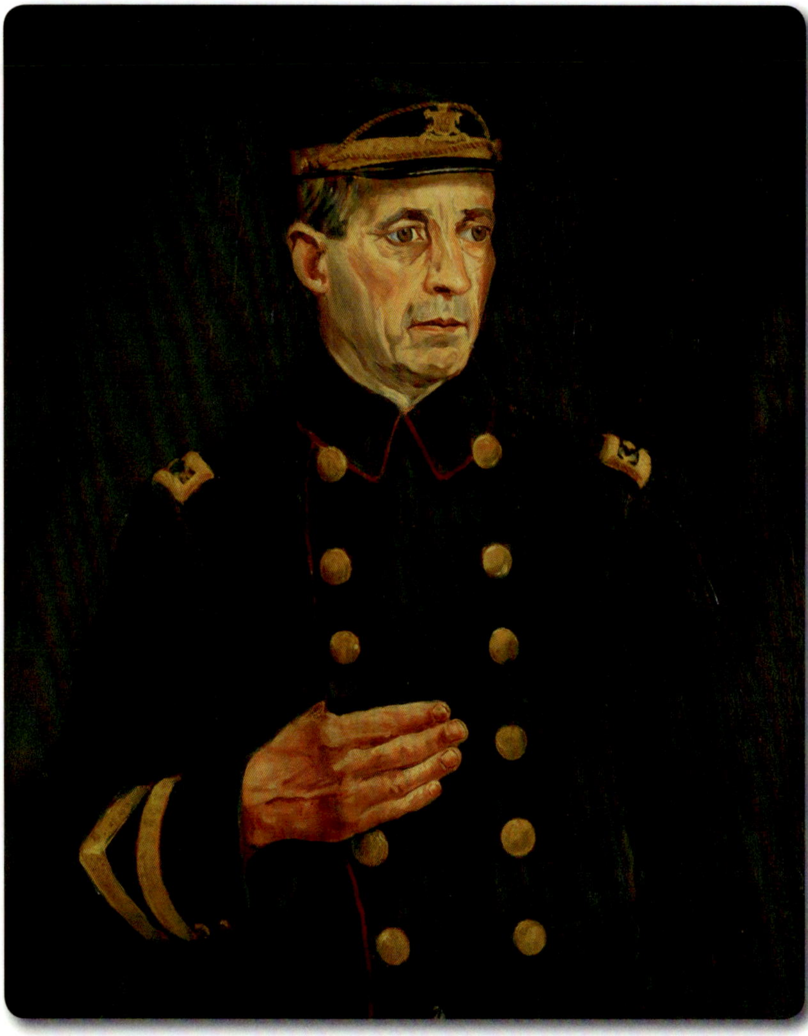

Colm's paternal grandfather, Dublin Fire Brigade Station Officer William O'Brien. The portrait is by James Conway, also a fireman, who was a pupil of Seán Keating, and exhibited at the RHA. The American-style uniform was adapted for the Dublin Fire Brigade by its founder, James Robert Ingram, who had served in the New York Fire Department. It remained in use until the early 1930s. (David Monahan, Courtesy The O'Brien Institute, Marino)

father's legacy, his daughter Bridget endowed a home for poor Catholic children, managed from 1888 by the Christian Brothers. The Institute was acquired by Dublin Corporation in 1982.

When William was growing up, his mother had had to take him out of school to help at home after his father's death, but the young man seemed to have made up for that loss of schooling. He loved poetry and was inclined to quote Shakespeare.

He and Dubliner Margaret Hill were married in 1904. The family income was secure, but the available live-in accommodation in the Chatham Row Fire Brigade headquarters happened to be extremely cramped. When the Tara Street station opened in 1907, they were transferred there and enjoyed ample space in up-to-date quarters that had the rare convenience of hot and cold running water. General living conditions there were very likely more comfortable than in the two-storey farmhouse William had left in Wexford. Conditions in his old home must nonetheless have been much better than in some parts of Dublin, where many were unfortunate enough to be living in overcrowded rooms of disease-ridden and structurally dangerous buildings. One report listed 786 houses on the south side of the river as being fit only for evacuation and demolition. They were noted as being occupied by 7,984 persons in 2,149 families using 2,982 rooms; 700 houses on the north side were similarly listed and noted as being occupied by 5,082 persons in 1,496 families using 2,401 rooms. Reports some years later stated that 12,042 families with an average of 6.1 persons were occupying one-room accommodation and that the tuberculosis death rate in Dublin was greater than anywhere else in Ireland or Britain. Occupants of Dublin tenements also lived in danger of being trapped by an outbreak of fire, despite Captain Purcell's innovative design and operation of mobile turntable ladders with telescopic extensions and add-on sections that gave a total reach of 100 feet.

About the time that William and Margaret were married, some new fire safety regulations came into force. Faced with consequent building upgrade costs, a small theatre in Abbey Street opted to close.

Annie Horniman, an Englishwoman who had already financed a number of drama groups in England, acquired the property and an adjoining one, combined and upgraded them, and offered their use, under conditions but with generous financial support, to the Irish National Theatre Society. They opened the Abbey Theatre there, presenting plays by W. B. Yeats, J. M. Synge, and Lady Gregory, on 27 December 1904. The actors in the Society were mainly young and amateur but inspired, and in turn they inspired the playwrights. Yeats's and Lady Gregory's short play *Cathleen ni Houlihan* went so far as to encourage young men to serve Ireland and to be willing to die in her service.

For a while Dublin went mad for the stage. Everyone was writing a play. Clubs had dramatic societies. Amateur groups staged productions wherever they could. There was extraordinary diversity. It was a time of general cultural innovation. A new wing of the National Gallery had just been completed. William Orpen was starting to influence a generation of Irish painters. Sarah Purser's co-operative, An Túr Gloine, was beginning to produce pioneering stained glass. The National Museum with its treasures of ancient art had opened its new Kildare Street building to the public in 1890. The Gaelic League, founded in 1893, now saw the Irish language added to the curriculum of many hundreds of schools.

Dublin, Belfast, and Cork had musical societies, and visits by the Hallé Orchestra had encouraged the founding of the Dublin Orchestral Society. The Belfast Philharmonic Society had long enjoyed modest orchestral resources. Public interest in opera had increased significantly, and some composers of opera chose Celtic themes and styles. Cork, apparently not content with an Opera House, had seen a 2000-seater concert hall with a four-manual organ built at the Mardyke for the International Exhibition of 1902. The Catholic Church was continuing to recruit continental musicians as organists and choirmasters to improve Catholic sacred music practice throughout Ireland. A popular 'bible' of traditional musicians, *O'Neill's Music of Ireland*, had just been published, offering a repertory numbering 1850 tunes, collected mostly from Irish emigré musicians and their descendants. The Feis Ceoil had begun in 1897, and the Gaelic League was also holding musical feiseanna, although some felt competition injurious to the morale of competitors. Cork had had a Pipers' Club from 1898, and Dublin from 1900, even though since the Famine the uilleann piping tradition had been in decline. The old tradition of the harpers had disappeared. Fiddling and flute playing were on the rise. The concertina had come to embrace Irish traditional and globally popular dance music alike, becoming such a favourite that many hardware and bicycle shops stocked it.

The O'Briens were to have twelve children, an exceptional tally even at the time. Their seventh child was Colm's father, Peter. He was born in early 1914 next after my own father, Andy, who had arrived in late 1912. In 1913 the family was transferred to Dorset Street Fire Station, where William was to take charge as station officer a few years afterwards. It turned out that the emergency services were then about to face their busiest and most dangerous years. A decade of severely disruptive civil unrest and revolution was beginning. Fire and ambulance crews were already in the business of taking necessary risks and continued to do so but were forced to leave scenes where the danger from shooting and shelling was disproportionately great. They sometimes had to abandon emergency vehicles until they could either retrieve them or resume work in greater safety.

During Easter Week in 1916, William suffered a foot injury and was on sick leave for a day. The Fire Chief reported that during that week 196 properties on almost 100,000 square yards of central Dublin were destroyed by a combination of fire, bombardment, and looting. Andy heard it said that on occasion retreating rebel activists were disguised as firemen. Turmoil and tumult were to break out again during the War of Independence and soon the Civil War when the Free State was coming into being in 1922. In Paris that year, James Joyce published his lengthy celebration of Leopold Bloom, fictional hero of ordinary happenings on a day in 1904 Dublin. Had his novel been generally available in Ireland, its deeply innovative and engaging writing about commonplace concerns of the recent more settled past might have offered some slight relief from the continuing hold of unrest, war, and revolution on people's attention and imagination.

In 1926 it probably seemed a small incremental token of changing times that Dublin Fire Brigade finally bade farewell to the last of its horses, which, together with firemen's gleaming brass helmets, had long impressed youths and small boys with the glamour of a fire-fighting career. In the same year, the Free State started broadcasting publicly from a studio in Little Denmark Street in Dublin.

About eighteen months previously, Northern Ireland had begun a BBC service in Belfast. Money for broadcasting was so scanty that

Dublin Station Director Séamus Clandillon and his wife Máighréad Ní Annagáin sometimes sang songs to fill a programming slot, both being good vocalists despite detractors calling her Máighréad Ní On-Again. Dublin broadcast a symphony concert as early as 1927, for which the Station Orchestra of only seven players was heavily augmented with musicians from the Dublin Philharmonic, successor of the Orchestral Society, and with resident musicians from theatres and silent cinemas. While symphony concerts have always been less popular than country dances or step dances or music for any kind of dancing, popularity is unlikely to have been the prime motive of Ninette de Valois and W. B. Yeats in establishing the Abbey School of Ballet, in 1927, but others followed their lead, notably Joan Denise Moriarty in Cork, who commissioned music by Irish composers and went on to draw upon folklore and local dance steps so as to include an Irish form of ballet among many original works for her amateur company.

Meanwhile, a vast trove of folklore and folk tales began to be collected from the countryside, and after some years this work was officially conducted by the Irish Folklore Commission. From 1928 Mícheál Mac Liammóir and Hilton Edwards began to present European works in Dublin's Gate Theatre and Irish-language drama in Galway. More new creators of stories, poetry, and drama were just beginning to make themselves known, many of them bilingual in ability but writing mainly in English. The best were independent of mass market influences but equally showed little sign of excessive local sentimentality or the parochialism that some patterns of thought or feeling seemed to encourage. With much to say of universal significance, some of it in strong opposition to prevalent habits and notions, an array of writers from Sean O'Casey to Patrick Kavanagh to Edna O'Brien documented previously little-aired realities of life, each in a uniquely personal way. At the same time, the Censorship of Publications Act of 1929 was being over-zealously interpreted, and many works by both Irish and other writers were officially prohibited. Sad to say, moreover, sometimes published reviews of plays, musical events, exhibitions, or films exhibited xenophobia.

Margaret was a quietly but actively charitable woman who attended Mass daily. William was a man of action and a free thinker. Later, with an air of philosophical resignation, Peter would remark that all his own children turned out to be free thinkers. 'Everything in moderation, including moderation' was one of William's mottos. Being a Dublin Corporation employee, he remained financially independent of market ups and downs and had not been affected by the industrial strife of 1913, except when he and all emergency workers were overstretched to cope with the scores of citizens and police who were being injured in street battles, or when there was deliberate incendiarism.

While Margaret and he were raising the children and living in their own quarters within the fire station, they had no rent or mortgage costs. William remained comparatively well-off throughout his career, even during the economically grim years of the 1930s. Buying a house in Home Farm Road, he retired in his early sixties on a comfortable pension and joined the committee of Home Farm Boys' Football Club. At that point the country's modest industrial sector was being supported by government stimulus and tariffs. There was improved assistance for the unemployed and provision for widows and orphans, and an average of 12,000 houses a year were built with State aid, but from the early 1930s the combination of the world economic depression and the Irish-British tariff war caused a serious decline in the volume of Irish exports and the prices they fetched, especially in the important cattle trade. As the decade continued, unemployment and hardship increased. The percentage of single persons in society remained high; 26,000 people left Ireland in 1937, the year the new Constitution was ratified.

The Catholic *Capuchin Annual* for many years helped to nurture an appreciation of the arts. Church organisations generally encouraged a rising standard of stained glass and fittings. In 1932, at which time 93 per cent of the population of the Free State were Catholics, the Church marked the 1500th anniversary of the coming of Saint Patrick by hosting the international Eucharistic Congress. A powerful new Irish radio transmitter broadcast the events of the Congress countrywide.

Listeners could tune in to High Mass from the Phoenix Park with John McCormack singing *Panis Angelicus*. The new radio transmitter in Athlone came into full-time use in the following year, making broadcasting an important resource for national self-communication. As a collector and arranger of Gaeltacht songs, Carl Hardebeck and others over many decades served music in the same way that scholars and writers like Standish O'Grady had served literature. Their conservation work in traditional music was now extended by broadcasting and by the record player, which could reproduce traditional performances more directly and more exactly than could musical notation.

Gradually, traditional musicians from different parts of Ireland and from the diaspora began to hear something of each other's repertoire and style. Meanwhile, the number of players in the Station Orchestra increased from seven to nineteen. By the end of the decade, Raidió Éireann was regularly providing a schools programme of music and the appreciation of music. Orchestral concerts now began to enjoy more success than they had at first. In 1941 Raidió Éireann began an orchestral series that lasted throughout the war years ('the Emergency') and beyond, and this was looked back on as a golden age for concerts. An Irish work by a contemporary composer was usually included. Local and semi-local composers in the first half of the twentieth century—Hamilton Harty, John F. Larchet, Arnold Bax, Ina Boyle, Elizabeth Maconchy, Aloys Fleischmann, E. J. Moeran, and many more—had modest audiences among a total population even smaller than today's. Their compositions deserve to be remembered. Performance and recording were greater hurdles than they are today.

During the war years 1939–45, batteries for radio sets became scarce. Public libraries lent out more books than ever. Amateur dramatics abounded. Remarkably, drama on Raidió Éireann itself still depended on part-timers and amateurs: the full-time professional Raidió Éireann Players were not established until a couple of years after the war. The Dublin Grand Opera Society was formed in 1941. Irish painters and sculptors who shared European artistic concerns started the Irish Exhibition of Living Art in 1943. The same year saw the Modernist architecture of the new airport serving Dublin at Collinstown. Politically, a policy of neutrality for the fledgling Irish State had very broad support at home, but Irish writers consequently found their work less welcome in wartime Britain, where there was, moreover, a paper shortage, so that life was doubly difficult for writers who were enduring censorship at home. Sean O'Faolain campaigned against censorship in his monthly review, *The Bell*, and an Appeal Board was eventually set up. During the war years many basic commodities were in short supply and were rationed. Despite unprecedented State intervention in the economy, some people endured real hardship.

Peter married Brídín Nic an Bhaird in 1942, and Colm was born to them in 1943. Margaret died in 1945. William made a trip back to Oulart with Andy and Peter. The old house was still standing, but Andy reported that William was visibly moved to see that it was no longer in use as a habitation. When William died in 1947, Ireland had come to an important juncture in its affairs. People were voting with their feet, mainly leaving for Britain, at a rate of about 25,000 a year, despite the immediate post-war period being one of rapid Irish economic growth. In the 1950s, emigration would rise to 45,000 per year, declining only in the 1960s with the *First Programme for Economic Expansion*.

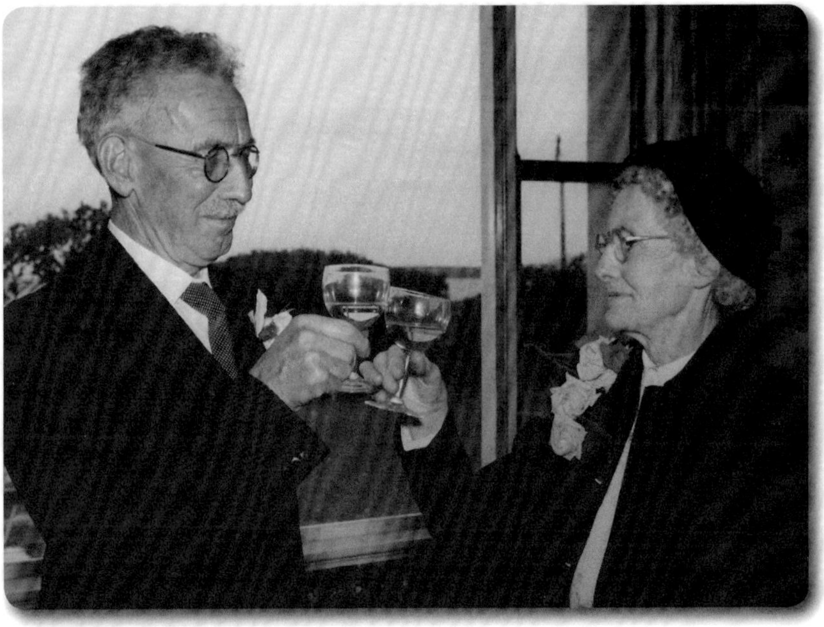

Colm's maternal grandparents, Art and Bríd Ward, celebrating their 50th wedding anniversary, Holmpatrick Hotel, Skerries, Co. Dublin. (Barry Mason)

There was a mixture of motives for emigration. Some left to escape poverty and hardship. Others could have stayed but desired a style of life that the cinema in particular now routinely showed them (22 million cinema tickets were sold in 1943). People were attracted to the life that workers returning periodically with money in their pockets seemed to be enjoying, especially workers in the British war- and post-war economy. Work in towns and cities abroad generally seemed to offer better living standards and often to be available for less competition. There was a hope of a more glamourous cosmopolitan culture or at least freedom from domestic oppression and stuffiness.

Colm himself recalled decades later that when his aunts Del and Moira were heading to America in the 1950s they wore fur coats as if to declare that they were footloose and fancy-free and not facing any economic ultimatum. It is an open question what range of options their father William had when he was about to migrate from Wexford to Dublin. It was not always out of dire economic necessity that the path of migration or emigration was taken. But very many had no real choice and this was overwhelmingly the case in the days of the 'coffin ships' at the time of the Great Famine.

Nonetheless, amongst other evidence, Padraic Colum's well-received Abbey Theatre play of 1905, *The Land*, offers a clear illustration of circumstances in which other motives could be at work.

Colm's mother, Brídín, was a stalwart enthusiast for the Irish language, bringing up her six children as Irish speakers. Peter had learned very little Irish at school. Vernacular use of the language had been declining since the middle of the previous century. Reflecting a widespread anxiety to distinguish the country culturally as well as politically from Britain, in 1922 the Provisional Government moved to phase the teaching of Irish into all national primary schools, but this took time to implement. It was in 1934 that Irish became a mandatory pass subject in the new secondary Intermediate and Leaving Certificate examinations. The Government gave financial assistance to some Irish-language projects and established An Gúm to produce high quality publications in Irish. By the 1940s, however, it had become evident to many people that the State's policies would be insufficient to bring the language to a point where it would be even moderately widely used outside Gaeltacht areas, which moreover were in chronically continuing shrinkage.

In 1941 Brian O'Nolan's masterly novel *An Béal Bocht* simultaneously lamented and laughed at an outrageously oppressively self-deluded impracticality that he perceived in official policies. Enthusiasts for Irish then began to take preservation and revival into their own hands. During the 1940s they established intellectually open journals and a newspaper in Irish, founded An Club Leabhar, and organised book publishing in Irish, in spite of a growing acceptance that English would remain culturally dominant as long as it remained economically so. For ten years, starting in 1945, Raidió Éireann broadcast the very successful Irish-language lessons series *Listen and Learn*.

With Peter's blessing, Brídín, the original 'Gaelgóir' of the extended family, sent Colm and their five other children to a section of the Marlborough Street Model Schools where all subjects but English were taught in Irish. There were then 523 similar all-Irish schools in the country. In 1960, about ten years behind Colm, I likewise attended Marlborough Street. Its physical location near some very poor parts of the city at the time added to my out-of-school education and presumably to Colm's. Pupils came from all districts of Dublin and from a variety of backgrounds. The mix was to us children only a normal part of the world's novelty but it likely contributed to broadening our perspective in a natural way.

Girls and boys were separated, however, from age six or seven onwards, with the girls having women teachers and the boys men; and a class was likely to retain the same teacher from year to year, and he or she would cover most or all subjects with them.

Years later, it would be one of Colm's first objectives as Arts Council Director to put the arts on a firmer footing in schools. His teacher at school in Marlborough Street had been Tomás Luibhéid. The same man later taught me. He happened to have a great love of the arts. Indeed, few seemed so versatile or eager to impart that love. He was a native speaker of Irish from the Dingle Peninsula, could command the attention of the class merely with a look, wrote Irish story books, a children's history book and an autobiography, broadcast occasionally on Raidió Éireann, and sometimes entered pupils from his class in an annual children's drama festival in the Gate Theatre. At one point he set us to learn a few verses of an epic poem dating from about 1750, by Mícheál Coimín. Its lines are full of internal assonances, and they rise to delicately rich imagery:

'Ag seilg dúinn maidin cheoidh
Ar imeall-bhorda Locha Léinn
Mar a raibh crainn ba chumhra bláth
's ceol gach tráth go binn ag éin . . .'

In music, Luibhéid found little difficulty in teaching us Dub boys songs like '*Thugamar féin an samhradh linn*' and '*Slán go deo le brón 's buairt*' and a Wren Boys song of his own youth in Kerry, '*Dreoilín a fuaireas-sa thíos ar an inse*'. Along with its melody, this song had two simultaneous harmony parts, all of which we picked up quickly and sang—even with musical feeling—in a city classroom in the middle of winter. Imagination flew from the smoky streets to mountain and stream. What a relief from sums and spellings! Actually, he was sometimes engaging even as a teacher of sums. He introduced negative numbers by asking the class whether a big number could ever be subtracted from a small one, and began by canvassing our opinions. Then he promised to explain the rationale and how to manage the thing, but rang the bell for a break. We argued among ourselves in the schoolyard, and by the time we were back in the classroom we were all agog.

It would be wrong to leave an impression that our schooldays were filled with nothing but liberality, sweetness, and light. It was widely accepted that teachers should blend instruction with any necessary disciplinary action and that on occasion this necessity might extend to corporal punishment. Almost all pupils felt that teachers used it excessively.

* * * * *

Colm, his parents and siblings, the 'Clontarf O'Briens' as we called them, seemed larger than life. My sister Aisling and I stayed with them for two weeks in 1960. Colm's schooling was then within a couple of years of finishing in Belvedere College. Peter had a hardware business and a shop in town, owned a large house on Castle Avenue, and drove an American car that could carry a whole squad of children, not necessarily all his own, typically to or from a summer holiday over winding country roads not much wider than the car itself. Aisling and I found that the Clontarf O'Briens had a fridge and a toaster, conveniences we had previously seen only in commercial advertisements.

Such novelties seemed an ordinary part of the Clontarf scheme of things, and nobody appeared to be promoting any grand notions about them or indeed about anything. There would anyway have been a ready supply of Dubliners to deflate any ideas of that sort, especially in those days, but it didn't feel like that kind of family anyway.

Peter and Brídín seemed to me always willing to offer a personal contribution to the gaiety of life. Peter, enterprising in business, found himself in a position to support the arts and did so generously, at one point even becoming patron of a foundry for sculptors in Dublin. In addition, he had a gently-spoken but rather genial manner and, prompted by Brídín, was willing to stand up and entertain relatives, friends, and on occasion even charity-event audiences. In typical fashion for Peter, he had purchased a baby grand piano at a bargain price because it sounded oddly tinny. He got it home, had a good look inside, and fished out some loose scrap metal, instantly restoring its tone. Brídín played it and Peter sang party pieces, often in comic music-hall style. They could be extremely funny. I remember Peter protesting that he felt embarrassed to be doing this kind of thing, but he managed it so well that people generally discounted any protests as all part of his act.

Colm took piano lessons, and played Beethoven at some of the parties in the house on Castle Avenue. Invitations to do a party piece evoked different responses. Some guests simply professed to lack the necessary appetite or skill. A few souls were uninhibited 'naturals' and nobody could stop them rising to an occasion, whether invited to do so or not. Some others felt equally happy to present a party piece or not to. A few others seemed to feel or believe that any kind of artistic performance attempt was really only indulging a weakness for 'showing off' and was therefore not to be encouraged.

Even if Peter felt any occasional diffidence about performing or entertaining, Brídín was his unflagging supporter, perhaps even something of his driver in this respect. More than that, she herself could be a witty writer and performer. She offered the complete antidote to inhibitions if a person was even half-willing to present themselves in any way.

In retrospect, it seems to me that Peter and Brídín were creating an environment in which self-presentation, performance, and self-expression could thrive as a natural and desirable feature of life; that their stalwart encouragement of this spirit was simultaneously a natural desire and a deliberate choice of theirs; and that in this endeavour they were evidently successful. Colm met a noble challenge to do the same in his own intrepid way, in many ways bringing greater fulfilment to a wider world.

A Family

Máirín Ní Bhriain

Brídín was on her bike, lost at night in the wilds of Donegal, when she first encountered Peter.

It was late, and the warden at the An Óige hostel at Trá na Rossan was worried that the group of Dublin girls he was expecting had not turned up. Concerned for their safety, he asked the lads who had settled into the hostel to get back on their bikes and head out in search of the girls.

The girls were more than happy to be found, and in the course of that rescue, a spark flew between Peter and Brídín.

Their relationship developed slowly over their years in An Óige. When Peter proposed they were on a cycling holiday in Scotland. It was September 1939 and World War II had just been declared.

An Óige was to have a profound influence on our family. Peter and Brídín had walked or cycled virtually every corner of Ireland and knew it intimately. They had a love of the land, an affection for its people, and respect for its culture. In An Óige, a spirit of self-reliance and mutual co-operation was encouraged and, in particular, the ability to create and perform one's own entertainment was brought to a fine art.

Growing up, we witnessed Peter and Brídín's parties with their An Óige friends—hilarious celebrations of poetry, doggerel, music, song, and skits. People enjoyed themselves with glorious, unselfconscious abandon. And everyone contributed. Everyone had a party-piece. This is something we inherited.

Peter was the son of a fire chief and was born in Dominick Street fire station in Dublin, one of twelve children. He left school at fourteen and served his time as an ironmonger, working firstly in Gleeson & O'Dea, then in Baxendale's Hardware Store. Brídín was one of four children, her father was a civil servant and both her parents were fluent Irish speakers. She went to London to train as a nurse but when she got called to the civil service, she returned to Dublin and abandoned her nursing career. She worked in the Department of Education, but because of the regulation at the time, once married she had to give up her job.

They started out their married life in a new house in Coolock. Brídín was delighted with this house and put a great deal of effort into making it a real home. Just when it was all coming together nicely, Peter sat her down one day to share his news. He had bought a shop! She was incredulous. 'With what?' she asked. 'With this house,' he explained. He had traded in the house for a shop, without consulting her. She had a real struggle to process what was happening and to know how to respond. Eventually, when she had recovered from her initial shock, she realised that she believed in him, and that she trusted him. She decided therefore that she would wholeheartedly support him.

From the comfort of their new-build in Coolock, they moved into Talbot Street, Dublin 1, to live over the shop—O'Brien's Hardware, under the bridge. It was old and draughty. And it was very noisy. From the upstairs back window an outstretched arm could almost touch the trains as they passed by into Amiens Street (now Connolly) Station. But business thrived.

Colm, their first-born, arrived in 1943 during what was called 'the Emergency' in neutral Ireland during the war. Piaras came next, followed by Art. Around the time of Art's arrival they moved out of Talbot Street to a house in Drumcondra—No. 5 Sion Hill Road—where they completed their family: Garry, the fourth boy, then me—the first girl, and finally Bairbre, the youngest.

We were like steps of stairs, two years between us all, except between me and Bairbre where Brídín had suffered a miscarriage.

Irish was our first language. It was how we always spoke to Brídín and it was what we spoke at home. Peter was not initially an Irish speaker, but he picked it up reasonably well as he went along. However, whenever we spent time alone with him on a one-to-one basis, the conversation usually reverted to English.

* * * * *

Our neighbourhood in Drumcondra felt like a wonderland when growing up. There was a strong sense of community and it was teeming with kids. At the bottom of Sion Hill Road, next door to the pub, was the all-important sweet shop. Across the road was what we called 'the dump'—an overgrown plot of undeveloped land which served as our adventure playground. There were clumps of bushes at the back providing dens and hidey holes for playing games and holding secret meetings. Sometimes it was worth searching for a discarded glass bottle or two to take across the road to the shop to claim a penny refund.

The roads were a hive of activity, with kids on their bikes or trikes, and gangs of girls lined up each side of skipping ropes, chanting skipping rhymes: 'vote, vote, vote for de Valera . . .' Chalk markings decorated the pavements for hopscotch and the thunderous sound of steel roller skates on concrete filled the air. Boys raced up and down the hill on carts, cobbled together from bits of old prams and spare wood. There was added excitement when some of the older kids put on a show in someone's garage. Colm was at the heart of organising these performances, as a producer and a performer. To us kids, it felt like we were getting the real deal, complete with stage curtain and a young girl with a tray selling sweets—inspired by the Lyons Maid ice cream lady who would appear at intervals in the Adelphi Cinema.

The sight and sound of horses was a common feature of everyday life. Bread and milk were delivered daily by horse-drawn carriage. Once a week the 'pig man' would arrive in his horse and cart to collect our food waste which he fed to his pigs. This meant that horse manure was a regular sight on the roads.

Brídín would get very excited at the sight of fresh droppings and would rush into the house, calling out the names of one or other of the boys, or all four in succession if she was flustered, with instructions to grab a bucket and shovel to collect the manure. With every nerve, fibre and cell of their being they dreaded and resisted having to do this, especially in full view of their friends. But Brídín simply dismissed all their protestations and told them to get on with it, saying that horse manure was the best thing ever for her roses.

In the 1950s, corporal punishment at school and at home was considered normal. It didn't feature heavily in our house, but it did feature. There were different degrees. You might get a few slaps on the hand, on the bum or across the back of the legs. A step up was when you heard the sound of the kitchen cutlery drawer being pulled open, with lots of rattling and rummaging in search of the wooden spoon. It was wise then to scarper if you could, but it wasn't always possible. The worst was when the kitchen door flew open and there was a rush into the garden to extract a bamboo from the beloved roses. You knew then you were in for a few stiff biffs with the cane which were very painful. But there were other, more creatively conceived punishments too. Colm in particular would forevermore describe as traumatic having to carefully unravel a whole jumper and then roll the wool back into a ball. We never heard what his crime was, but we never heard the end of that punishment.

Peter had a different style, but he liked to teach a lesson nonetheless. He was a pipe-smoker and very attached to his pipe. He kept his plug tobacco in an earthenware jar that sat on the windowsill in the dining room. About once a week he conducted the ritual of preparing a fresh batch of tobacco. He would carry the earthenware jar to the table, unscrew the mechanism that fastened the lid and remove the dark, aromatic block. Then, with a razor blade he would begin methodically

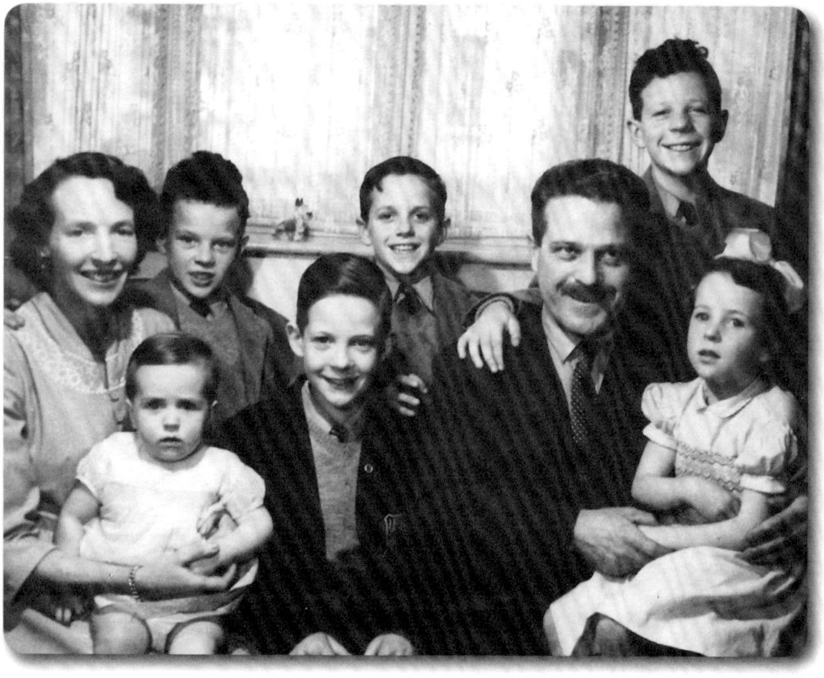

The O'Brien family c. 1955. (Left to right) Brídín with Bairbre on her knee, Garry, Colm (centre front), Art, Peter, Piaras, Máirín. (J. B. Cafferkay)

and rhythmically shaving slivers of tobacco from the block. These in turn he sliced into thin strips, then cut again horizontally to create a fine mixture. About half of this mixture he would gather up and place in his tan leather pouch which he placed in his pocket, and which imparted an unmistakeable aroma to his clothing. The other half would be returned to the jar for his next refill and placed back on the window sill. It was a calming, hypnotic procedure which we liked to watch.

On one occasion he summoned all four boys into the dining room. They were asked to line up in order of age, like a military inspection parade. They suspected they were in big trouble. He stood before them, his hands in his pockets, and told them he had noticed that someone had been at his tobacco.

Silence.

He wanted to know who it was.

More silence.

He said that someone had gone to the jar, taken the blade and chopped up his tobacco, and he needed to know who had done that.

Still more silence.

He walked up and down, looking at them, then eventually he asked them one by one:

'Colm'?

'*Níor dhein mise é, Dada.*' (I didn't do it, Dad.)

'Piaras'?

'*Ní mise.*' (Not me.)

'Art'?

'*Níor bhaic me leis.*' (I didn't touch it.)

'Garry'?

'*Ni raibh me in aice leis.*' (I wasn't near it.)

He continued to look from one to the other, allowing the tension to mount. He repeated that he wanted to know who had chopped up his tobacco, he wanted the truth, and again asked which of them had done it. They all shook their heads.

He continued to walk up and down then finally he produced a shilling from his pocket and flicking it in the air said it was a real shame he couldn't find the '*buachaill maith*' (good boy) who had done him such a good turn because he wanted to give him a shilling.

A wave of confusion and dismay passed over the boys' faces as they struggled to understand what had just happened. The culprit never owned up.

* * * * *

Every St Stephen's Day, immediately following the indulgence of Christmas, Peter took the four boys on a character-forming, three-day hike through the Wicklow mountains. As Bairbre and I were not considered to be part of the wolf pack, we were left at home. To compensate, Brídín tried to make things special by having a girls' afternoon tea. She would unfold the green, felt-covered card table and cover it with a hand-embroidered table cloth. We had dainty buns and cakes, and were allowed to toast the bread on the open fire with the long brass fork. It made for a cosy scene and had its own charm, but there was always the underlying sense that something much more elemental and exciting was happening in the Wicklow mountains.

When the boys returned they were bedraggled and hungry and were welcomed home to a roaring fire, hot baths and a feast. There was always a lot of laughter and mutual slagging as they recounted tales of the challenges and hardships they'd had to face and overcome. On a particularly gruelling hike through bitter winds and snow, Colm, who was struggling to keep up was heard to cry out from behind 'Go on then, just go ahead and leave me here to die alone in the snow.' This was simply met with guffaws from the others who continued to press on ahead through the storm.

One Easter Sunday the whole family went to spend the day in the Wicklow mountains. After a picnic, the four boys headed off on a hike with Peter while the rest of us stayed behind relaxing at a river bank. But the afternoon began to drag—they seemed to be gone a very long time. Eventually, when Peter reappeared it was clear that something was wrong. They had lost Art on the mountain. They had retraced their steps twice but there was no sign of him. Peter had returned to let us know and to call for further help. Then, already exhausted, he had to turn around and head back up the mountain again.

It was black night when they returned, having failed to find Art. We drove to the nearest village, where Peter checked in with the local guards and publican and left his contact information. When he got back into the car and started to drive away, my mind filled with images of Art left alone on the dark mountain and I began to cry out in panic. I was quickly told to knock it off and we headed for home in stoic silence.

In the hours that followed, the unthinkable was held in the tension of our unexpressed emotions. Then the phone rang. He'd been found! There was an explosive sense of relief and an instant feeling of brightness, as if the overhead lights had suddenly gained wattage. Art had found his way to a remote cottage inhabited by a couple of sheep farmers.

When he arrived home, he was brought straight to a hot bath. Brídín, in her immense relief, kept repeating '*tú an buachaillín beag is fearr*' (you're the best little boy) as she washed his hair. Art, always the one to be in trouble, dropped his jaw in astonishment at such praise, only to swallow a full mouthful of soapy water. He was then fed, and allowed to tell his story. But before he could feel too comfortable, Peter took him aside and severely admonished him for having violated the mountain code he had taught him. He had done this by breaking away from the group and striking out alone. Peter conceded, however, that thankfully Art had at least remembered something he'd been taught: to follow the line of a river if ever disoriented or lost. This he had done, which had led him to the home of the hill bachelors.

*****

Next door to us lived an elderly couple called Mr and Mrs Lemaleh. They were German Jews who had come to Ireland for safety just before the outbreak of World War II.

Mr Lemaleh was an international businessman who had rightly detected how things were developing in Europe. He was cultured and wise and Peter admired and looked up to him as a sort of mentor. Years later, Peter sometimes quoted something Mr Lemeleh would say to him: 'Watch the trends, Mr O, watch the trends.' When Mr Lemaleh died, his wife was left completely alone in the world without any family support. Peter and Brídín helped in every way they could, with Peter sorting out paperwork she had no way of navigating. He discovered that she was completely dependent on her husband for everything; she had never paid a bill or done anything without his assistance. He was so appalled by the implications of her extreme dependency as a woman that he insisted from then on that Brídín had her own money, her own bank account, that she handled the family finances and that she learned to drive. This was very unusual in the 1950s.

Money was always treated with care and respect. Peter and Brídín were anything but mean, but they were both very frugal. Nothing was ever wasted. Peter used to joke that whenever he had the urge to spend money, he would lie down for twenty minutes and wait for the feeling to pass.

Brídín was an excellent seamstress and made a lot of our clothes. Fabrics from old dresses and shirts were remodelled and re-used. Not even the smallest bits of wool from old jumpers were thrown away, but were incorporated into making new, multi-coloured Fair Isle jumpers that for a time were our signature fashion statements as kids. Equally, food was never needlessly thrown out, leftovers always found their way into another dish, and everything was homemade. Marmalade was made in a huge vat, with the unmistakeable smell of bitter Seville oranges pervading the house. Eggs used for baking were bought in bulk and at discount, individually preserved with lard and then stored under the stairs.

Every month or so, Brídín would meet with her friends for what they called 'the sewing circle'. Taking turns in each others' houses, they would come together with their baskets of clothes that needed mending and socks for darning, nattering as they worked and making a social evening of it. Peter had a workbench filled with all the tools he needed for DIY, including an anvil on which for many years he mended our shoes.

We were given our pocket money every Friday in little brown pay packets that were made up with the wages in Peter's office. They had a lovely feel and smell to them and our names were typed on the front. We were given a modest and set amount, with a small raise with every birthday and were encouraged to save. Beyond that there were no extras ever given, and we knew not to ask—unless it was for books or for some educational activity.

As a businessman, Peter was well able to wheel and deal but he was also very honest. His attitude to paying tax was that not only was it a social obligation but it was an indication that he was making money, for which he was very grateful. His philosophy was that if your goal was purely to make money, you'd never be happy. He defined success as providing a service that people needed, enjoying the work which that entailed, and thereby making money in the process.

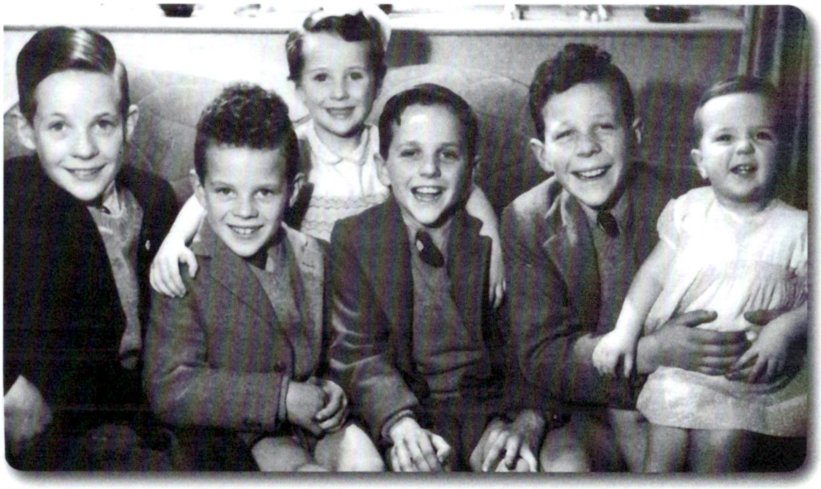

The Ó Briain siblings c. 1955. (Left to right) Colm, Garry, Máirín, Art, Piaras, Bairbre. (J. B. Cafferkay)

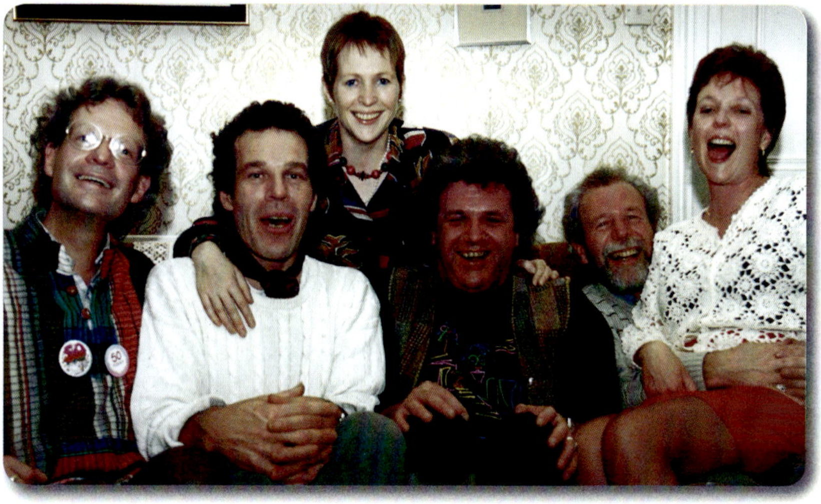

The siblings again in 1993—celebrating Colm's 50th birthday.

I learned a salutary lesson about financial propriety at a very young age. I called around as usual to play with my friend Kathleen and found her trying to slice a hole with a kitchen knife in the lid of an empty tin box. This, she said, was to collect money for the Black Babies. We were both in Junior Infants, and although we went to different schools, we were each familiar with the box that sat on almost every teacher's desk in the country. It was a collection box for the African missions and depicted an African baby on the front. She had a spare tin box and encouraged me to join her in this noble endeavour. Once the considerable challenge of slitting a hole in the top of the second box was overcome, we set off together down Calderwood Road. We found that people were very willing to part with a penny and before long our boxes were full.

Kathleen said that we had worked so hard and done such a good thing we probably deserved a treat. So we headed for the shop. Normally our pocket money might stretch to a small packet of fruit pastilles, but now our eyes wandered to the higher shelves where they displayed the family-size boxes. Why not? Hadn't we been very good? We wandered back to the bottom of Sion Hill Road and on the corner house wall we unpacked and counted our remaining pennies while enjoying the pastilles from our conspicuously displayed family box. A sibling rat caught sight of this spectacle, and, especially when refused a pastille, went straight home to tell Brídín. Word was sent that I was to report back immediately. I learned that I was in very big trouble and that a suitably severe punishment awaited me. But firstly, I would have to retrace my steps and give back every penny. The very thought of it immobilised me with fear and dread. Colm was selected to accompany me and to supervise the hand-over of the money.

Colm walked me down the hill in complete silence. He never spoke a word except to eventually ask me to point out the houses of my victims. We approached the first house, and as he prepared to knock on the front door, he put me standing behind him, obscured from view. When the door opened, the performance began. He threw himself into an animated display of verbal fluency, his body moving in synch with the flow of words that poured from his mouth. I couldn't understand a word of it, his vocabulary was far beyond me. But I heard mild, gentle laughter and my fear began to dissipate. The man at the door cast a benign glance in my direction and accepted the money back with a smile. This performance was repeated at every house, with me hiding behind Colm, until finally we headed for home. Still, Colm spoke not a word to me. But unmistakeably I had felt his heart, I had felt his protection, and I felt that he had thoroughly enjoyed himself!

*****

For many years our summer holidays were spent in Skerries. A trailer would be hitched to the car and piled high with our belongings for a month. The big white Kelvinator fridge would stand proud in the centre of the trailer, like Fitzcarraldo sailing down the Amazon. Brídín flatly refused to spend a month in Skerries without her fridge. As we approached Skerries we all got ready to sing excitedly 'Hello Scírí, Hello Scírí' as we passed under the railway bridge. When we were leaving at the end of the month, heading back to school, it was a very different feeling when we sang '*Slán leat Scírí*'.

For us it was a time of great freedom, but for Brídín it was still cooking and cleaning for eight people. Nevertheless, a whole community of Peter and Brídín's friends converged on Skerries every August so in that sense it was a very sociable time. Going for a walk with Peter up the harbour took ages as he would stop to talk to someone every couple of minutes.

Sailing was a big part of what being in Skerries was all about. Peter had built a boat for the boys, a Heron called *Optimus*. It was aptly named as it was a real winner. Piaras had a talent for sailing and although he was not the eldest, he was the natural skipper. The other three took turns in crewing with him, and the many racing cups and trophies that were won in *Optimus* decorated the sideboard at home for years to come. There was, however, an attitude that sailing was a purely male preserve and no amount of pleading for a girl to be allowed to learn to sail was successful. I was thinking to myself how unfair this was, not for the first time, while trying to teach myself to swim. At the moment I found I could float I had an epiphany. 'They don't own the ocean,' I thought. 'I'll swim instead.' And so I became a swimmer.

Colm's interest in sailing eventually waned. It really wasn't where his passion lay. His passion became crystal clear with the arrival in Skerries of Flash Parade, a travelling theatre troupe from England who set up their marquee at the edge of the village. The whole family went together to one of the performances, which was a great treat. But Colm became like someone possessed. He begged, borrowed and offered to do any odd jobs possible to make enough money to return to every single performance thereafter, including all the matinées. He couldn't get enough. He was completely intoxicated.

*****

In 1960 we moved house to a three-storey red brick in Clontarf. The house needed a complete overhaul and for months before we moved in we were spending weekends and evenings after school helping out. Colm was tasked with painting the intricate plasterwork in the sitting and dining rooms. He spent weeks up a ladder, wielding his artist's brushes like Michaelangelo.

Peter's hardware business had expanded from retail to wholesale and now included a premises in Lower Gardiner Street. Around the corner from his office there was a bridal car rental business. They found a willing customer in Peter when it came to selling off their secondhand American cars. So, with a fine new house in Clontarf, and a pale green Chevrolet Reg. MIK 707 parked outside, Peter's success in business was becoming evident.

The new house was elegant and very spacious. However, for us offspring, leaving our pals and our community behind in Drumcondra was a terrible wrench and left us with a sense of bereavement. It was as if a golden era had come to an end. There were no kids around on that leafy avenue in Clontarf. Bairbre, who was only four at the time, was so disorientated with the lack of children in the neighbourhood she went from house to house asking if there were any children she could play with, but found none. Finally, she called next door where old Mr McEvoy, one of nature's gentlemen, lived. He told her there were no children, but that he too would like a friend. He invited her in, and that was the start of a beautiful friendship. Whenever Bairbre could not be found we knew where to look. She would invariably be next door, sitting on a low stool chatting to Mr McEvoy, while he sat at the table with his cards playing Patience.

The following year, Peter arrived home one Friday with a TV set from Murphy's Rentals. We were beside ourselves with excitement. 'It's just on hire for the weekend,' he insisted. He left it sitting on a chair for a couple of hours before connecting it up. Meanwhile, word travelled through the sibling vine that there was a top secret meeting being held in the garage and a full attendance was required.

The garage was at the end of the garden, well away from the house. Art was sitting up on Peter's workbench, his legs dangling. Piaras sat astride one of the bikes and Garry pulled out a deck-chair and made himself comfortable. Bairbre and I sat on a couple of boxes. For quite a while we sat waiting and wondering what this was all about.

Then Colm made his entrance and took the floor:

'You'd all like to have a telly, would you?' he asked.

'Yes! Yes! Absolutely! Definitely! Of course!' we answered.

'Well, then, don't be fooled!' he said. 'This is a test! We're being tested, watched, monitored—to see how we behave having a telly in the house.'

He told us we had to be on our best behaviour and that no-one was to mess it up for the rest of us. Yet again, Colm was so far ahead of us, and we seemed so far behind, but we recognised that he had the situation sussed.

After our meeting, Brídín happened to ask Art to fill the coal hod for the Aga. Up jumped Garry : 'No! *Déinfidh mise é!*' (No! I'll do it!) he said. 'No, No! *Déinfidh* mise *é!*' (No, No, *I'll* do it) countered Art as they both made a lunge for the hod.

Later, when we'd finished our dinner, we set to doing the washing-up as if it were a pure joy, and left the kitchen gleaming. Then Art, feigning nonchalance, asked if it would be ok if we watched just a little bit of telly? Remembering not to rush, we headed into the breakfast room and sat enthralled in front of the set. The reception was lousy, lots of snow and lines moving up and down the screen, but we were not deterred. We could only pick up TWW, what we later referred to as 'Telly Welly Wales'. For us, even the ads were exciting. At every ad break we heard of the racey stories that would be revealed in *The News of the World* and *The Sunday People*. Brídín made tutting noises and complained that they were terrible English rags. She also warned about the insidious power of advertising.

The experiment was repeated the two following weekends and we continued to compete with each other for best behaviour. After the third weekend the telly was not sent back.

In December 1961, RTÉ broadcast for the first time. In contrast to Telly Welly Wales, the reception was fantastic and we were overjoyed to have a crystal-clear picture. RTÉ bought in a lot of American programmes. Every week we'd watch the police series *Dragnet* which opened with: 'This is the city, Los Angeles, California. I'm Joe Friday. I work here. I'm a cop'. And we heard lines like: 'You're a cop, a flatfoot, a bull, a dick, John Law, the fuzz, the heat, you're poison, you're trouble, you're bad news. They call you everything, but never a policeman.' It sounded better than poetry and we soaked up every word.

Then there was *The Twighlight Zone* which opened with 'You are about to enter another dimension, a dimension not only of sight and sound but of mind. A journey into a wondrous land of imagination. Next stop—The Twighlight Zone.' We were completely hooked.

On a lighter note, we watched the *Donna Reid Show* and *Father Knows Best*. And for a bit of spook we had Hitchcock and Boris Karloff.

The ads urged us to visit the Indian Tea Rooms because 'A cup of tea revives you'; to eat Galtee processed cheese to become 'Slim, trim and brimful of energy', and to buy Raelbrook shirts—'The shirts you don't iron' (made entirely of nylon they made the armpits of *Fir na hÉireann* stink to high heaven).

There was a particularly captivating ad for Horlicks, depicting a woman tossing and turning in her bed at night, and above the mesmerising music the voice-over asked 'Do you suffer from night starvation?' meaning no doubt, 'Do you have trouble sleeping?' Garry turned to me and said 'I get starving at bedtime, do you?' I agreed and followed him into the kitchen for a bowl of cornflakes. We felt we could do with a jar of Horlicks and asked Brídín if she'd get us some. She quickly replied that she most certainly would not and that this was proof of the terrible power of advertising. Still, we felt we were missing out, so we pooled our pocket money and Garry walked to Killester to get some. Anticipating a delicious, almost mystical creamy beverage, we both however gagged on the first mouthful and spat it into the sink.

Further evidence of the power of advertising was to surface a few months later and was treated as a major incident. Art was discovered on a Sunday morning, sitting in a shelter on Clontarf seafront happily reading both *The News of the World* and *The Sunday People*. The ads that weekend had promised to reveal the saucy secrets of an English convent.

*****

Every evening the telly got switched off when it was time to say the Rosary. We had always said the Rosary together as a family. Religion had a big presence in our home. As well as the usual Mass on Sundays, all through Lent we got up for daily Mass before school. And because November was the month of the Holy Souls, it called for daily Mass also. Then there was the First Friday of every month, as well as the random feast days of often obscure saints that warranted the early morning call. On Christmas morning we would be brought to Gardiner Street Church not just for Mass, but for three consecutive Masses—all on an empty stomach.

The Rosary beads were kept in an ornamental wooden box that sat on the mantlepiece in the breakfast room. It made an unmistakable sound—the lifting of the lid, the rattle of the beads within. It was our call to prayer. But times were changing and there was something else in the air—the sound of rock n' roll. The Beatles were singing 'Love Me Do', Colm's hair was getting longer and Garry was wearing Beatle boots. Art was spending most of his pocket money on building a record collection. Perhaps Brídín felt she needed to employ a different approach to ensure her adolescent brood stayed in line. She took us completely by surprise one evening when, holding the wooden box in her hands, she made the following announcement:

'*Éistigí liom. Táimíd chun an Paidrín a rá anois. Tá sé tábhachtach é a rá, an chlann go léir le chéile. Agus tá súil agam go dtigeann sibh chomh tábhachtach atá sé. Ach . . ba mhaith liom go mothófadh sibh go bhfuil sibh á rá as bhúr stuaim féin . . . go bhfuil sibh á rá mar gur mian libh é a rá.*' ('Listen to me. We're going to say the Rosary now. It's important to say it, the whole family together. And I hope you understand how important it is. But . . . I'd like you to feel that you are doing it out of your own volition . . . that you're saying it because you want to.')

There was a stunned silence.

Eventually, Colm spoke up:

'*Agus muna mían linn . . . an bhfuil muid saor chun imeacht?*' ('And if we don't want to . . . are we free to leave?')

An usettled Brídín answered: '*Bhuel, Colm, bheadh sé sin ana bhrónach ar fad . . . ach . . . bhuel . . . is dócha go bhfuil . . . sibh . . . saor.*' ('Well, Colm, that would be very sad indeed . . . but . . . well . . . I suppose . . . you are . . . free.')

With that, Colm sprang to his feet and left the room. He was quickly followed by Piaras. In the tension-filled room, Art and Garry eyed each other, trying to assess the situation, then leapt up together and rushed out the door. A shell-shocked Brídín stood holding the Rosary box, struggling to comprehend what had happened. Peter sat quietly looking on. Only Bairbre and I remained—too young and too scared to be so bold. There was little energy or volume in the Rosary that evening and it was never restored to its former glory.

In time, my own religious doubts began to surface. I had a burning question, but who could I ask? I couldn't ask a teacher, most of them were nuns, and there was no way I could ask Brídín. I wondered if I could ask Peter, but then he just went along with matters religious and kept his own views firmly to himself. Eventually I decided that Colm was my best bet.

I decided to seize my opportunity when Colm was alone in the breakfast room apparently doing nothing. I should add, however, that Colm could often be seen, sitting or standing, 'apparently' doing nothing, when actually he was always extremely busy—thinking. He had a rich and engaging inner life which I suspect he often found much more interesting than making conversation.

Aware that I was probably disturbing him, I approached him a little gingerly.

'Colm,' I said, 'can I ask you a question?'

'Mmmmm?' he responded.

'Do you believe . . . I mean, do you think . . . you know the way . . .'

He gave me a steady look, waiting for me to become more articulate.

'Well, what I was wondering . . . is there such a . . . is there such a place . . . I mean . . . do you actually believe . . . in hell? . . . Do you really believe that hell exists?' I finally blurted out in a full sentence.

As was characteristic, he inhaled slowly and looked away slightly. He pursed his lips and his nostrils flared.

He had my full attention.

Then he got up, and moving towards the door he said with a flourish:

'Well, Jean-Paul Sartre said "Hell is other people!"' And he was gone.

I was left standing, completely dazed and confused. He had thrown a grenade into my young mind, blowing open the walls onto a whole new paradigm.

* * * * *

On the first occasion that Brídín accompanied Peter on one of his overseas business trips, Colm was left in charge. It was a really big ask!

He was delighted to have the run of the kitchen to develop some culinary skills. Brídín was extremely territorial about her kitchen where she was the supreme ruler. Nor did she share her knowledge. Though she was a master of most of the domestic arts, neither Bairbre nor I left home knowing even the basics, and had to learn everything from scratch.

Colm proved himself to be a brilliant cook and we were treated to gourmet meals every single evening. He changed the status quo forever by making roast potatoes with olive oil, at a time when olive oil was bought in tiny bottles in the chemist for treating an earache. They were such a hit that when Brídín returned we insisted she adopt Colm's method.

Mealtimes were the hub of the family's energies. Brídín ran a tight ship and meals happened to schedule.

On weekdays we ate in the evening, and at weekends we ate in the middle of the day. On Saturdays we ate lunch to the radio sounds of the Walton's programme, often parroting the phrases 'Jimmy Magee and his Merry Banjo' and 'If you feel like singing, do sing an Irish song'. The Jacob's programme, following a musical intro by Frank Sinatra, doled out advice by agony aunt Frankie Byrne. We would often laugh or roll our eyes or even shout at the radio when she attempted to offer guidance to some poor unfortunate.

On Sundays Brídín's parents came for lunch, as well as her bachelor uncle and a cousin who was studying in Dublin. A three-course Sunday lunch for twelve was some operation and Brídín pulled if off for years. We listened to our favourite radio comedy programme *Round the Horn* from the BBC which we found absolutely hilarious, made even funnier by Art's infectious laughter.

When it came to washing-up, Brídín would remove herself from the kitchen and we offspring would take over—one person to clear the table, one to wash up, two to dry up, one to put away and one had a day off. There was no question of skiving off, it wouldn't be tolerated.

Dinner time was heralded by the sound of the pressure cooker hissing and the smell of scorched coffee as the percolator overflowed onto the Aga. Sometimes Brídín would also call us by giving the brass gong in the hall a strong belt. She was a good cook and she expected us to eat whatever she put in front of us. If anyone grumbled that there was some gristle in their meat she would dismiss that out of hand saying that she had given them 'the choicest piece'. We learned to receive that with some humour, wondering how many choicest pieces there could possibly be—it was the stock answer.

Mealtimes were filled with conversation and, for the most part, good-natured banter. Whatever the topic, we were expected to be able to laugh at ourselves and never to take ourselves too seriously. That was considered a cardinal offence. The downside of that was that it was not safe to show any vulnerability or sensitivity whatsoever. There was a lot of slagging, some of it very funny but some of it went very close to the bone.

The older we got, the more opinionated we became. The '60s were in full swing, and revolution was in the air. The dinner table became a forum for emergent ideas. It was a place to try them on, try them out, and even risk potential ridicule. If anyone offered a pessimistic view, we would jeeringly turn around and point at the plaque hanging by the window: 'Blessed is he who expects nothing for he shall not be disappointed.' When discussions began to overheat, one of us would point to a poster on another wall that said: 'Those of you who think you know everything, are annoying to those of us who do.' Sometimes, Colm and Art would lock horns. When that happened, the spirit of dialogue departed and it became a battle of wills. It was difficult to witness at times.

Peter would often arrive home either halfway through or towards the end of the meal and the energy would change. We quietened down and we'd watch him eat his dinner with gusto as he chatted in English with Brídín about the day's events. His business was continuing to develop and grow. He was now the Irish distributor for quality products from the UK, Germany, the US and Japan and he regularly had to travel abroad. He was very active within the Irish Hardware Association and was particularly interested in the provision of training within the industry. Increasingly, he was invited to join committees that were not confined to the hardware business: the Prices Commission, the Guaranteed Irish Board, the Decimal Currency Board and others.

Brídín was also active in her own right. She initiated and ran a very successful community-based service in the city centre providing meals for the elderly. She dealt with the suppliers, beating them down in price, balanced the books and co-ordinated teams of volunteers. In another era she could have run an efficient government department. Together, they also attended the Adult Education Institute twice weekly for years, studying a range of subjects, including economics and politics. They adopted a policy of never revealing to us how they voted in elections, to encourage us to think for ourselves and to avoid the Irish tradition of families perpetuating civil war politics.

They went to the theatre very regularly. Peter's all-time favourite play was Arthur Miller's *Death of a Salesman*. In later years, he also developed a great appreciation for sculpture. This led eventually to him collaborating in the establishment of the Dublin Art Foundry, the first foundry in Ireland, in response to a situation where Irish artists had no option but to send their work abroad to be cast.

We were all given the privilege of a musical education. Brídín was a good pianist and had a fine musical intelligence but she made light of her ability. In her youth, she had conducted the An Óige orchestra when they performed a musical show in the Olympia Theatre to full houses.

Peter did not play an instrument but he was a great lover of Beethoven's music and would like to conduct in his mind's eye, waving an imaginary baton while listening to his records. Beethoven formed the sound track to our days in Drumcondra. In later years, Peter and Brídín would get a season ticket for the RTÉ Symphony concerts. The ticket allowed three to attend so every week one of us would have a turn to accompany them.

We had a piano teacher who came to the house twice a week. We were always at the dinner table when she arrived and there was usually a dispute as to whose turn it was to go first. The poor woman could sometimes be left five minutes before being let in. Her style of teaching was to painfully rap you on the knuckles with a pencil when you made a mistake. We were expected to practise for half an hour a day. Any messing or dossing at the piano would incite Brídín to bang a radiator with a metal spoon, sending the message through the pipes to 'get on with it'.

By far the most musically talented of us all was Garry. At twelve he taught himself to play guitar. He then taught Piaras a few chords and Piaras took off in his own right. This added a new dimension to our all-important family parties. Brídín would usually get things going by playing a medley of tunes on the piano—she could play anything by ear. Then the guitars and the singing would follow. For a time, we also loved to play 'Murder in the Dark', giving whoever had pulled the short straw to be the murderer the delicious opportunity to reveal capacities for ruthlessness, deviousness and cunning, normally taboo in any other setting.

Over the years, our piano lessons became increasingly frustrating and unfulfilling. Garry took the initiative by buying the sheet music of Gershwin's 'Rhapsody in Blue' and bringing it to his lesson. The teacher was horrified, considering it to be less than proper music. Then I asked to play some Beatles music which made matters worse. In the end she refused to teach us, believing our family to have completely lost the run of ourselves.

Our primary education was through Irish. We attended the Gaelscoileanna in the grounds of the Department of Education in Marlborough Street, in the city centre. We survived that, suffering varying degrees of misery. National schools in the 1950s were not typically the seats of child-centred or humanistic education. Our secondary education was through English. Colm, of course, was the first to go to secondary school. He wore his Belvedere blazer with pride and seemed to love every minute of it. He thrived and he excelled. He always had the air of someone who found learning very exciting. He even made friends with one of his teachers and brought him home to meet the family. This was a phenomenon that was incomprehensible to the rest of us. Hubert Delaney was still a young novice, but they remained friends for life, and later Fr Hubert officiated at Colm and Muireann's wedding.

Belvedere at that time put on a musical show every year, and for several years running they performed Gilbert & Sullivan operettas—*The Mikado*, *The Pirates of Penzance* and others. For Colm this was pure heaven and he shone in his leading roles. He put so much effort into learning 'Model of the Modern Major-General' that it became his party-piece for years until he replaced it with 'First Born' by the McGarrigle Sisters.

Brídín got very involved, helping to sew costumes and providing food during rehearsals and performances. In time, Piaras also performed in these musicals, but his greater interest was in rugby. Both Colm and Piaras enjoyed what seemed to be a golden era in Belvedere. However, by the time Art and Garry arrived, things had changed. They experienced something very different and were on the receiving end of the dark side of that institution. This had a very negative impact on both of them, and Art in particular was tormented by his experience for most of his life.

Bairbre and I both went to Loreto on the Green. But for fifth and sixth year Bairbre was sent to a boarding school in Arklow. The rationale given for this was that, as she was now the only school-goer in a family of adults, it would help her education to be in a more studious environment. But for Bairbre it was very hard not to feel that she had been singled out for abandonment.

In UCD Colm studied law but most of his time and attention was taken up with Dramsoc. He was usually home on the last bus, and took a very dried-up looking dinner from the oven. He would sit alone in the kitchen, eating slowly, staring straight ahead, thinking, thinking.

Sometimes he would bring home a bag of chips, a terrible tease for the rest of us, and stand in the kitchen eating them with a glass of milk. We had to learn not to ask him for a chip.

Even though he was now a college student the reins of family discipline were still kept very tight. He was, for example, forbidden to attend the annual King's Inns' dinner, for no satisfactory reason other than it was deemed to be possibly not quite suitable. It infuriated him and in his exasperation he would sometimes yell at us that he was struggling at the front lines, opening up the path for the rest of us. As happens in many larger families, parental over-consciousness and control waned over time and Colm saw the rest of us enjoy freedoms that he couldn't even have dreamt of.

To earn some money as a student he got a job as a waiter in the Trocadero Restaurant. He arrived home one day holding a Cassidy's paper bag with some black silk fabric and stiffner and asked me if I'd help him make a cummerbund. I'd never heard of such a word and had no idea what he meant. He explained that it was a wide, stiff waistband with pleats. He felt it would help him look the part as a waiter. We dispensed with needle and thread and used Copydex glue instead, a new invention that could be used on fabric and which Peter's business had begun to distribute. Neither of us had a clue what we were doing but between us, we turned out a garment he was happy with. I used to imagine him wearing it while waiting at tables, flicking a cloth and serving plates like a matador.

His hard-earned cash financed his trips to London. He would leave with an enormous 'emigrant's' suitcase that was almost empty and would return, sporting a very natty haircut, with the case filled to the brim. I remember staring at the case lying open on his bedroom floor—filled with exhibition catalogues, theatre programmes, admission tickets, posters and books, so many books. There were plays, novels, critiques—most of them from the edge, pushing the boundaries, some of them banned. I wondered how he even knew such stuff existed. And then there were the clothes, beautiful, ultra-trendy clothes that could never be found in a Dublin shop.

For his twenty-first birthday, perhaps as vengeance for being forbidden to attend the King's Inns' dinners, he asked to have a fully formal dinner party at home. His wish was granted and his friends arrived at the house, dressed like lords and ladies. We were all roped in to help out—Piaras was the head waiter and I was his assistant, Art and Garry were on wash-up, and Bairbre helped with plating up the food. Both Piaras and I wore dark suits for the occasion. It was an exercise in struggling to maintain poise and composure. Serving plates of hot soup was particularly nerve-wracking but we managed not to drop one in anyone's finely-clad lap. However, offering seconds was another matter. As a thirteen-year-old it was quite a struggle to manoeuvre the steaming pot and large ladle without scalding anyone.

Relieved to have managed it reasonably well, I cast a glance back over my shoulder before heading back to the kitchen. To my horror I saw a row of dark dinner jackets, all of them with dribbles of thick soup down the back, their wearers oblivious. After a great release of nervous laughter in the kitchen and an emergency trip to the loo, enough equilibrium was restored to continue serving the food, surreptitiously flicking the soup off as I went.

*****

Colm stayed living at home till he married Muireann in his late twenties. During those years, although he had a good job in RTÉ, he was completely broke. This is because most of his income went on repaying the debts incurred through some aspects of his creative initiative, Project '67. He carried that financial burden alone and fully discharged all debts.

In time, we all began to leave home, some of us returning for a period when our circumstances changed. Peter and Brídín could always be counted on to provide a stable base if needed.

The first grandchild to arrive, to great excitement, was Colm and Muireann's daughter Neasa, a golden-haired beauty who won everyone's heart. When she was about fourteen months old, the happy family joined Peter and Brídín on a boating holiday on the Canal du Midi in France. It was to be, quite literally, the holiday of a lifetime. Only a short few months later, Neasa died in a tragic accident.

I was in London when I received the telegram with the terrible news. When I returned home, everything felt completely surreal. People were calling to the house to offer their condolences. I opened the door to my Uncle Páidín, Brídín's eldest brother, who was barely past the threshold when he broke down into uncontrollable sobbing. He was recalling the death many years previously of his own little daughter who had died at four years of age. It felt as fresh to him as if it had just happened, his buried and unprocessed grief fully reawakened by the current tragedy.

At the funeral, Muireann, who was seven months pregnant, was in a state of complete shock. Colm appeared to be in performance mode. He read and he spoke with dignity and composure. Then at the end he walked towards the little white coffin and lifting it into his arms, carried it from the church.

Back at the house, where friends and family gathered, Colm continued to circulate, talking with one person after another in a display of extraordinary strength. Then as people began to leave and the clearing up began, I saw him sitting in a corner all alone, slumped over in the armchair, crushed with grief.

For Art and his wife Nuala, it was a roller coaster of extreme grief alternating with extreme joy. Their first child Oisín was born on the same day that Neasa died, causing them to experience a collision of the mysterious realities of birth and death.

Two months following Neasa's death, Colm and Muireann's daughter Aisling was born. Her safe delivery was greeted with much relief during what was such an intense time.

The Christmas that followed was a strange affair. During Christmas dinner, Peter, a man of great resilience who loved his grub, pushed aside his barely eaten meal, left the table and took to the bed. Never before had I seen him so affected by anything.

Within a year, Peter and Brídín organised a special family holiday by hiring a large boat on the Shannon.

We moved slowly together through calm waters, learning that the land that we inhabit and think we know can appear different when viewed from the perspective of the river.

We all took turns in preparing leisurely family meals which were enjoyed with characteristic family humour and banter. Except now I felt the benefit of having feisty and articulate sisters-in-law who were more than able to hold their own. On the upper deck there was a playpen for the new grandchildren and a clothes line permanently hung with cloth nappies. These had to be washed daily, by hand, down by the river bank in what felt like a timeless ritual. Gradually, the energy of the river and the solidarity of family combined to bring about deep, much needed healing.

On a very sunny afternoon when the boat was docked, I sat up on the top deck near the playpen having volunteered for babysitting duty. From below deck I could hear the sound of squealing and muffled laughter.

Then off jumped Colm and Muireann onto the quay, skipping along, hand in hand, laughing and giggling till they disappeared into the long grass. I had my suspicions about what they were up to and sure enough, nine months later, their daughter Seóna was born.

*****

When Peter retired he finally bought a boat of his own, a wooden river boat called *The Lady of Dublin*. Brídín, unlike Peter, had never been interested in sailing, but she could enjoy a river boat where she could create a cosy interior and make full use of the kitchen. They were now free to spend a lot of time on the Shannon, and the *Lady of Dublin* became a home away from home.

Brídín was very partial to, and a great believer in, the health benefits of Guinness. She said her obstetrician had told her early on that the best tonic for a nursing mother was a pint mixture of 50 per cent Guinness and 50 per cent milk to be taken at bedtime. When the days of nursing six babies were behind her, she dispensed with the milk and enjoyed a pint of Guinness before retiring for the night. This habit she maintained till the end of her life. She had never frequented pubs, not till her days on the Shannon with Peter. After a day on the river, they would dock the boat and head for the local hostelry to quench their thirst.

It was now the '70s and Brídín was about to do her bit for Women's Liberation. An issue that was exercising the women's movement was the prevailing culture of publicans refusing to serve women with pints. Any woman wishing to consume a pint had to buy two glasses which were more expensive than a pint. Nell McCafferty and others were openly challenging this practice but things were slow to change. In Dublin there was still less than a handful of pubs willing to serve a woman with a pint.

In rural Ireland, Brídín took up the cause. Given her natural frugality, she considered it the height of nonsense to have to ask for two glasses at extra cost when what she wanted was a pint. With the same assurance with which she could discipline a bold child, she reprimanded every barman she encountered and simply insisted that they stop their nonsense and serve her a pint. No one had the nerve to refuse her. She became a Shannon legend earning the title 'The Lady of the Pint'.

*****

In 1991, at the age of seventy-seven, Peter suffered a fatal stroke. He was unable to speak or communicate as the speech centre of his brain had been damaged. It was painful to wonder how much he could understand or not. As I sat by his hospital bed, desperate to make contact, I started to quietly sing what I could remember of one of his favourite Beethoven pieces for violin, 'Romance No.2 in F major'. Then up shot his arm and he started to conduct the music. The part of his brain that responded to music was intact! The news travelled through the family and later that morning Colm's daughters set up their music stands at the end of his bed and gave a musical performance—Aisling on flute, and Seóna on clarinet.

He died three weeks later, with Brídín at his side saying ' Let go, Peter. Let go. You've taken great care of us always but you don't have to worry about us any more, we're fine, we're all fine. It's time for you to go. Just go, Peter, go.' And he went.

Brídín outlived him by nearly twenty years. As she grieved she struggled with feeling she'd have to downsize to a smaller house, that it would not be right for her to be rattling around in a big house on her own. But with time she began to reconsider. What about the parties?, she wondered. Where would the family stay? And what about the piano—there would be no room for it in a small house. No. She would stay.

The family parties continued through the years, with in-laws and grandchildren greatly swelling the pool of creativity and talent. No party was complete without Brídín singing 'The Village Pump' or finishing with the Hokey Pokey. And it was simply not an option to be absent.

When Colm was working as special adviser to Michael D. Higgins when he was Minister for Arts, Culture and the Gaeltacht, on one occasion he rang to explain to Brídín that due to an exhausting schedule and some extremely pressing matters of State he would unfortunately be unable to make it to her party. She was not impressed. When I arrived at the party I was surprised to see Colm. He shrugged his shoulders and with a resigned look explained to me that he'd had a return call from Brídín telling him to get his priorities straight. What matters of Government could possibly be more important than a family party? she asked. And there he was. Now that's *real* power!

Brídín died in 2010 at the age of ninety-six. When the undertakers were removing her body, we gave her a rousing chorus of 'The Village Pump'. And when they were loading the coffin into the hearse, we did the Hokey Pokey out on the road. We divided her ashes in six, for each of us to scatter or keep. She's been scattered over mountains and valleys, in lakes, rivers and streams all over Ireland. She's also been scattered in Machu Picchu, Peru, over the native flower *Winay Wayna* meaning 'Forever Young'. And still there's more to scatter.

* * * * *

All of us made our way in the world in our own unique fashions. Nothing more needs to be said of Colm whose life achievements are well documented elsewhere in this book.

Piaras was the only suitable heir to Peter's successful businesses. Peter was very wary of offspring thinking they had an automatic right to a family business, claiming that many a good enterprise was destroyed by the second generation. Both Peter and Piaras played 'hard to get' with each other. After graduating, Piaras headed off to Australia, taking advantage of the Government-assisted 'free' passage (£10) at the time. In Australia he trained and gained experience in business management. He returned having earned his own stripes to a delighted Peter who welcomed him into the business with open arms. To a cautious and prudent Peter, Piaras proved to be a safe and capable pair of hands who creatively developed the business far beyond Peter's vision.

Art taught drama in Ballyfermot and became involved with community projects together with Dr Ivor Browne. He went on to direct theatre, as well as television, working for RTÉ and T na G. He directed amongst other things, Brian Friel's *Translations*, *The Riordans*, *Pajo's Junk Box*, and *Ros na Rún*.

Based in remote but beautiful Conemmara, in later years he focused on his independent documentary making. Notably, his last work was a documentary on the life of traditional musician Martin Hayes. He died soon after Colm, in September 2020. It was six weeks to the day.

Garry, after his travels in Europe, the Middle East and Canada, returned to Ireland with his wife Helen and their first child Tadhg and settled in County Clare. There he made his life as a traditional musician, performing, composing, arranging, producing and conducting. He also provided music for stage, film and television.

His many albums and collaborations include *Carolan's Dream*, an interpretation of Turlough O'Carolan's music and *When I was Young* with Pádraigín Ní hUallacháin and Len Graham, a collection of Irish children's songs, used extensively in Irish schools.

Gifted in woodworking, he also became a musical instrument maker.

For my part, in my late twenties I encountered and embraced Nichiren Buddhism, which caused shock to Peter and Brídín, but in different ways. Peter got flustered, saying I should not consider myself unique—that this had been trying to come out in his family for generations. His own father, who had read volumes on all the religions on the world, had concluded that it was the Buddhists who seemed to know what was going on.

Brídín, on the other hand, invited Fr Hubert Delaney SJ to lunch to put me through my paces. After an energetic but genuine dialogue, he gave her the thumbs up, telling her not to worry, and she relaxed. Both Peter and Brídín became very supportive of my practice when they saw its transformative effect on my life. They also respected my pioneering efforts to establish the S.G.I. Buddhist movement for Peace, Education and Culture in Ireland.

In my working life, after various twists and turns, I established a fulfilling career as a psychotherapist.

Bairbre and her husband Derek both worked for the family business. They followed in Peter and Brídín's footsteps by making their boat on the Shannon their home away from home. Bairbre also discovered a latent passion and talent for painting.

At the very end of Brídín's life, Bairbre wrapped her wings around her and brought her into her home where she and Derek gave her the love, care and respect she deserved. They provided her with everything she needed and more. It's where Brídín wanted to be when she passed away. For this, the rest of us are eternally grateful.

As a family, our bonds are strong. Following the sufferings and privations of the Covid lockdown era, the whole extended family met recently and spent three days together in an Irish hotel—almost fifty of us. We talked, walked, cycled, ate, argued, laughed and made our own entertainment.

Peter and Brídín's great-grandchildren, now blossoming into their lives, were there in full force—strutting their stuff, flexing their creativity and gloriously pushing the boundaries.

Long may it continue. All the way down the line.

The Other Colm Ó Briain

Derek McCann

Colm Ó Briain is well remembered and honoured for his contribution to the arts in Ireland. From the 1960s through to the time of his death in 2020 he was instrumental in the development of arts policy, theatre practice, arts administration, arts finance at governmental level, the development of arts education and understanding in schools and the Lord only knows what else.

An all-round good guy and heavy hitter, no doubt.

My contact with Colm missed all of this.

In 1975, I married Colm's sister, Bairbre, in a classic example of one partner (Bairbre) making a terrible mistake and the other partner (Me) getting lucky. At the time, I was working in Dublin city for a very large food-manufacturing factory, and Bairbre worked in the family businesses. This gave us the income and the room to have a ball (which we did) and also, over the years, allowed me to develop certain basic skills in DIY.

Now, Colm was a true-blue behemoth of the arts world, respected, admired, possibly feared in certain circles and definitely widely known in the arts and governmental worlds. However, he couldn't change a light bulb. That led to a couple of interesting phone calls.

In about 1977 Colm and his wife Muireann moved their family into a rather splendid Edwardian mansion in Rathmines, in Dublin. One Saturday afternoon, Muireann phoned our home in Tallaght, usual pleasantries, then: 'Are you free at the moment? Help! We have eight important guests for dinner in two hours. Colm went to hang a painting on the dining-room wall. AARGH! Water squirting out of the wall! HELP!'

I arrived twenty minutes later, with enough parts to sort the problem, to discover the Director of the Arts Council, in all his pomp and glory, patiently standing in his dining room with his finger on the hole in a copper pipe which really ought not to have been there. We fixed the pipe, dried up the water, re-hung the painting, packed up the tools, patted down and hugged the Director of the Arts Council and nipped off. As far as I know the posh dinner went off well.

Some years later, Colm, Muireann, Bairbre and I invested in a rental property on Dublin's South Circular Road. In buying the property we realised that it would require some considerable work to bring it up to lettable standard.

Colm volunteered to handle the construction process, managing the design, carpentry, wiring, plumbing, roofing and decoration that were required. In fairness, the project was a constructional (and commercial) success, but the process brought him to the edge of his sanity. That is to say nothing about the sanity levels of the decorators, carpenters, plumbers and so on, as Colm's vision of what he wanted really bore very little resemblance to the tradesmen's visions of what ought to be required.

The point of all this, I suppose, is that it is possible to see people in very different ways. The same man who cannot be trusted with a screwdriver can be a powerful player in the life of the State, the bumbler can be incisive, the inept can be strong and really rather wonderful.

These things are true of Colm Ó Briain.

A very fine gentleman, intelligent, well-read, articulate, influential at several levels, charming, rapier sharp as required, pleasant and friendly, competent and capable and yet incompetent and incapable in some corners of our joint existence.

I loved him, respected him, and continue to miss him.

Ar dheis Dé go raibh a anam.

The Trip of a Lifetime

Bairbre McCann

We came from a large family. I was the youngest and Colm was the eldest. An age difference of twelve years. Colm was always much posher than the rest of us for some reason but was loved as much as us all.

The age difference meant I didn't have a lot to do with Colm but there is one childhood memory that is still with me.

It was Christmas-time and all the fuss was a'going on in the house. I was the youngest and more hyped up than the rest. Not quite sure what age I was—six, seven or eight.

The usual thing was for Mam to bring me into Santa in Henry Street. But for some reason things were different this year—Colm was going to bring me into town—wow!—unheard of.

Off we set. Not Henry Street but to O'Connell Bridge. I'd never crossed the bridge without holding Mam's hand but Colm wouldn't hear of it.

We reached Grafton Street and Switzers and in we went. I had the time of my life. A real toy!

And then Colm brought me into Bewleys—Oh, what a treat.

By the time I got home I was exhausted.

THANK YOU, COLM, FOR THE TIME OF MY LIFE.

Dramsoc, UCD and Life's Diversions

Thérèse Brennan Boissé

Home—parents rushing to the theatre—Mum powdering her nose—Dad being sent upstairs to put on a tie—'You can't go out looking like that.' The excitement and preparation remain with me today. Also, later in the '50s, late night productions in the Pike Theatre with the closing down by the police of *The Rose Tattoo*—what a story.

The piano—climbing up to reach the keyboard—the piano being brought down from the sitting room (upstairs) to the living room with a constant fire, and thus the warmest room in the house behind the shop and storeroom. Recommendation of a music teacher from Cork, living in a lovely cottage beside the canal, behind the old school house. Crunching leaves underfoot going to school up the canal past Boland's Mills, Sir Patrick Dun's Hospital onto the canal banks into Haddington Road.

School—a big open fire in the classroom. Tennis courts in front of the old school building. Piano lessons; drill displays with beautiful ribbons and bells; choir practice; plain-chant lessons; school productions with lavish costumes arriving in huge chests from 'Kings'.

Yes, a very rich background to schooling. On reflection, an early childhood brimming with activities to delight a little girl trailing behind her adored older sister who appeared to know everything.

At some stage, I overheard my father exclaiming to a very nice rep that he didn't know what to do with this little person who was full of energy and obviously attracted to the stage. It so happened that the gentleman in question was Brendan Smith's brother-in-law. He recommended the Brendan Smith children's classes in Speech and Drama. So off I trotted with my loving sister into George's Street, every Saturday afternoon, where indeed I learned the rudiments of stagecraft, while Clare sat on the steps patiently waiting to bring me home. I so enjoyed the classes, making new friends, and end of term performances in the Royal Irish Academy of Music on Westland Row.

When asked to audition for a radio commercial I was delighted to embark on my first steps into the acting world as a Bisto Kid with Jonathon Bell as the other Kid. The radio commercial was recorded monthly in the Éamon Andrews Studio. On overcoming my initial shyness it became part of my normal routine for several years. Other commercials were also recorded but the Thursday morning Bisto Kids remained a constant.

Meanwhile, piano studies continued, having had a little exposure on a children's programme recorded in Portobello House for Raidió Éireann, and Feis Ceoils. Miss Owens, my loving encouraging music teacher, so wanted me to concentrate on the piano, filling my head with ideas of a possible future in performance.

Indeed, life was brimming over with extra-curricular activities.

My patient mother was persuaded to allow me to go to ballet classes in the Irish National Ballet School with my best friend Grace Meagher who was my loyal and trusted school friend from the age of four and a half. I was interested to learn about ballet but I had no desire to pursue it, just to taste it, unlike Grace who would have loved to continue to dance.

In spite of a prolonged childhood illness at the age of eight (one year out of school) my memory of that period was, I suppose, idyllic. I have a clear picture of Mum and our life-long housekeeper Nancy, sitting indulgently clapping hands in pretence at being a real live audience as I performed goodness knows what. I can hear Mum saying 'I knew her as a little girl, you know,' with Nancy exclaiming 'Really? Imagine that and look at her now, so famous.'

The horrible jolt to all this period came when I was thirteen years of age and my darling mother died. Of course this was the beginning of another chapter. My father, broken-hearted as he was, took on the care of his two girls, devoting his life to being an excellent and loving parent.

A particular aunt and uncle, Doreen and Stanley, took on the role of my mother, wherever possible, attending every performance I was ever in, while showering me with love and encouragement and bouquets of flowers. They too were huge theatre fans. Not to forget my biggest fans, my father, Clare, and Grace.

UCD 1962—the encouragement and support I received in the Holy Faith Convent helped shape me into believing I could achieve anything. Again, my father, seeking advice from friends, encouraged me to go to UCD and pursue an Arts degree as this would be a foundation for many careers.

Dublin city in the '50s and '60s appeared to me to be a rather dreary place—all grey and brown with huge poverty in the city centre. Going to Earlsfort Terrace that first morning was really stepping into an exotic world. I was intoxicated with the idea of being educated.

At seventeen I was really too young and naive. Nonetheless, I entered this high place of learning on my own, being the only girl in my class to go to UCD in that year. In those days, a Leaving Cert with Latin and your fee were the only requirements to apply for an Arts course. English and French were my chosen subjects but having a *grá* for German I persuaded Professor Cunningham to accept me into her class, although Leaving Cert German was a requisite, and I hadn't learnt German before.

Freshers' Day was a Pandora's Box with so many interesting possibilities presented by students advertising their societies. My eyes fell on Dramsoc and—click your fingers—I found myself sitting on the stairs in 86 Newman House, joining a queue to audition in the Little Theatre.

Looking back, it wasn't long before I found my place in UCD, in Dramsoc. It was certainly a coming home, a sentiment echoed by Máirín Cassidy, in the sense that the students involved in the running of the society all appeared to be so dedicated. Before long, friendships were formed with like-minded students all in the pursuit of drama while getting involved in plays, both one-act and longer productions.

This really is the pivotal point—lectures, tutorials. Studying was seemingly allotted to second place as the next production took precedence. The first time I recall seeing Colm on stage was in a play of voices, *Under Milk Wood* by Dylan Thomas, produced by Hugh Keegan and Éamon Grennan with Macdara Woods, David Jordan and Colm.

'A green leaved sermon on the innocence of men.'

I think my first role was in *Hello Out There!* by William Saroyan, produced by Jimmy O'Reilly and Donal Mooney.

The first big production was our entry to the student drama festival in 1963 under the patronage of Professor Roger McHugh. *Easter* by August Strindberg was produced by John Lynch, an insightful and talented director. The cast was Máirín Cassidy, Margaret Harrington, Colm, David Jordan and myself. To my recollection this was a highly recommended and successful production. Two other plays come to mind from 1964. The first was *Luther* by John Osborne, produced by Colm, 'assisted by Thérèse Brennan and Carol Gill' (or so the programme shows).

The second was *Ross* by Terence Rattigan produced by Patrick Cosgrave with Anthony Glavin, Jim Rogerson, Liam Hourican, Colm, Joe Lamont, David Jordan and James Macken.

At this stage Colm had come more and more to the fore in the continued development of Dramsoc. He had clearly a fully formed personality from the outset, being focused on what he wanted. Gerri Murphy feels this was evident in the self-assured persuasive manner in which he ran for director of Dramsoc. On achieving this goal he showed himself to be an ideas person, among his other talents.

His own acting morphed into directing plays. His attention to detail in every aspect of a production became the hallmark of his direction. I remember watching him place tin soldiers representing all the characters in a play on a huge table, tracing each move of every scene; then, at rehearsals, like the conductor of an orchestra, guiding the actors along with detailed precision.

Rehearsals were magical!

He inspired and encouraged each actor to achieve their best in their role, all the while recognising their ability to interpret and develop their character in great detail, no matter how insignificant this role appeared to be to them. This added to the excitement and preparation for a performance.

In 1965, undertaking the staging of *The Devils* by John Whiting was a mammoth task. It was the first Irish performance and reported as being the largest and most elaborate production ever staged by Dramsoc. It could have been controversial as there were concerns that it might not be approved by the College. Nonetheless, Colm went ahead with directing it, with Anthony Glavin, myself, and a score of other actors all contributing to making it an outstanding success.

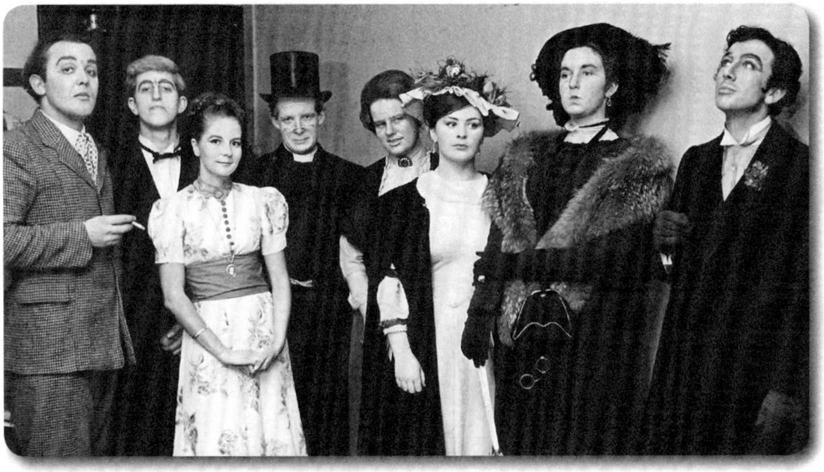

The Importance of Being Earnest UCD Dramsoc 1964. (Left to right) Martin Rogerson, Declan Burke-Kennedy, Máire McHugh, Colm Ó Briain, Mary Churchard, Noirín Ní Scollain, Una O'Dwyer, David Jordan. (Michael O'Reilly)

On a lighter note, Dramsoc staged a revue titled *You should have gone before you came* directed by Mícheál Ó hUanacháin and written by Joe Lamont and cast members Helen O'Meehan, Henry Kelly, Colm, Joe Lamont, and myself, with a number of backing musicians. It was full of fun and laughter. We took it to the Gas Company Theatre, Dún Laoghaire, for a very successful one-week run.

We were also invited to participate in a mime show hosted by Maureen Potter on RTÉ. We competed against Trinity Players, being the winners on two occasions. Máirín, Colm, Joe and myself enjoyed this so much.

Another event we greatly enjoyed was 'the Dramsoc outing' to London, instigated and organised by Colm, right down to the smallest detail. The aim of this trip was for us to experience professional theatre in London. Only a small number were interested and free to go, but it was an enormous success.

Off we went, having booked into a B&B, attending plays in the evening and films in the afternoon. At that time, art and foreign films were difficult to find in Dublin.

I recall one morning Máirín and myself being treated to breakfast in bed, delivered by Colm announcing the times of Mass as it was Sunday! The landlady was perplexed at this little group of mainly male students, with two females among them, heading off to Mass before continuing on their way.

Towards the end of our stay we treated ourselves to an Indian meal, whereupon Colm, wishing to taste an authentic Indian version, against the advice of the waiter, ordered the house specialty, which was a very hot dish. Well, his reaction was very dramatic indeed, having to suffer the consequences of his venture into Indian cuisine.

Around that time or shortly following it, Máirín produced *Endgame* by Samuel Beckett, hugely encouraged by Colm. Joe Lamont, Anthony Glavin, Henry Kelly and myself revelled in the language of Beckett.

'Nothing is funnier than unhappiness. It's the most comical thing in the world', exclaims Nell. Not sure how much I understood of that!

Máirín had written to Beckett requesting permission to enter the play in the UDA competition which went on to win the best one-act play award. Having given his permission, he was delighted to hear of the award and sent Máirín his congratulations.

Caligula by Albert Camus, directed by Donal Mooney, also won the best production award, with Macdara Woods and Jim Rogerson.

These productions and many more were made possible by the assistance and dedication of many other students. The following all spring to mind: Gerri Murphy, Annie Power, Tony Owens, David Binchy, Elizabeth Walsh, Helen O'Meehan, Declan Burke-Kennedy, Kieron Murphy, Joe Lamont, Sinéad Lamont, Piaras Ó Briain, Máire de Valera, Biddy Roden. Of course, many more were involved.

The Little Theatre on the top floor of 86 is where the rehearsals and one-act plays took place. A warm reception and cheery atmosphere greeted us from the porters. I admit to looking back through rose-tinted glasses. Of course there were times when things did not go according to plan and huge obstacles had to be overcome, but with Colm at the helm nothing was too difficult to achieve or too high to aim for. Many members before 1962 and after 1966 went on to carve out careers in the world of theatre and the arts.

Colm was still the director of Dramsoc when *The Glass Menagerie* by Tennessee Williams, directed by Hugh Keegan with Macdara Woods, and *The Maids* by Jean Genet, directed by Richard Callanan with Elizabeth Walsh, were performed.

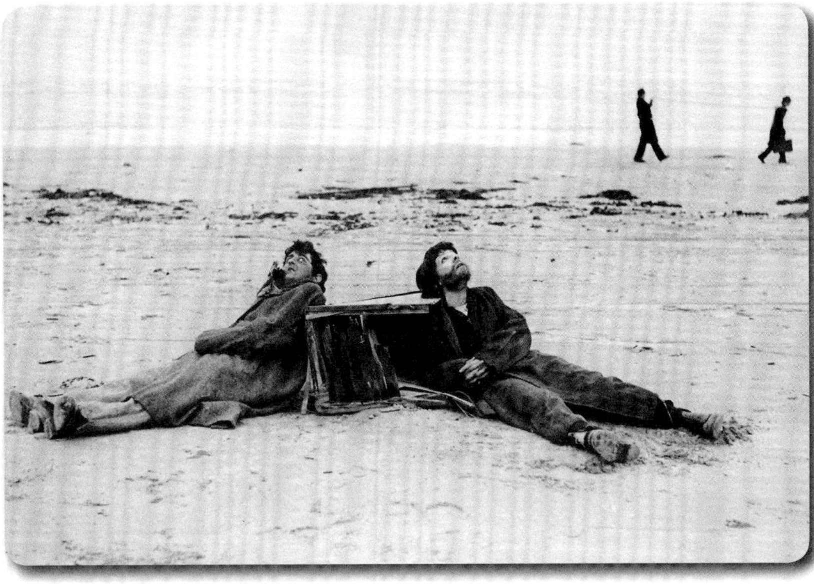

Waiting for Godot: Kieron 'Spud' Murphy as Estragon and Colm Ó Briain as Vladimir.

In 1966 Colm persuaded Máirín to produce *Waiting for Godot* by Samuel Beckett in the Gate Theatre under the auspices of Dramsoc. At this stage, Richard Callanan was the director. This was a huge undertaking as finances had to be secured. The unenviable task was aptly managed by Piaras Ó Briain. According to *The Irish Times*, Colm's Vladimir was of McGowran quality! What an accolade. Peter Walsh, Chris O'Neill, John O'Conor and Kieron Murphy also gave excellent performances. Máirín received huge praise for her direction, being regarded as being as good as any professional.

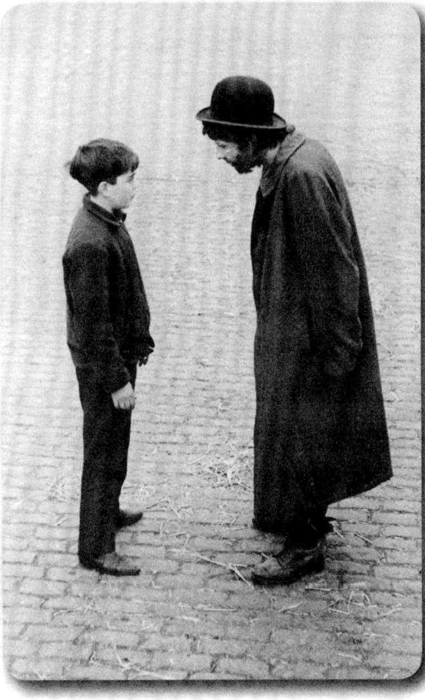

Vladimir and The Boy.

For myself, I can safely say my time in Dramsoc gave me the confidence to taste life further afield.

Following a year as an exchange language assistant in a Gymnasium in Nuremburg, I spent two to three years teaching English in the Rudolf Steiner School which was part of an educational system which embraced, broadly speaking, teaching and learning through music, art and drama. I really loved it there and fitted in so well.

However, having been urged by Joe Lamont to return to Dublin as there was an interesting development taking place in the Vocational School system, embracing a communicative approach to teaching, I found myself working with Anton Trant, the principal of Ballyfermot Vocational School. His interest in this area attracted a host of diverse people to join his staff. It wasn't theatre in the strict sense as I had known it but it wasn't teaching in Ireland as I had envisaged it.

Among the staff, I was very pleased to work with Art Ó Briain, Colm's younger brother. He had a great empathy for the students and interest in education in the real sense of the word. Helping out with plays, I saw this in action with shades of Colm, his total dedication to their well-being.

A certain time in Dramsoc certainly influenced my life and I'm sure others alike. I can only express my huge gratitude to Colm and all the truly wonderful people I met through Dramsoc.

The Early Days of the Project Arts Centre

*Colm Ó Briain**

In September 1966, having obtained the degree of LL.B., I decided that I would build on connections I had made with the Gate Theatre. I asked Jim FitzGerald to direct my production of *Who's Afraid of Virginia Woolf* at the Gate. Jim announced our plan as 'making a statement which is unprecedented . . . trying to establish a theatre based on an aesthetic, rather than box office, to make a theatre where you have room for every cross-fertilisation process there is . . . a theatre in which everything happens all the time.'

Unfortunately, I did not succeed in acquiring the rights to *Who's Afraid*, and I had still rented the Gate Theatre. So we had to come up with another plan. With Jim as director, we put on three one-act plays—Pinter's *The Lover*, *The Tiger* by Murray Schisgal, and a play by James Saunders called *Double Double*, in which all of the actors played two roles. I engaged Bob Carlisle who was a full-time actor, and three students from Trinity Players, Gillian Hanna, Dinah Stabb and Ian Milton, and they, along with myself, were the cast for the productions.

The sessions were moderately successful in terms of box office takings, and excellent from a critical perspective. And since we had the theatre every day, all day, for three weeks in November/December 1966, we decided to extend the use of the theatre for teach-ins, seminars, readings, music sessions and an exhibition of art. We called the endeavour Project '67, and that was the beginning of the Project Arts Centre. The artists who put in work to the exhibition included John Kelly, Michael Kane, John Behan, and others, who all then continued their connection with the Project.

One of the events was a seminar on theatre for young people, and the interest it generated gave rise to the establishment of the National Association of Drama for Young People. Two people who came to the seminar were Grainne O'Flynn and Anne Leonard, who was later Anne Gill, and my friendship with them has lasted all our lives.

* Compiled by Muireann Ó Briain from press and personal interviews

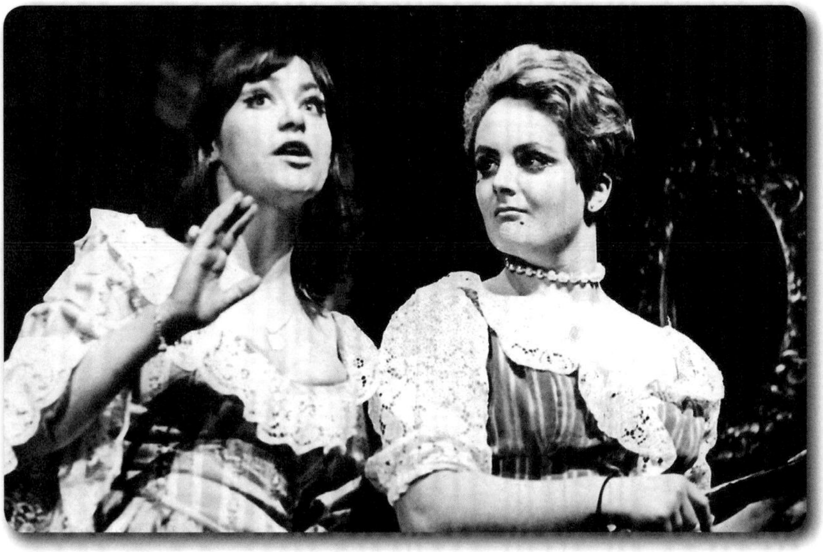

Dinah Stabb (left) and Gillian Hanna in *Double Double* by James Saunders, a Project '67 production at the Gate Theatre, 1966.

Another seminar we held was on the topic of censorship. Edna O'Brien, whose books were banned in Ireland at the time, was the guest speaker. Edna had declared that she was carrying her books when she arrived at Dublin airport from London, and they were seized by the Customs officials. The press was tipped off and queues to get in stretched around the corner. 'Fionnuala Flanagan and T. P. McKenna read extracts from O'Brien's work to a packed meeting, highlighting the absurd situation whereby words that could be freely spoken in public could not be read in private.' (*Irish Times* obituary of Jim FitzGerald 20 Sept. 2003)

When I did the accounts at the end of the Gate season, despite our moderate success at the box office, we had lost money on all of the activities. It fell to me to pay off the debts, which I duly did with a loan from the Bank of Ireland.

My father had some space in Tuck & Company on Abbey Street, and I asked him if I could use it to set up an exhibition space there. The rooms were on the second floor. I showed them to John Kelly and John Behan, and they were enthusiastic, so we set up the Project Gallery there in July 1967. It was launched by Donogh O'Malley, the charismatic Minister for Education, who died within the following year. It is a sign

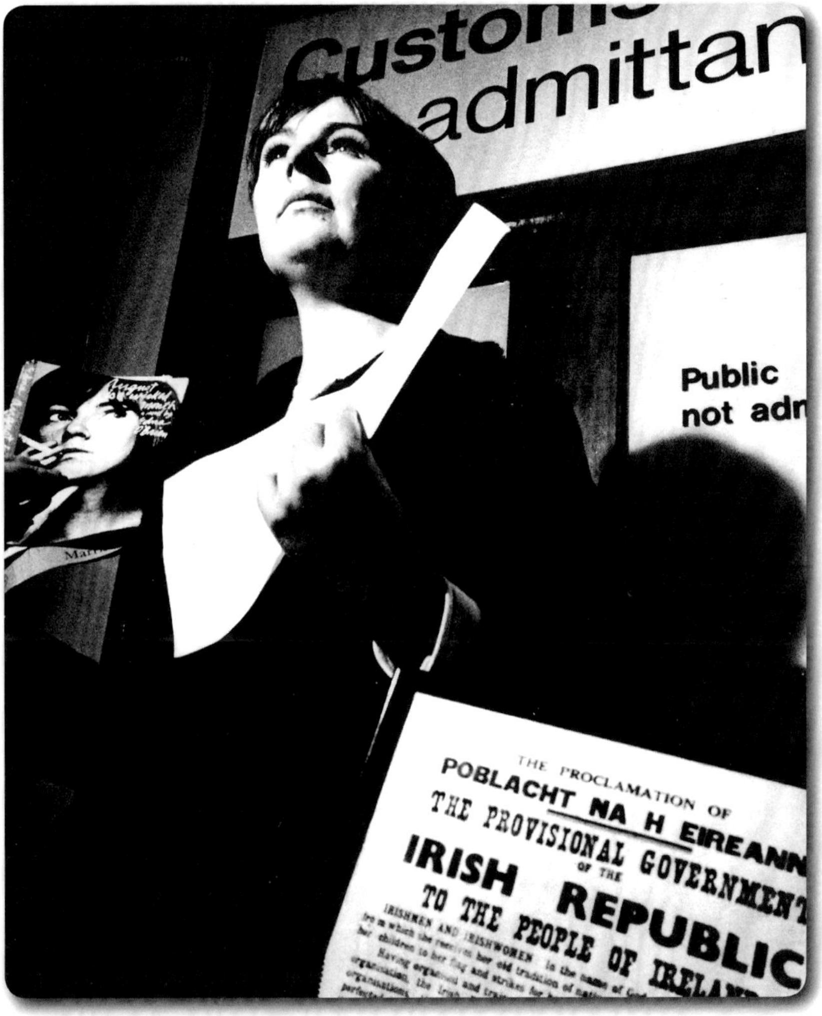

Edna O'Brien speaking at the 1966 Gate Theatre seminar on censorship organised by Project '67. When she arrived at Dublin Airport from London, she declared that she was carrying her books, then banned in Ireland, and they were seized by the Customs officials. The press had been tipped off and queues to get in to the seminar stretched around the corner. (Fergus Bourke)

of our self-importance that we were not fazed by inviting a government minister to open two rooms on the second floor of an engineering shop as a gallery. James McKenna, one of the group, was outraged at us inviting an establishment figure, and resigned from the Project committee in protest. He later rejoined.

On 15 July 1967 an editorial in *The Irish Times* criticised a 'self-appointed group' for an 'attack' on the Arts Council. In a letter to the editor, dated 17 July 1967, I wrote:

> In thanking the two commercial firms M/s Tuck & Co. and Phillips Electrical for their help in establishing the Gallery, I sought to emphasise the importance of their support, since so far, no positive support was forthcoming from the Arts Council. This was the only mention of patronage whether from the Commercial sector or the Arts Council, made on that occasion, yet your leader asserts that 'an exhibition in Dublin recently was used as an opportunity to attack the Arts Council for not setting up an Art Centre.' The facts do not warrant the accusation.
>
> Again, assuming that the 'self appointed group' which would 'exercise a central control over all the Arts' refers to the musicians, poets, novelists, theatre people, painters, sculptors, and educationalists from the primary, secondary and university levels, working together in Project '67, your statement is a serious inaccuracy totally at variance with the aims set out during the Project '67 season last Nov/Dec, with the statements made in our press release of last week, and with the observations expressed by the Minister for Education when he launched the Project Gallery.

By the time of the gallery's first anniversary we had extended our space, and were able to maintain a permanent collection as well as the exhibition space. We identified our group as Project '67, a collaboration between the National Association of Drama for Young People (NADYP), and artists involved in a movement towards the ultimate goal of establishing an Arts Centre which would provide facilities for all the arts.

The artists who collaborated with the Project Gallery included Michael Byrne, John Behan, Charlie Cullen, Michael Kane, John Kelly, James McKenna, Eamon O'Doherty, Paul Funge, Michael Bulfin, Constance Short and Lee Gallagher. Jonathan Wade, who tragically died in a motorbike accident in 1973, aged only thirty-one, was a very important influence in the early years of the Project. When we would have great rows on the committee, Jonathan would be the pragmatist and the down-to-earth person.

My father,who was colour blind, appreciated sculpture as an art form. He became friendly with John Behan. In later years they set up the Dublin Art Foundry together, with capital investment from Peter who also did the book-keeping for many years. This was the first art foundry in Ireland; previously the sculptors had to send their work to Britain to be cast. Being able to do it in Ireland meant that it was much less expensive and supervision of the work was much easier. When Peter was retiring from all his activities in his seventies, he offered the foundry to me. But I was unsure that I could manage the responsibility at the time, as I was quite busy in my own career, so I turned it down. He handed the enterprise over to a workers' cooperative of the foundry workers instead.

To set up the Project Gallery, I approached Phillips Electrical in Clonskeagh, and the company donated lighting equipment suitable for an art gallery. Constance Short, Patricia Phillips, Suzn Sweetman and some others helped to manage the space. In later years, Rachel Doyne and Rhoda McManus were secretary and manager. We were extremely fortunate in having the active collaboration of several wonderful women who worked for small wages and kept the organisation going.

We tried to benefit young and emerging artists by showing their work; in fact we wanted to bring artistic works around the country to factories and school canteens. We managed to bring exhibitions to Cork and to Dundalk, and formed a collaboration with Ballydehob West Cork Pottery, and the Manchester Community College of Connecticut in the USA. We brought an exhibition of graphics by some Dutch artists to Dublin, and our first anniversary was celebrated with a group exhibition of works by Irish-based artists. We also promoted business involvement in the arts, an idea which was a forerunner of the Business to Arts organisation which I established many years later.

In late 1968 my father moved Tuck & Co. from Abbey Street to Upper Gardiner Street, and the Project moved across the street to the Metropolitan Hall, thanks to one of my father's business colleagues, Eric Webb. The bigger space allowed us to put on theatre productions, and we also held poetry readings. We even wanted to make films, but that never happened. The visual artist, Lee Gallagher, joined our organisers once we could do theatre, as he was also writing scripts for drama.

The Arts Council supported us to some extent by providing grants against losses on exhibitions. Mervyn Wall was the secretary to the Council at the time; there was no full-time director. Exhibitions by Michael Kane and Michael Byrne as well as group exhibitions were supported. The Council also purchased some of the artwork for its own collection. Artists who exhibited their work in individual or group shows included Brian Bourke, Jan de Fouw, John Behan, Fergus Bourke, James McKenna, Charlie Cullen and Michael O'Sullivan.

Bord Fáilte also supported the Project, giving it a three-year grant in 1968, probably through the assistance of T. J. O'Driscoll, who was Bord Fáilte's director general at the time. His daughter, Sarah Horgan, was an artist who in later years co-founded the Black Church Print Studio, and was friendly with many of the Project artists.

The finances for the Project were run through a personal account of mine with the Bank of Ireland, and were later operated through its own business account. We were all pretty amateur in the matter of running a business. There were no computers in those days, and letters were typed individually. Many people wrote to us by hand, and we had a lot of difficulties in managing overseas sales, of which there were a few. In 1969 we decided to form a company under the Companies Act so as to have a professional identity. Eventually, in December 1971, Project became a non-profit company limited by guarantee. What we created was a new type of company, that later became the norm for arts bodies that wanted to limit their liability while being non-profit associations. Donal Barrington (who later became a judge of the Supreme Court) prepared the Articles and Memorandum of Association.

In 1972 the Project had to leave its Abbey Street premises. We found another premises on South King Street, alongside the Dandelion Market, a space now occupied by the Stephen's Green Shopping Centre. We were there for a couple of years until moving to Temple Bar, into an old printing works. This move was a real turning point for the Project. Ann O'Driscoll was the person who made the link for us with the accountants who were acting for the printing company, which had vacated a building on Essex Street at the back of the Olympia Theatre. We managed to buy the building, which gave Project a stable base for the first time, although of course the financial worries always remained.

After I was employed by the Arts Council in 1975, I resigned from any involvement with Project, as it would have presented me with a conflict of interest. However, in 1989, the then chairman of the Project, Dr Joe Long, asked me to rejoin and to assist in finding a new home for Project.

In 1991 we celebrated twenty-five years of Project. Many of the people who had put on drama or art exhibitions there showed up. It was great to see them, and so many of them who had done well. Project had provided an environment in which artists of different disciplines intermingled, where the managers understood and respected artists, irrespective of the financial value of their work. It functioned on the basis of the principle that artistic endeavour deserves to be nurtured.

I remained as head of the Venue Development Unit (Venue Development Officer) until 1993, working in collaboration with Temple Bar Properties.Ultimately Project got a new building on its site in Essex Street in Temple Bar, where it remains to this day. Rooney O'Carroll were the principal architects.

There was a huge amount of work to be done with architects, quantity surveyors, theatre furnishers, lighting designers, theatre designers, sound engineers, planners, etc. It was quite a complex matter, because there were a number of ways in which the site could have been developed, but each option carried serious financial implications, and each option also either addressed or could not fully address the original idea for the Project which was for a multi-art venue. Initially the hope had been that the Olympia site and the Project site, which are back-to-back, could form one major site, but unfortunately this could not be ultimately agreed.

Temple Bar Properties was the company for the development of the whole of the Temple Bar area as a cultural quarter, and it was that company that assisted the redevelopment of the Project, and also assisted the provision of new premises for a number of cultural entities, including The Ark, the Black Church Print Studio, Music Base, the Photographic Centre and others. Laura Magaghy was the manager, and Patricia Quinn, who later became director of the Arts Council was the cultural director. I had great admiration for both of them. The new Project building was opened in June 2000.

In 2001, Project was in serious financial difficulty again, and I was part of a group, including Joe Long and Kieran Owens, which worked to restructure the organisation and its activities so that it might become sustainable. There were huge liabilities which Project had no means of paying, and it was at risk of being wound up. The board had to find a new director and ended up micro-managing the Project for many months. During these months, the board managed a massive re-structuring of the legal entity to a company which more fitted the times. I headed the membership review committee which proposed the changes that had to be made. Eventually the problems were resolved and Project survived—again! Around the time that we were resolving the problems (June 2002), Willie White was appointed as artistic director and really the Project never looked back after that. He was inspirational.

Project was Ireland's first arts centre. It provided an alternative venue to the established exhibition and theatre centres; in this way it achieved its objective of working in the interests of all artists, especially those struggling for recognition. People like Neil Jordan, Gabriel Byrne, Jim Sheridan, Peter Sheridan, and Liam Neeson did experimental work in the Project Theatre. Artists like John Behan, John Kelly, Manus Walsh, Michael Byrne became established through their involvement with the Project, and then made way for younger artists. Project was a magnet for talent and to this day remains an adventure. I am proud of my contribution. I stuck with the enterprise through thick and thin, to make sure that it could become a serious institution in the Irish arts world, and that is where it arrived.

Two Score and a Leaking Roof

Constance Short

From a booklet produced to mark Project's fortieth anniversary, 2006

When I bump into Rhoda McManus, Rachel Doyne, Colm Ó Briain, John Kelly, John Behan, Anne O'Driscoll, Peter Sheridan, John Stephenson, Tim O'Neill over the years I have such a strong surge of affection for them like long-lost relations that it always shocks me into the realisation of how strong my bond with Project is. I know we had plenty of screaming matches (do you know that theatre people don't know what a diary is for and they think that the lavatory bowl is for stuffing cotton wool make-up balls into!!) but all that has long faded.

The Gate event was over when I met my future husband in the Studio Club in Molesworth Street, well actually Schoolhouse Lane. John Behan told me about their dream of finding a building that would house all Arts disciplines and be for all the people. I loved it. Soon we were all cleaning out a couple of rooms over Tuck & Co., generously given by Colm's parents, Peter and Brídín O'Brien. There would have been no Project without them. The doors of Project both there and across the road in the Seaman's Mission were kept open by their financial help plus Colm's RTÉ salary and the sale of works of art, especially John Behan's lithographs.

We lived on little to keep the money in Project's account. For me this was to be a socialist alternative to the capitalist system. This view was not shared by all; some saw Project as a way in, a stepping stone. That came later and was more manifest when we moved to South King Street, and my involvement ended until, with Rhoda, we put on the male nude show in 1975, I think, at any rate in East Essex Street. And more recently with Grant Watson, Niamh, Willie et al, who keep 'my' spirit of Project alive and well. I feel, they make me feel, as though I had never left.

No money; we lobbied for grants, we lobbied for a renewed Arts Act, for a fairer distribution of government funds for the arts. All our actions came from experience. We learned on the job. We discovered that it wasn't possible to make art and run an Arts Centre. Project remains open to new ideas; it's in good hands. The independent artist will always remain in the margins of society. Happy 40th Birthday, my darling.

14 November 2006

Conjuring Colm

Fiona McHugh Sankey

Colm appeared to me out of the blue one day in Paris.

Was it in that misty autumn of 1968? No, more likely it was spring, the spring of '69.

A telephone call preceded him. The voice was brusque. A crisp, officious, no-nonsense voice, a voice telling me instantly in tone alone there was absolutely no point in arguing with it. It belonged, I now believe, to someone who worked with Colm, a co-worker on some committee or other. Or someone's secretary—possibly his own. Colm Ó Briain, the voice announced, was on his way back to Dublin from somewhere else. He would arrive at my place in the Latin Quarter on such and such a date, at such and such a time. He would stay overnight and leave in the late afternoon of the following day.

The news caused my heart to nosedive. Colm Ó Briain? What earth was I going to do with Colm Ó Briain, I asked myself, glancing around my very basic living space.

It hadn't been that long since I'd been lucky enough to land a job in the Paris office of the Irish Tourist Board—or Bord Fáilte, as it was then known. Luck had played a part too, in helping me find not only this apartment on the rue Soufflot, but also my agreeable flatmate, Nancy from New Jersey. And now, surely, surely, I argued with myself, as I wrestled with panic, my luck seemed to be still holding, didn't it? Because Nancy was away. So at least that solved one major problem: I could stick him in Nancy's bed for the night.

But still, much as Nancy and I appreciated the apartment, clearly it'd be way too shabby for the likes of Colm Ó Briain. Wouldn't he be far better off in a hotel? Our place wasn't just faded and pokey and entirely *derrière-garde*. It was on the seventh floor of an old, rather down-at-heels building. No lift. A consistently cranky concièrge. And the light on the stairs worked on a begrudging timer, that plunged one into darkness as soon as one set foot on the first few steps.

The fact of the matter was: I hardly knew Colm Ó Briain. His name was familiar because he was a friend of my elder sister, Muireann. They'd studied law together in College. But although I'd never met him, in the pantheon of college personalities his was a name to conjure with—a name uttered with awe by those in the know at UCD's Dramsoc, where I'd volunteered on and off as an Arts undergraduate.

He sounded intimidating. A great man for an argument, people said. Articulate, people said. Flamboyant. Impatient. Avant-garde. Not one to suffer fools gladly. I was already aware of his talent as an actor and director. But more than that—he seemed someone with a brilliant mind, a profound grasp of the law, and the courage to question it. Surely to God a man of his distinction would be much MUCH happier in a hotel?

But No. Clearly, I didn't know Colm Ó Briain. Up, up he came, on the appointed day. I had stepped out onto the seventh-floor landing in anticipation of his arrival and could hear him, bounding up the endless uncarpeted stairs, bags banging from both shoulders. He dropped them as soon as he saw me and to my surprise threw his arms around me in an open, generous hug. That hug is what remains with me still, like a light, when I think of Colm. No matter how troubled or complex life later became, he was capable always of flinging his arms wide and drawing you to him with unconditional warmth and affection.

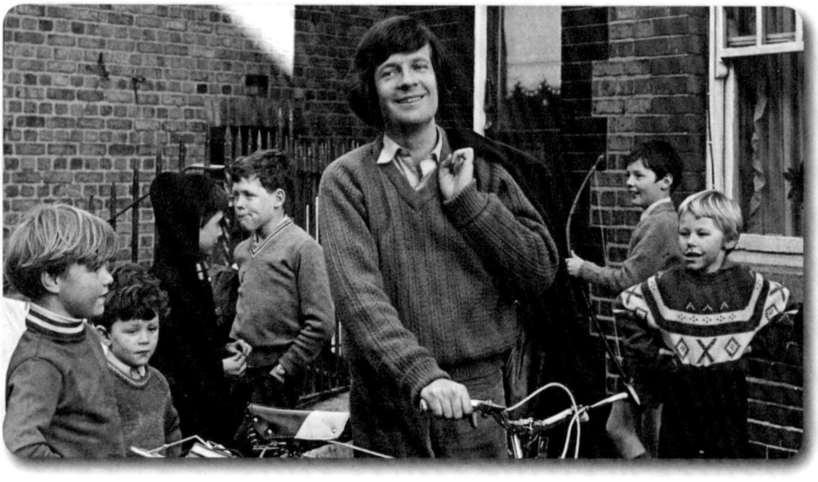

Colm Ó Briain plays a sixteen-year-old in RTÉ's drama *The Glory and the Dream* 1971. (RTÉ)

I don't remember much of what we did during Colm's brief visit to the City of Light. Paris, it seemed to me, was astoundingly resilient. Barely a year had passed since the student uprising of May '68, when young people had poured into the streets in protest and workers had flooded out of factories to join them. All over the student quarter, where I was now living, trees had been uprooted and formed into barricades. Students had torn up cobblestones to hurl at *les flics*. And the police responded with tear-gas, brutal beatings and arrests. The pavements became battlefields. And then, within less than two months the turbulence subsided. By the time of Colm's visit, the barricades had vanished and bistros were back.

Quite possibly I may have suggested a walk in the Luxembourg Gardens which lay just down the street from the apartment. Colm might have preferred to check out what remained of Zola or Voltaire, or Rousseau, or even Victor Hugo, all of whom were languishing in the Panthéon, a stone's throw from where I lived. But to reach the Panthéon one had to pass the Commissariat de Police, which at that time occupied the building almost next door to ours. Given their reputation, French police made me nervous. The way they stood around, too close to the entrance to my apartment, fingering their truncheons, eyeing passersby. The way they parked their long, predatory vans all over the sidewalk and street, and often sat inside them, playing cards, uniformed and armed, as if itching for trouble.

Most likely we spent most of our time at one of the crowded cafés on the Boulevard St Michel, where the smell of tear-gas had long been replaced by the heady aroma of garlic, cigarette smoke and talk.

Strangely, where conversation was concerned, Colm didn't seem in the least bit interested in discussing the labour strikes of '68. Nor in probing the causes of May's widespread student unrest. Nor even in analysing the character of Charles de Gaulle. He had, it slowly emerged, only one topic on his mind: my sister, Muireann.

His voice warmed when he mentioned her name. And he mentioned it constantly. He wondered aloud whether Paris might be just the right place to find exactly the right gift for Muireann? Was I aware Muireann had an excellent brain for the law? That she was a consummate organiser? Efficient and tireless, capable of working her fingers to the bone? Muireann was reliable and responsible. A marvellous knitter. Muireann liked to cook. And bake. Muireann spoke a dizzying number of languages. Why, Muireann even knew some Irish.

Every word he spoke was true. My sister was genuinely an amazing person, gifted in countless spheres. As I listened and agreed with him, it gradually dawned on me: Colm Ó Briain was no mere casual friend and colleague of my sister. Whether he knew it or not, this man was head over heels in love with her!

This discovery surprised and relieved me. My sister had already known too much sorrow. A year or so earlier she'd been just about to marry her quiet, gentle, Belgian fiancé, Francis Cornut. The invitations to the wedding, due to take place in Dublin in 1967, had already been sent out, when Francis, who had been doing his compulsory military service in Belgium, collapsed, due to an improperly diagnosed heart condition. Muireann, barely into her twenties, flew to Brussels to be near him in the hospital where he was scheduled to have by-pass surgery. She lived in the apartment they had found together, the apartment they assumed would be their home after they married. And there she stayed, alone, for several months, her distress and worry over her fiancé's condition compounded by having to hold down three jobs, in order to pay the rent on the apartment.

Francis appeared to be recovering after the operation. But something went wrong. He was twenty-six when he died. Muireann was twenty-three.

She had to face not only the loss of the man she most loved in the world, but also the heart-breaking task of dismantling the apartment and all the hopes it embodied. If anyone deserved to be happy, it was the sister I dearly loved.

Granted, Colm seemed the complete opposite of the reserved, perceptive Francis, whom I had met only once, and had taken to instantly.

But Colm was here now, in the present, brimming with life and energy.

Clearly he loved Muireann, and admired and respected her. If all went well, I reflected, if Muireann felt the same way, they might marry. I realised I hoped they would, that I really liked this excitable, warm-hearted, interesting man and would be delighted if he became a member of our family.

All did go well.

They married in the autumn of 1970, a quiet, family wedding in the chapel behind the Pro-Cathedral. Muireann reflective in a simple ivory-coloured dress, a Tudor-like head-piece framing her heart-shaped face. The groom sported a rich brown velvet jacket and brown flowing tie—similar in style to one favoured by W. B. Yeats. Afterwards we all went back to Glenart, our parents' house, to celebrate with champagne and cake.

By early 1971 Colm and Muireann had found a house in Dublin's inner city and were in the process of renovating it. While the work was being done they moved into Glenart. Around that same time I was planning to emigrate to Canada in the hope of finding work in educational television.

It was a bleak day as I was leaving for the airport, a desolate wind blowing in through the open basement door, where my heavy suitcase stood. The uncertainty of what I was doing weighed me down.

In Canada the War Measures Act was still in effect, invoked in response to a series of terrorist attacks, the kidnapping of a British trade official and the murder of a Québec Labour Minister. The crisis was over. But how would its consequences affect ordinary life?

Would I be able to get a job? Would finding a convenient place to live be difficult? I knew by her silence my mother disapproved of what I was doing. Would I be welcomed if I had to come home again? As if he sensed my growing apprehension, Colm stepped towards me and wrapped me in a reassuring hug, wishing me luck, telling me I'd be fine. It was a gesture I've never forgotten.

As it turned out, I did find a job in Toronto with an organisation called the Ontario Educational Communications Authority, a name later changed to the simpler TVO, or TV Ontario. I also met my wonderful husband, Tom Sankey, a playwright and singer from Wisconsin. Muireann and Colm came to visit us after we married. I remember Colm impressed us all by cooking a wonderful veal Stroganoff. It may have been his culinary swan song, because I never knew him to cook another meal after that!

On our first visit to Dublin together, Tom and I were invited out to dinner by Colm's parents, who emanated the same warmth as their eldest son. Indeed we discovered that not just Colm, but all the O'Briens were enormously welcoming and inclusive.

We also discovered that Colm's younger brother Art Ó Briain, a passionate theatre-lover, had already, by some fluke, met Tom's younger brother Brien Sankey, years before Tom and I even knew each other. As a student from the States, Brien had been travelling with his guitar through Europe, and in a Dublin bar chanced to strike up a conversation with Art. When Art heard Brien's last name he asked if Brien had ever heard of Tom Sankey, whose play, *The Golden Screw*, had won an Obie Award in New York. Discovering Brien was Tom's brother, Art immediately asked him home for a meal.

It might have been on this same trip home that Tom and I went to see a children's play Colm was directing in one of the Dublin theatres. Written by Robert Bolt, *The Thwarting of Baron Bolligrew* tells a comical tale of knights and dragons. I'd read excerpts from it but never seen it performed on stage. The theatre was packed with children bursting with laughter and delight. Grown-ups too seemed to love it. It was brilliantly done, a theatrical tour de force, one of the most memorable productions of a children's play I've ever seen.

Where his own children were concerned, Colm seemed to have an emotional umbilical cord binding him to them in a close, instinctive way. Living in another country as I did, I missed most of Aisling and Seóna's childhood and growing up, something I still regret. But on several occasions when we were all together I noticed this deep attachment.

One instance returns vividly when I think of him. We were at the airport in Toronto. The whole Ó Briain family had been visiting. By this time both girls were adults and we were all gathered to say goodbye to Seóna, who was returning to New York, where she was then living. The fact he was going to have to part with his youngest daughter seemed

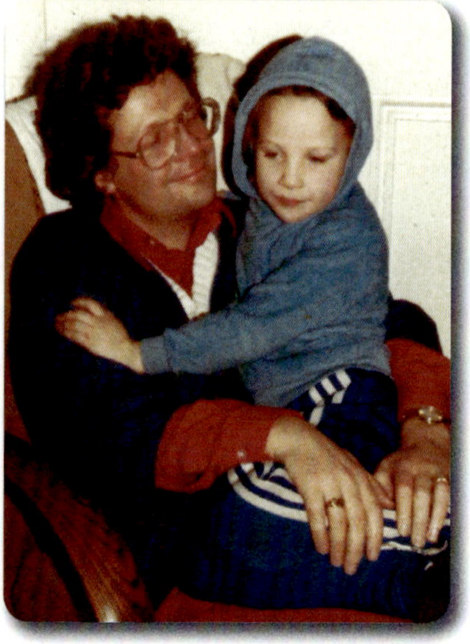

Colm Ó Briain and his youngest daughter, Seóna, 1979.

to hit Colm suddenly. While everyone else stood around talking, he moved away and sat down. Tears in his eyes, he seemed as if on the verge of collapse. as he repeated incredulously, over and over, how long it would be before he set eyes on Seóna again.

Gradually, during his seventies, as his health eroded and deafness grew, Colm began to withdraw. His energy dissipated. For hours he would sit silently on the sofa, the radio on, but unheard; a book or newspaper in front of him, often unread.

But without fail, a magical change would occur when one of his daughters or grandchildren approached. Then, as if conjured, the real Colm, Colm of the generous heart and genuine smile, would reappear. The light would return to his eyes as, standing, he opened his arms wide to embrace those he loved.

Married Life

Muireann Ó Briain

The one consistent description I could always give of my life with Colm Ó Briain was that it was never boring. There were hard times, and good times, times of joy, times of dreadful sorrow, and times of exhaustion and loneliness, but I could never say that I was bored. Which, with one day short of fifty years married life together, I consider a serious achievement.

We were friends from our college days in UCD, both of us studying for the BCL, and then attending the King's Inns. I ended up a year behind Colm, because I went to Nice for six months in 1966 to study European institutions, and Colm stayed in Dublin and did an LL.B as well as his Bar finals. There were some of his productions in UCD with which I helped, mostly as the 'props person' or the 'gofer'. But I missed out on all of the Project '67 adventure in 1966, the multi-art events at the Gate Theatre, which led to Colm setting up the Project Arts Centre, and I never saw the Beckett *Waiting for Godot* show earlier that year, in which he played the part of Vladimir, which won rave reviews, and was Colm's first public success as an actor.

In 1970 Colm's suggestion that we marry came as a complete surprise to me. I had come back from Geneva where I had been working for Seán MacBride at the International Commission of Jurists, and Colm had come back from Scandinavia and Russia where he had been exploring children's television. He telephoned and asked me to meet him for a drink. We met in a pub near Busáras, as a midway point, he being from the north side and me from the south side of the city. He presented me with a lovely little red shawl from Sweden, which was the first surprise, as, apart from his twenty-first birthday, when I had given him the complete works of Shakespeare, gifts had never featured in our relationship.

As we shared our experiences of living at home again after time abroad he said he was thinking of buying a house. He had some savings from his work in RTÉ, and was getting freelance work in the theatre.

I told him that my mother was also trying to persuade me to buy a house, as I now had a steady job and some savings too from my work in Geneva. That was when he suggested we buy a house together, and followed that suggestion with a proposal that we marry. And we did, a couple of months later.

My mother, Patricia (Kelly) McHugh, was quite surprised at the decision. I think she expected me to marry an accountant, or at least someone who had a steady—preferably well-paid—job. She did find it very frustrating that Colm never sought her advice on anything to do with interior design, for which she had a remarkable talent. He, on the other hand, completely respected another of her talents, which was for the provision of good food and hospitality to all-comers. Patsy did enjoy having a famous son-in-law, and in her later years invited Colm to join the Art Committee at the Royal Hospital in Donnybrook which took over the curation of the amazing art collection there, which she had established and managed for many years. My father was a respected academic, Roger McHugh, with a great love of theatre. So he and Colm got on very well and always had plenty to talk about. Roger was not particular who I would marry; I think he was just glad to have his eldest child settled. The good conversation was an added bonus.

The relationship between Colm and myself was one based on mutual trust. I knew him to be a good and kind person, and I also knew him to be interesting and extremely intelligent. I'm not sure what he thought of me except that I was reliable and supportive. He wanted to settle down and he wanted a family. Three years before this I had been bereaved when my then fiancé, who was Belgian, died within weeks of our intended marriage. I needed a safe harbour.

With our combined savings and a cash wedding present from Colm's father, Peter, we bought a little house on Lower Rutland Street in the centre of Dublin. We could not have raised a mortgage because Colm did not have a reliable income, my income didn't count because I was a woman, and the address in the heart of Dublin City was not considered 'suitable'. After buying the house with all our cash, we had very little money, and did a lot of the work on the house ourselves. Colm was quite handy, having been taught by his father how to paint, hang wallpaper, and clean surfaces. During periods when he was not working, he did the cooking. If he was working, it was in the theatre or in television.

Being part of the Ó Briain family was wonderful to me. Father, mother, five siblings, all—with the exception of Peter, my father-in-law—speaking Irish at home. All moved happily to English when outsiders, like myself, were present, but never addressed their mother, Brídín, in anything but Irish. I did a Gael Linn course in those early days, and even enjoyed occasionally pointing out the correct word for something for which Brídín had used a version in *Béarlachas*. They were amazing people. All talented, opinionated, talkative, musical. Sunday dinners at No. 46 Castle Avenue, Clontarf, or holidays on the Shannon, or special celebrations when songs and verses were written and performed, stories were told, old favourites were chorused—every occasion was full of wit and wisdom. If Colm was doing a 'party piece' it was always hilarious, but as he got older, he performed less within the family, and preferred to enjoy watching his children, and his siblings and their children, provide the entertainment.

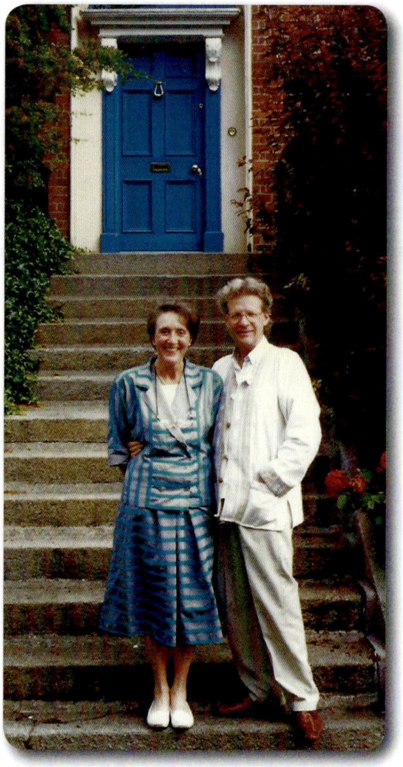

Colm and Muireann in front of their family home in Rathmines, June 1996.

What was completely different between our families was that while my siblings all emigrated, with the exception of my younger sister, Niamh, who never married, none of Colm's siblings remained out of Ireland after they married and had children. The Ó Briain family simply got bigger and bigger as the children married and started their own families. Even after Peter died, Brídín refused to 'downsize' from the family home because there had to be a place where Christmas and important events could be celebrated, a temporary home could be available, and the parties could accommodate all comers.

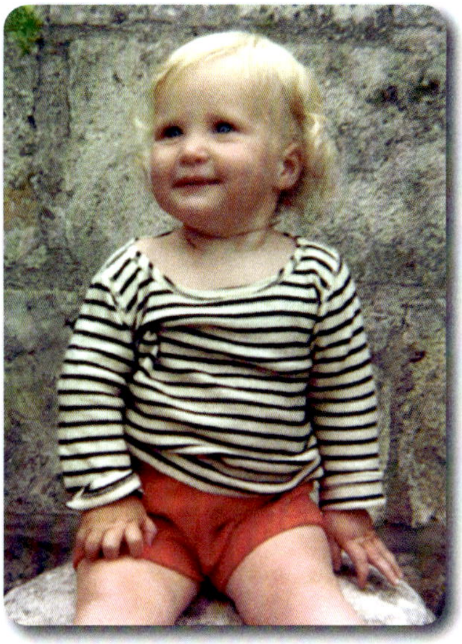

Colm and Muireann's first child, Neasa, in 1973, aged fourteen months.

It was the family that carried us both through the worst time of our married lives, when our first child, Neasa, died by accidental drowning, aged just sixteen months, in August 1973. Without his father's wisdom and kind support I don't think that Colm would have been able to manage his own sorrow and to help me through the guilt and horror I suffered from our child dying accidentally in my care. His resilience was extraordinary. He buried himself in his work, he was tender and caring at home, and a few months later our second daughter, Aisling, was born. Her birth allowed everyone to focus on a small new life. Oisín, the first child born to Art, Colm's brother, and his wife Nuala Hayes, had arrived a few months earlier, the day after Neasa died. Now there were two grandchildren for Colm's parents, and a new one for mine. We had another daughter to care for, and all the engagement that a new baby brings to a household. Aisling was followed eighteen months later by Seóna.

I continued to be surprised by Colm all our married life. It was not for nothing that he was frequently referred to as 'a Renaissance man'. He had a capacity to absorb information and retain it, and there were many times I would listen in amazement as he came out with facts and figures on some obscure subject; it was like opening a filing cabinet and finding the exact information that was relevant to something under discussion, without understanding how he ever came by that information. He read widely, but it was politics and history that interested him more than novels or poetry.

Whatever Colm was engaged with, he gave it all his energy and commitment. The work would take precedence over everything else, to the extent that during much of his working life he spent little time at home. In fact, I could guarantee that as soon as we went anywhere on holiday, Colm would become ill. His reserves would be depleted, and his immune system compromised; the first week of any break he would spend in bed, recovering. Short holidays were therefore a waste of time, and summer holidays would have to be not less than two weeks in duration in order for him to enjoy at least one of those weeks.

His religion was very important to him, and he rarely failed to miss Mass on a Sunday; but he did not engage in discussion about religion or religious observance. He was even critical of the obligatory saying of the Rosary upon which his mother had insisted for many years. He told me how his colleagues were mystified if they discovered his adherence to the Catholic faith while holding what they considered as Marxist views. The Irish language was also important to him, and he had even made it a condition of his marriage proposal to me that our children would be brought up speaking Irish. Our children were indeed brought up with Irish as their first language, and they always conversed with him and, following the family tradition, with his mother, through Irish. I was let off the hook when language became more complicated as they got older.

Colm didn't speak about me or his children to others; there were many colleagues who did not know he was married, and our girls never knew what to tell their teacher or friends if they were ever asked what their father did. The only sacred time as a family was Sundays. Sunday newspapers were banished as they took up too much time, and late and long Sunday breakfasts became *de rigueur* as the children got older. (It used to make me laugh in later years when Michael D. would call up on a Sunday, furious at something that had appeared in a Sunday newspaper and want to speak to Colm. I first had to find an excuse to hold him on the call, as Colm would still be in bed, and then Colm would have to throw on some clothes, rush out to buy the offending paper, and later call Michael D. back with soothing words about the piece, and how it really wasn't worth bothering about.)

Colm had strong opinions on how the children should be educated; no private school would be considered. He also insisted that they had to learn to play a musical instrument. But it had to be an instrument they could carry—so the piano was out. A piano did eventually enter our house, and was much appreciated by both girls, but that was when Colm was directing an opera, and needed to work out the score and his stage moves. I used to joke that Colm took all the important decisions about the children, like where they would go to school, while I took the unimportant ones, like how they would get to school, what they would eat, what time they went to bed, who would supervise their homework.

I was the one mostly at home when they were around, and they also had the daily presence of Mrs Darcy, from the inner city, who minded them when I was at work. It was Peter who had introduced Mrs Darcy to our lives; one of her sons had worked for him, and he knew the whole family. 'Darcy', as we called her, was like a third grandmother to our girls, utterly loved and treasured.

In 1975, when Colm was appointed as the first full-time Director of the Arts Council, our lives changed utterly. This time he was surprised, as indeed were many of the artistic community intelligentsia. He had seen the advertisement himself, and wondered about applying, but was cautious about how an application from him would be perceived. In his efforts on behalf of Project he had often been critical of the Arts Council. But he did apply, and the rest, as they say, is history. From my point of view, we could now consider looking for a bigger house—one with a garden instead of a small yard, and one where Mountjoy Square would not be the only available nearby green space to which I had to push a pram.

In 1976 we moved to that bigger house, in Rathmines, with a dauntingly large garden. Colm decided on the house; he fell in love with a small stained-glass window on the landing return, and came back out to the car where I was sulking and fed-up with house-hunting and hungry children, and announced that we would buy it. We did buy it, but it was in such a sorry state that living there with small children was quite difficult for many months. Interestingly, we would still not have been given a mortgage by any building society, as Colm's new job was only a contract one. His father's bank stepped in and gave us a twenty-year mortgage, on the strength of Peter's reputation as a businessman, and his significant accounts with the bank.

Colm decided everything about the renovation and decoration of the house. I was allowed only to choose the colours and décor for my study and for the tiny laundry room. That was it. He even designed the kitchen, having acquired a certain amount of expertise from a television programme he had directed. The garden had to wait several years before we could afford its makeover, but again, Colm was the one who decided how it would look. I was allowed a vegetable plot at the back.

The eight years Colm spent at the Arts Council were exciting and productive. Colm felt supported by his team in the office, and by his council. He had enormous respect for the arts practitioners on the council. He also admired the chairmen he had, from Professor Geoffrey Hand, to Pat Rock, to James White. Pat Rock was particularly important in reinforcing the need for a business attitude to the management of the arts, and indeed to one's personal life, such as ensuring a pension for one's later years. James White, beloved of everyone in the arts world, stood up to Taoiseach Charles Haughey, who wanted Colm fired from his position because he was becoming too dominant in relation to artistic policy.

While Colm did become a national figure during his time as Director of the Arts Council, there was nothing he ever did for personal credit or gain. He was not interested in being famous; he was interested in making things better in the arts and for arts practitioners. In order to make things better he was willing to promote his own image, and enjoyed whichever part he was playing. He caused quite a stir one time by giving a lecture while dressed in a bathing suit and a pair of goggles. He had me working the slides he had arranged for the lecture, and had given me the list of prompts that would indicate where I was to change each slide. Of course I was completely befuddled with getting the order of each slide done correctly and I had no idea at all of what was the intent of the lecture, and I still haven't a clue. All I do know for sure is that there had to have been a serious intent, because otherwise it would not have been done.

From Colm's own point of view, his biggest achievement in the Arts Council was the creation of Aosdána. The one thing in later years that infuriated him was the attempt by Anthony Cronin to claim Aosdána as the sole creation of Charlie Haughey and himself. Since his days of involvement with Project, a living concern for Colm was the situation of artists, many of whom found it extremely difficult to make ends meet. While he himself had rarely been out of work, and he was always the consistent earner in our family, he felt for artists like Jonathan Wade or Manus Walsh who had to take up work outside of their art to feed their families, or who depended on the income of their working spouses. Aosdána grew from the initial extension of the Arts Council's bursary scheme, known as Ciste Cholmcille, with the support of the Council. Colm developed all the structures and procedures for the new organisation, and then made a proposal to government for its funding. Luckily, the proposal fitted exceedingly well into the then Taoiseach Charlie Haughey's own vision, and so came to fruition. For the remainder of his life, Colm was very proud of Aosdána.

Colm left the Arts Council in 1983. It was entirely his decision, and he had no 'Plan B'. He simply believed that one should not remain too long in a job which required creative thinking. He was quite prepared to go back into freelance work, and by that stage I was earning sufficient money so that he knew there would be food on the table. Then, within a day or two, the job of General Secretary of the Labour Party came up, and I said that he was always talking about politics, and here was a chance to actually do something, so he applied, and got the job.

Dealing with politicians, and aspiring politicians, was quite a change. He worked terribly hard in setting up structures and training to enhance the image and the effectiveness of the party. But although he had the support of many people within the organisation, the trust of some of the main players eluded him, and he resigned after about two years. As John Horgan wrote about Colm: 'He arrived in the Labour Party like a breath of fresh air—his perennial irreverence and good humour was a tonic to us all, especially in the most difficult of times. It was, indeed, unfortunate that so much of his extraordinary talent had to be expended in fire-fighting and damage limitation, at some cost to his ability to deploy his radical and creative gifts.' He did remain a member of the party all his life, and in later years managed the election campaign of Eithne FitzGerald to the Dáil with huge success and worked on Michael D.'s campaign for the presidency.

Immediately after his resignation as General Secretary of the Labour Party, Colm was at work in the Gate Theatre with Barry McGovern, Bobby Ballagh and Gerry Dukes on a production that would become *I'll Go On*, based on the works of Samuel Beckett. That show became a major hit at the Dublin Theatre Festival in 1985 and remained popular, with revivals in Ireland and tours in several countries. Colm continued to receive small royalties as director for years, but he was never offered work again at the Gate Theatre. He had fallen out with Artistic Director Michael Colgan over the payment of expenses when presenting the show at the Barbican in London, and had the temerity to issue proceedings against the Gate for the money he was owed. Michael paid the overdue expenses, but that was the end of the working relationship between the two. In a way it was an example of how stubborn Colm could be over a principle, to his own detriment. If he had overlooked the insult at not being paid what he was due, he probably would have continued to get work at the Gate.

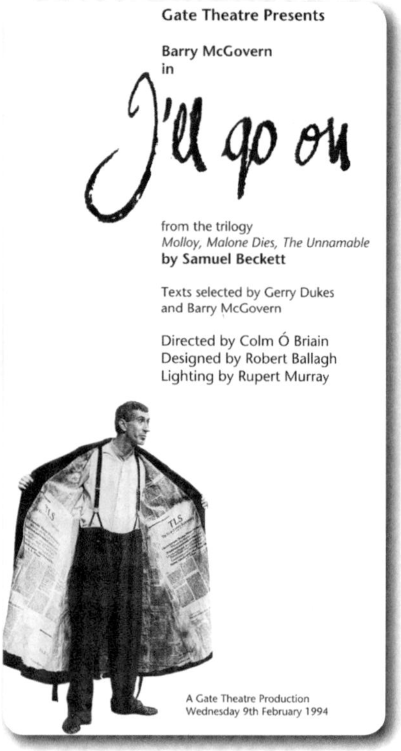

From the programme for the 1994 Gate Theatre production of *I'll Go On*, based on the novels by Samuel Beckett.

Between 1985 and 1993 Colm was freelance. He made television programmes, established the Arts Administration course in UCD, set up Cothú, now known as Business to Arts, chaired book awards, helped with Labour Party elections, and worked on the Millennium programme with Dublin City Council as well as on Dublin City of Culture 1991. There was always something going on. He asked me to help him with the management of the Celtic Film Festival in Gweedore in 1990. I was in charge of arranging the accommodation for the attendees and otherwise being a 'gofer' again, like back in our College days. Apparently the event was a big success, but I only got to see one of the 43 entry films, and even that was standing at the back of the room before rushing back to other duties. Colm expected anyone working for him to work at least as hard as he did.

Then in 1993 the Labour Party was in coalition with Fianna Fáil and Michael D. Higgins was appointed Minister for Arts, Culture and the Gaeltacht. He appointed Colm as his adviser. Colm was in his element in that position. He was a huge admirer of Michael D., and of course he had experience over all the aspects of the arts—from theatre to visual arts, to literature, to television, to arts administration; Colm had opinions and experience on everything the new minister was taking on. He thoroughly enjoyed the challenge; here was a chance to influence legislation, and set up new structures.

One early highlight of the years in government was the repeal of Section 31 of the Broadcasting Act. The section had empowered the Government to forbid the broadcasting of material by simple Order specifying what was prohibited. Broadcasters working on political programmes lived in fear of it. Colm had been working on the RTÉ programme *7 Days* when the Section had been used to restrict his and producer Muiris MacConghail's work; it gave him particular satisfaction to be involved with its repeal.

There were many other initiatives undertaken during the years from 1993 to 1997, through two coalition governments. The marvel for Colm of working with Michael D. was that both of them were totally passionate about the primacy of culture in State policy, and between them they developed an extraordinarily cohesive relationship. Every issue that came up was addressed in both intellectual and practical terms. They realised that no government can legislate for talent, but that with Michael D. as a government minister they could create or support the frameworks in which talent can develop and flourish.

By the time Labour was out of government in 1997 Colm was in his fifties. It was back to freelance work. But the mortgage was paid, the girls were raised and starting to earn their own money, and the urgency had gone from earning a living. He did miss the excitement and productivity of working in government, but he was also at a stage in his life when he was able to appreciate leisure and not having to be always in a rush and in demand. Going to the theatre or to a concert or to an art exhibition was no longer 'part of the job', it was pleasure. It was in those years that I was offered a job in Thailand, and I said to Colm that it was my turn at an interesting career. He was completely supportive of me, and remained in Ireland while I spent three years abroad. He took responsibility for ensuring the well-being of my widowed mother during that time; I was the only one of my siblings living in Ireland (Niamh having died in 1995) and I could not have taken up a full-time job in Asia otherwise. He also enjoyed visiting me there, and we did some wonderful travels together in Thailand and in China.

In 2002 Colm was persuaded by his good friend Niamh O'Sullivan to apply for the position of Director of the National College of Art and Design, and was appointed. He remained as Director until the age of retirement in 2008. As usual he gave his all to the job, but he no longer had the same energy to fight for what he felt had to be done. The major problem was space at the Thomas Street premises, and Colm felt that the only option was co-existence with another academic institution. With Philip Nolan, then Registrar at UCD, he started to explore the possibility of moving the College to the UCD campus. However, with a change in board membership and under a new chairman, Joe Mulholland, there was not sufficient support to develop the idea. There was even antagonism to his exploration of any such option. Colm became more and more depressed as time went on. He could have resigned, but was too stubborn to do that, and was just determined to leave with as good a pension as possible by staying until he was sixty-five. After retirement, he never again wanted to enter the NCAD premises. I don't think he had any understanding of how many staff admired and appreciated him, and of his achievements during his term of office. He was tired, and he felt a failure.

For the next few years Colm stayed at home. He read and he listened to music. He enjoyed the company of his grandchildren, particularly the two who lived in Dublin. His memory started to deteriorate, but he never forgot any arrangement involving them, and I would find him waiting for them outside their school or on the road where he knew they would pass. He was content. He even liked the idea of travel, and looked forward to the day when I would retire from my job as the Legal Manager at St James's Hospital—a day which I kept postponing. When we did travel he did not have much energy, so that it became a challenge to decide what he would be able for, or work out how to do what he was interested in doing. Yet he was still able to surprise me. In December

2019 we went on a cruise on the Garonne for Christmas. Colm wanted to go to Midnight Mass in the cathedral at Bordeaux. To my horror, 'midnight' really meant midnight. But Colm stood through two hours of a ceremony without flinching. It was his last Christmas. He died in July 2020 of heart failure, one day before our fiftieth wedding anniversary.

I consider myself a fortunate woman to have married such an interesting man, and to have been the support that encouraged and enabled him to achieve what he did in his life. In his later years he would tell me that marrying me was the best thing he ever did. Compared to his life achievements, that sentiment is clearly an exaggeration. I don't think Colm ever fully realised the extent and value of those achievements. For the most part he had enjoyed whatever job he was doing, and always set himself goals, which, when they were achieved, gave him great satisfaction. But then he moved on to the next job, and new goals. He did appreciate that he had been looked after and supported in whatever it was that he took on, and that home was a safe place to be.

Colm's first love was the theatre, and if a long-term career as an actor had presented itself, he would have wanted to follow that path. But he had realised the difficulties of supporting a family as an actor, and instead took whatever opportunities presented themselves, using them to the best of his abilities. As things turned out, those abilities were legion, and Irish society is the richer.

In all our fifty years together, we were blessed by the support of our families, and especially the encouragement of Colm's parents, Peter and Brídín O'Brien, and the wider Ó Briain family. My mother-in-law used to be congratulated on how her four daughters-in-law loved her, and she would always reply that the best thing was that they all loved each other as well. Despite much arguing and disagreement over the dinner table, there was a consistent love and admiration of their parents, and a mutual respect between Colm and his siblings, so that action and decision-making in any family crisis was shared between them, with the support of their spouses. It was, and remains, a wonderful environment of which to be a part.

The White Box
(For C. and M.)
Hayden Murphy

Twin sides of a wound
Are stitched by the tinyness
Of the body gone cold
In the white box between them.

They were stitched
Into lonely parenthood
By the change in a season
No human, animal or god provided;

A season of whiteness;
Not a time of invigorating snow
Or green licked lilac, but the time
Embraced by the cold white ribbon

Round the white box. Here is love
Wrapped up by an impudent innocence.
Outside white hands, laying fingers
On cold pennies shrouding white eyes,

Caress adult fears with their icicle touch
On the throb of a parent's pulse.

Bird of Paradise

Lelia Doolan

It's a rather formal affair; wine and morsels of nothing much. The men stand around in grey suits, the odd dark blue; the women sway on heels and black with maybe a flash of glitter. Sober, you might say. Waiting. The staff circulating in black and white. The rise and fall of murmuring chat. Not everyone present knows for what chore, for what guest appearance, for what impressive blather they are waiting. Ah dear God, how long more . . .

Wait, though:

What's that? A flash of dark green velvet, a flowery handkerchief, a head of bobbing curls, a glint of silver-rimmed glasses . . . what colour are his pants today?

Thank God. Rescue. Talk. Laughter. Maybe a minor altercation on some esoteric frivolity.

The corduroys gleam crimsonly!

Who is this bird of paradise?

A Northsider *le neart gaeilge*!

A wha'?

Himself, *is ea*.

About to express a considered view on the fatuous goings-on of capitalism, culture, art, the play, the environment.

Brains to burn. A steady temperament. Courage.

Gas.

In 1973, when I was Artistic Director, I asked him to come to the Abbey to co-ordinate training and to direct plays, taking over from Roland Jacquarello who had been directing for a year and having challenges with the more 'settled' older actors. Roland's sartorial eccentricities were more pronounced than Colm's, concentrating more on the long frayed flapping black overcoat and a Raskolnikov demeanour. He was a sweet and gifted director, wholly engaged in and loyal to the work in hand and to his insights. Too original by half.

Ah, well . . .

Colm has been weaving in and out of my mind, a fellow flashing past with determined ideas, UCD, the early Project—a staging post in those days, in Abbey Street, not far from your actual Abbey.

He came over to say hello, in relatively pedestrian garb, head to one side, enquiring. We'd lean on the window-sill of the rehearsal room, looking down on The Flowing Tide to consider the state of the world and eventually he stayed to direct and think and talk and plan about new ways of refreshing the work.

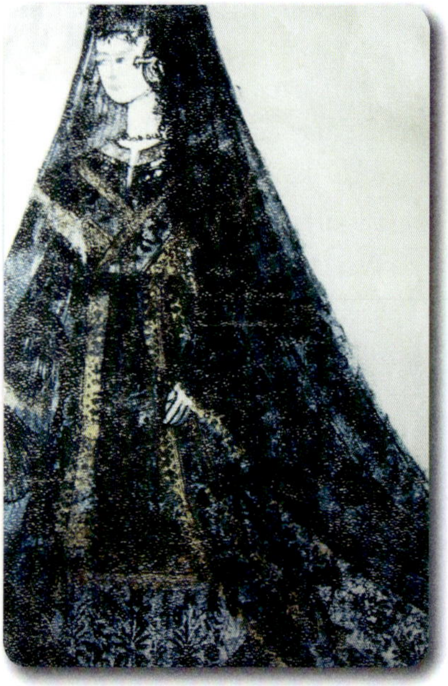

Colm Ó Briain directed a production of Federico Garcia Lorca's *Blood Wedding* at the Abbey Theatre in 1974. The wedding dress for The Bride was designed by Alastair Livingstone.

There was much to repair and renew: a board of old men were in charge, keepers of the flame; actors of old; old poets and writers, the still influential and decidedly opinionated Ernest Blythe; a decent chairman in Micheál Ó hAodha. There was a valuable company, some of them tired from want of new work and praise; writers in need of enthusiasm and support, a band of young eager actors, ready for challenges.

The board (I often wonder at their foolhardiness in taking me on at all, especially after the great Hugh Hunt) agreed to my proposal, with John Slemon, at their August 1973 board meeting, to have Colm as a new recruit. He was to be a play director and 'to act as co-ordinator of training and workshop activities for the acting company'. Pat Mason, our newly appointed voice coach, (and later distinguished Artistic Director), was to partner him in the workshop activities. Colm had already directed (courtesy of RTÉ) Pádhraig Ó Giollagáin's Irish-language musical, *Johnny Orfeo*, in the Peacock. This was a lively piece of gyrating and warbling by Jimmy Bartley and cast, on which Colm decided to involve me as fairly hapless assistant. He was in full form and the production had verve and energy, whatever about narrative coherence in the original script.

We had made a plan to replace the Abbey School of Acting/Junior Theatre Workshop (later called The Young Abbey) by offering one-year apprenticeships in technical and acting departments to half a dozen young hopefuls. The idea was that they would be modestly paid and could form working relationships and see, and at times, assist, in the work-in-progress.

We also chose a Theatre-in-Education group to work in schools—Joe Dowling, John Olohan, Garret Keogh, Angela Harding, Marianne Hardie and Siobhán Cleary. They did impressive work then—as they do to this day.

Colm was easy to work with; a fastidious, punctual being; stimulating, enquiring, always creative, seeking agreement and solutions. Rarely fussy. A good listener, head to one side, fixing you with a level stare.

I recall all these good and comradely qualities and the enjoyment of our encounters but they are as nothing to my really strongest remembrance of those days with Colm in the Abbey. That haunting remembrance is of the death of Muireann's and his beautiful child, Neasa. She was a small bundle of delight. The image of Colm carrying the small white box down through the gathering at the church is one that I will never forget.

Colm came to say that he and Muireann must go away together for a time. They found the courage to keep going—and Colm to direct Crístóir Ó Floinn's *Mise Raifteirí an File* later in the autumn.

With characteristic generous thoughtfullness, it was Colm who presented a complete set of Beethoven's work to me shortly after that—as a gift from the company, he said. My departure from within those storied walls was greatly lightened by the high pleasure of listening to Ludwig's majesty in Belfast in the months that followed, and by the good memories of working with him and the other good spirits there.

It was also a great happiness to run into him from time to time and to see his astounding and ground-breaking work as Director of the Arts Council, the first of his long-term gifts to the world of Irish art, education and politics.

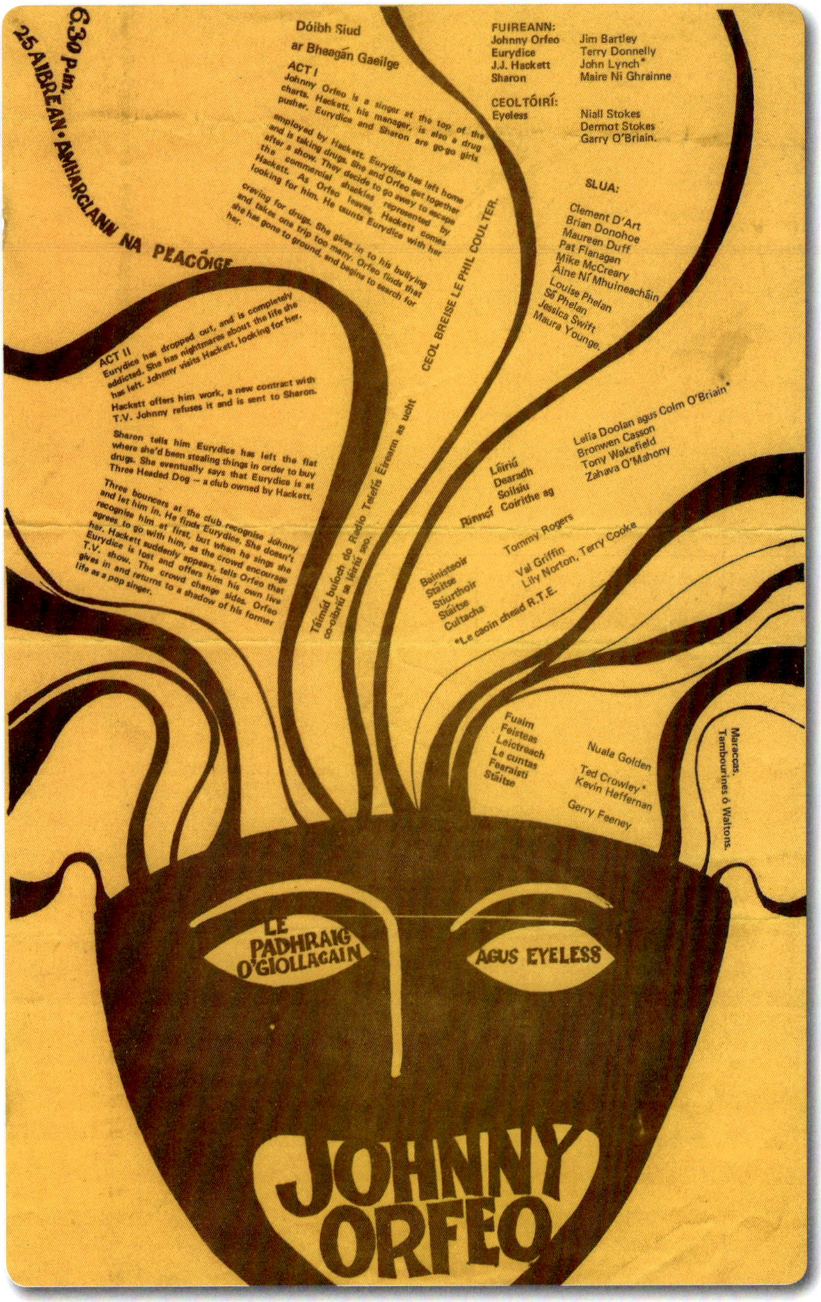

Poster for Pádhraig Ó Giollagáin's Irish-language musical, *Johnny Orfeo*, directed by Lelia Doolan and Colm Ó Briain, music by Eyeless, with Dermot and Niall Stokes and Garry Ó Briain, the Peacock Theatre, 1973.

I recall a phone call one fine spring Saturday, late morning in 1993, sitting in the kitchen with some family and friends.

It was Colm.

'Would you accept to be the chair of Bord Scannán na hÉireann?'

'What? You're joking!'

'I'm not'.

'Ah, Colm . . .'

'What do you say?'

'Hold on a minute. Can I think about it?'

'Yes, until two o'clock.'

'Ah, now.'

'I'm in Wexford. Michael D. wants to announce it this afternoon.'

Two o'clock! Chaos in the Saturday kitchen! I thought about Tiernan MacBride, Louis Marcus, the many great warriors who had campaigned in the long wars for a native film support. I called Tiernan. And David Kavanagh, director of the Irish Film Institute. Go on ahead, they generously said. We went ahead. Ructions, new talent, the wonder of new Irish story-telling on film . . . Colm grinning mischievously to himself.

We only had one major disagreement—he as special adviser to Michael D., mighty Minister for Arts, Culture (which included part of the Environment etc.) and the Gaeltacht, me as one of the Burren Action Group, opposing the Government's choice of Mullaghmore as the location for their interpretative centre. He was a Dub and simply 'didn't understand that the centre should be located in a village', I declared. Did I actually hear myself say: 'Sure once ye've begun the rape ye might as well continue, is that the policy?' However shocked, he remained calmly unflapped—and did not demur when our argument won the day.

One of my last happy memories is of meeting himself and Muireann, arm in arm, looking content, welcoming and debonair as ever.

But I'll never forget the bright flair and the panache!

Recollections of RTÉ

Ted Dolan and Tish Barry

Ted Dolan

I first encountered Colm in the late 1950s. We both went to school in Belvedere College, we were both about the same age, we were both Northsiders. I grew up in Drumcondra and he not too far away. Although close in age, I was a year ahead of him, so we did not really bump into one another until the school theatre productions were cast. There had always been a strong tradition of drama in Belvedere—a Gilbert & Sullivan operetta every year after Christmas and a play just around Eastertime—and we both took an active part in these endeavours.

Colm was truly gifted, and I well recall him playing Mad Margaret in *Ruddigore* as well as Sir Joseph Porter KCB, in *HMS Pinafore*. However, his tour-de-force was playing the role of Lady Bracknell in *The Importance of Being Earnest*. That cast also included John Bowman as Ernest, Niall McCarthy as Gwendolen, Colm's brother Piaras as Miss Prism and myself as Canon Chasuble.

Our paths diverged for a few years, Colm to UCD and the beginnings of an active public life, while I resentfully toiled in the dark satanic mills of Jacobs' biscuit factory. I joined RTÉ in 1965 as a studio trainee and then Colm joined as a producer/director in 1966/7.

He instantly made an impression. Television was still a relatively new medium and everything was up for discussion and debate. There was an energy about the place and Colm, never one to shirk an argument, would engage with anyone, at any time, on any subject, in the coffee bar, office or control room with passion and vigour. What I particularly remember from those early days was, that no matter how polarized the positions, Colm had the ability to move on without the slightest trace of rancour. This was not a characteristic all that common in RTÉ.

I have few memories of his work in children's programmes. Around that time, I had become a floor manager, working mainly on drama and entertainment and frequently away from Montrose and so I remember little of *Brogeen* or *Motley*.

However, in 1969 I was assigned as floor manager to the current affairs programme *7 Days* and consequently saw at close range how highly Colm's contribution was valued when he joined the team. The programme's young and energetic editor was Muiris MacConghail and it was obvious that a special professional rapport existed between himself and Colm. They shared many of the same political views and cultural aspirations. Importantly, they both possessed abundant energy and courage.

The late 1960s was a time in Ireland when the revolutionary generation was fading from the scene and they were being replaced by those cast from very different clay. The power of the institutional Catholic Church was largely unchallenged and, although we did not know it then, the Knights of Columbanus had insinuated themselves into positions of power and influence throughout the State sector, not least in RTÉ. It was against this background that when the opening bars of Sibelius' *Finlandia* crashed out twice a week after the News, the powers-that-be at the time gritted their teeth and snarled. They pounced after a *7 Days* programme on illegal money-lending caused a stir. A full tribunal of inquiry was set up to investigate, not the criminal underworld or the hardship it inflicted on communities, but the television programme itself that had the temerity to reveal the extent of the scandal. The inquiry was vigorously defended (Muiris was represented by John A. Costello, no less) and dominated the news cycle for weeks. In the end the programme's researcher, Janet Moody, was unfairly pilloried and bore the brunt of the judicial odium. It was a defining moment in Irish broadcasting and the fall-out lasted many years.

In 1970 I was appointed producer/director and, after a spell in Religious Programmes, I found myself the following year working in the TV Feature Department under its new head, Dick Hill. I was asked to start up a new business programme *Enterprise* which I felt was hardly playing to my strength; instead I had wanted to start up an arts programme.

By way of compromise, I was allowed initiate a monthly programme *Aurora*, provided that I also produced the weekly *Enterprise* (two for the price of one!). I knew from the start who I wanted to present the arts programme; the problem was that Colm was a full-time producer with *7 Days* and, although it was clear he would love to do it, he felt that Muiris would not allow it. To our surprise, after much sucking on the editorial pipe, Muiris agreed to a limited release, one day's filming a month with the proviso that it would cause minimal interference with the 'day job'.

One of the first programmes we made coincided with the International P.E.N. Conference held in Dún Laoghaire and it highlighted the difficulty of such an arrangement. It featured substantial interviews with two writers, Heinrich Böll and Richard Hughes. Hughes was a bearded man of the sea, who had sailed his yacht, crewed by his daughters, all around the Mediterranean. He had written *A High Wind in Jamaica* and the short novel *In Hazard*, described as being the most authentic maritime writing since Conrad. Böll was the embodiment of post-war Germany. He had served as a conscript in the Wehrmacht during the war, had been wounded and imprisoned. He began writing after the war as a prominent exponent of the 'literature of the rubble'. He later lived on Achill Island and his *Irisches Tagebuch* for many years formed the romantic German view of Ireland. The day before we were due to make the programme, Colm confessed to me that he had never heard of either of them. I hastily provided him with copious background notes and, like a good senior counsel, he absorbed the brief overnight and conducted two magisterial interviews. Böll received the Nobel Prize for Literature a few months later; the honour was no doubt as a result of the interview, as we said to each other at the time, with as straight a face as we could muster.

The programme in this series that will be forever associated with Colm was the one we made on Seán Keating. We filmed him in the painter's studio in Rathfarnham and Colm took him through his early years in Limerick ('a medieval dung-heap'), as a pupil and devotee of Orpen, of his time as an iconographer of the revolutionary period, of his social-realistic phase that chronicled the construction of Ardnacrusha. Then, more confrontationally, Colm conducted an interrogation of Keating's role as a long-serving President of the Royal Hibernian Academy and a defender of ultra-conservative values in general. By any yardstick, I thought that the interview had gone well but Colm instinctively knew that there was more, much more. He said, 'keep the crew for the day, try and get it for tomorrow as well and let's take him down to ROSC.' I was a bit doubtful, thinking that we had achieved what we had set out to do, but

Colm convinced me otherwise and so in the afternoon we took ourselves down to the RDS. What followed was a classic piece of television.

The exhibition itself, ROSC 71, featured paintings and sculptures by the leading figures on the world scene. As well as major European works by Gerhard Lindner, César, Niki de Saint Phalle and Josef Albers there were also works by Rothko, Stella and Oldenberg from America. It was a snapshot in time of international cutting-edge art.

The camera followed the two men into the large exhibition space. It was as if both had been cast for parts in a drama. Keating's small frame bristled with indignation. His eyes blazed beneath beetling eyebrows as he dismissed one work after another as either incomprehensible, meretricious, or just plain bad. Colm, playing the young aesthete, pointed out the merits he saw in the works and then, playing the part of toreador, coaxed and goaded the Grand Old Man into further reaction. The culmination of their tour came when Colm stopped in front of a tableau of soft sculpture by Eva Aeppli called 'The Table'. Keating said it reminded him of 'Totentanz' ('Dance of Death') at the bridge in Basel. Then Colm drew his attention to the fact that there were thirteen figures all seated at one side of the table à la Leonardo. 'Ah, now I get it, she's making fun of the Last Supper.' *Fin*!

When that series ended our paths diverged yet again. I stayed in the Features Department making documentaries. Colm left *7 Days* and was asked to set up a nightly magazine programme. Tish worked closely with him during this time, and these are her recollections.

Tish Barry

The difference between a current affairs programme and a magazine programme became quite controversial in 1972. The colourful, feisty, and talented Colm Ó Briain was charged with the task of producing a magazine programme. This might have been, and indeed was, considered a downgrade for a producer of Colm's quality and track record.

But Colm took it on with verve and courage. I was assigned as his production assistant. I would not have been viewed as a calming influence but as fate would have it, we gelled together and worked our socks off.

Colm called the programme *Tangents*. I can imagine he meant it to convey energy and sometimes danger. Michael Garvey, the controller of programmes, hated the name. Colm said he waved his cigarette holder in the air, looked out the window of his office and very slowly said 'Tan . . .gents' a few times. 'It sounds like a bad holiday programme,' but in the end did not interfere with the choice.

We went on air in September 1972 with John O'Donoghue as studio anchor, joined by Cathal O'Shannon and Doireann Ní Bhriain. *Tangents* was transmitted five nights a week after the early news from the tiny Studio Three (considered to be yet another slight on the potential of the programme).

Colm wanted to have a current affairs element in the programme and of course this brought him into conflict with the 'Controllerate' on many occasions but, by deftly including music and arts and coverage of 'country' affairs such as farming and festivals, the powers-that-be were quietened down. The fact that some of the non-controversial items were hilarious had to be overlooked.

So, there we were working away and then our luck was in. In 1973, a general election was called. Fianna Fáil had held the reins of power for too long. Fine Gael and Labour struck up an alliance which could possibly topple them.

Colm consulted his muse. He came up with an item which I think affected the outcome of the election. But could he evade sanction? It was seemingly innocent: 'How does Proportional Representation, or, as it was commonly called, "PR", work?'

Colm got the graphics department working at full tilt. A fantasy constituency 'Ireland's Eye' was drawn up. Then a list of fantasy candidates with names that were close to, but differed from, the real runners and riders, were inserted. Then they were all assigned party representation. There were about thirteen candidates in this mythical five-seat constituency. Then we came to the nub of the matter: how to cast one's vote so that one could elect those parties that would mean change. Simply, vote for every candidate of every party on the ballot paper except—and this is crucial—those of the party you want out.

Election results night was fantastic. The whole *Tangents* team went to Kiely's of Donnybrook to watch the count on our big sister programme *7 Days*. At 10 o'clock it looked like Jack Lynch and Fianna Fáil would romp home but at around 11 o'clock things started to change as the

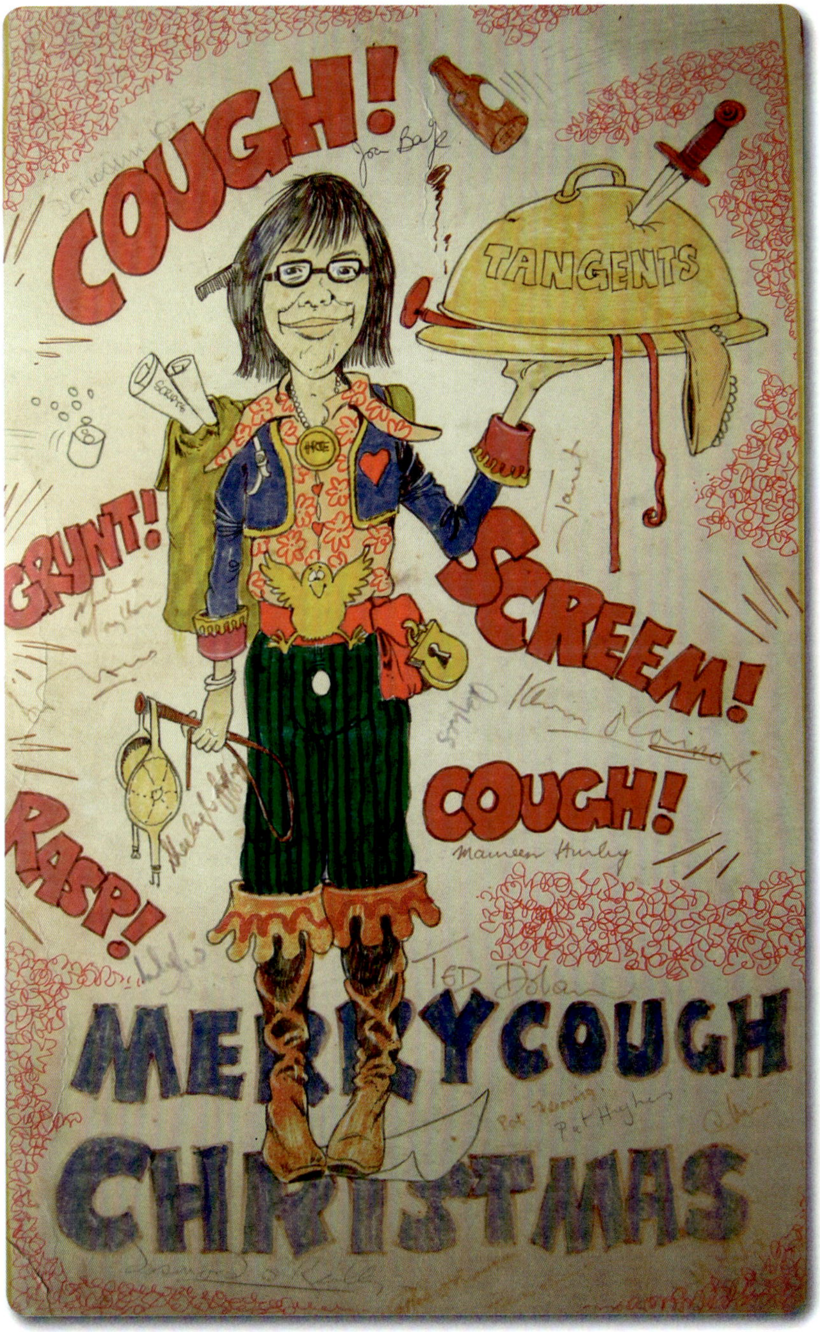

In 1972 Colm Ó Briain began producing the five-nightly RTÉ magazine programme *Tangents*. This Christmas card is from the team.

counts continued on around the country. Slowly but surely candidates of other parties started to pick up votes and put the squeeze on the favourite. The drinking stopped as we looked in awe. PR was working for change. By 2 a.m. Taoiseach Jack Lynch had conceded. A new era in Irish politics was born. In my view, Colm's dogged determination to show the country how to use the system prevailed.

Ted Dolan

It was many years later when Colm and I worked together again and much had happened to both of us in the interim. I had left RTÉ in 1989 and set up my own production company, Orpheus Productions. This company was principally set up to make music programmes and it made a good few such programmes with RTÉ, BBC Wales and ZDF, but it also made some programmes on archaeology and literature. From time to time, I was asked by RTÉ to come back on a freelance basis and direct the RTÉ Proms with the Symphony Orchestra, and vocal and choral works with the Concert Orchestra. In 1999 I was asked to come in and help out on a books programme, *Undercover*, being produced by Colm and Michael Garvey. The following year, RTÉ decided that it would put it out to tender as an independent production. We three decided that we would pitch for it and, as Orpheus was in existence, use that company as a flag of

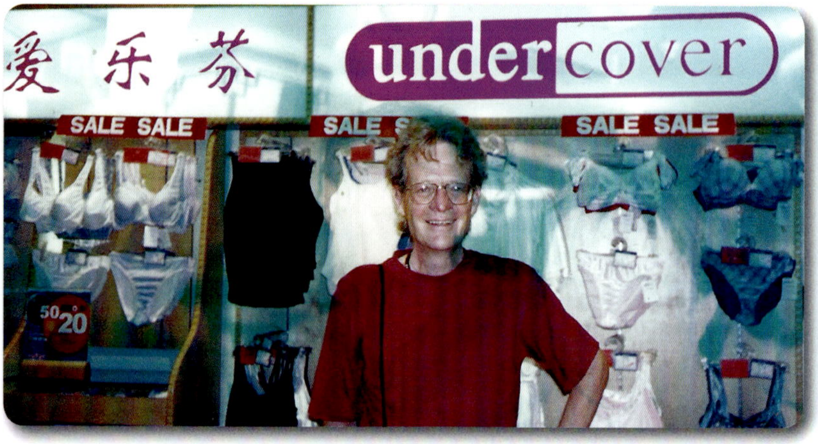

On a visit to China in 1999, Colm Ó Briain, then producer of a book programme for RTÉ called *Undercover*, was delighted to find this Beijing underwear shop with the same name.

convenience. We were successful and had two more happy and collegial years making full documentaries on Irish writers such as John McGahern, Eavan Boland, Anthony Cronin, Dermot Healy, Francis Stuart, J. P. Donleavy, William Trevor and Jennifer Johnston, as well as ones on genres as disparate as children's literature, crime and science fiction.

We were all privileged to know Colm, all energized by his presence, all impressed by his conviction and vision—even when we were irritated by his unwavering conviction that he was right. The most irritating thing of all was that usually he was just that: right.

Muireann Ó Briain adds:

One of the programmes Colm made for *7 Days* (in 1971) was based on the scandal of the felling of the trees at Lissadell in Co. Sligo in the 1950s. An article in the English *Sunday Times* sparked the interest of the programme team, so, together with Denis Mitchell, a journalist on the team, they researched the issue, and met with the family, the Gore-Booths. They contacted an expert in trees from the UK, and went with him to Lissadell where he reviewed the stumps of the trees that had been felled many years before.

The expert was a scientist named Barry Richardson, who concluded that the huge forests at Lissadell had been grossly undervalued, and that essentially the owner, Sir Michael Gore-Booth (who was a Ward of Court), and his family, had been robbed under the management of those who were supposed to be protecting his interests.

Colm filmed the programme in March when the grounds at Lissadell were covered in daffodils, and Denis interviewed the two Gore-Booth sisters who lived there, Gabrielle and Aideen. Colm used Elgar's elegiac cello concerto music throughout, and the result was a scientifically argued but highly emotive programme demonstrating a terrible wrong done to a vulnerable person and his family.

There was a significant public reaction to the programme, as a result of which the Gore-Booth family's solicitor, Charlie Brown, contacted Seán MacBride and, on behalf of the family, asked him to seek to re-open a case that the family had lost back in 1957 when they had tried to show the losses inflicted on the estate and their brother by the agents of the Irish State.

When interviewed about the Lissadell programme by John Bowman many years later, Colm expressed disappointment in how television could awaken interest in an issue, but did not change things. In fact, that programme did effect enormous change, a change that would never have happened were it not for the tragic story that he had told in the *7 Days* programme.

Following on Charlie Brown's request for a review of the 1957 case, Seán MacBride and I discovered that the most elementary mistake had been made by the judge in the trial. Where the Gore-Booth side had given evidence of the width of the tree-trunks at breast-height—less than the height of a person, the evidence on behalf of the Ward of Court Office, which had managed the estate, had given the width of the tree-trunks at mid-height—which is halfway up the tree. These were mature trees, so the difference in the evidence meant that the enormous trees in the Sligo forests literally had been sold for the price of Christmas trees.

A few years later, the Ward of Courts Office wanted to sell the one remaining wood at Lissadell (the Western Wood) to support the upkeep of the Ward, Sir Michael. An application was made to the High Court, and the remaining Gore-Booth siblings living at Lissadell were put on notice of the application. Charlie Brown again contacted Seán MacBride, but Seán was not in the country at the time, so Charlie asked me to represent the family. Instructed by him, I contacted Barry Richardson who came over once again to Dublin and gave evidence to the High Court on the value of the wood that was about to be felled. The President of the High Court, Mr Justice Thomas Finlay, accepted Barry's evidence and decided that only half the wood needed to be felled to provide the required funds. He also concluded that there had been a 'frailty of management' in the earlier sales of the woods.

From then on things were different at Lissadell. Judge Finlay agreed to transfer the estate at Lissadell to Josselyn Gore-Booth, the nephew of the Ward, Sir Michael. Barry Richardson became an adviser to Josselyn, and helped restore the gardens at Lissadell to productivity. After the remaining family members had died and no longer needed to be housed, Josselyn sold Lissadell. It was bought by Edward Walsh and Constance Cassidy who live there with their family, and now open the house and grounds to visitors.

Pearsa Ildánach

Seán Ó Mordha

'Tá pearsa imithe as an saol' a scrí an file Seán Ó Ríordáin.

Pearsa ildánach a b'ea Colm Ó Briain. Is trí Gaeilge a chuireamar aithne ar a chéile. Gaeilge a labhramar le chéile. Bhíomar beirt cairdúil le Muiris MacConghail, athair baistí Seóna Ní Bhriain. Cultúr na Gaeilge, craoltóireacht, na healaíon an ceangal a bhí eadrainn.

Colm Ó Briain was a serious person with a great sense of humour. His acclaimed film documentary on the Gore-Booth family, 'Lissadell House and Estate', is a serious television programme. A classic of its kind.

His interview with the artist Seán Keating is a seriously funny television programme. The elderly outspoken dogmatic Keating in a dialogue of confrontation with the young sceptic Ó Briain is a jewel of comedy and art. Pure gold. A candidate for *Reeling in the Years* in any year.

Colm was steeped in broadcasting and the arts. His brother, Art, was a noted TV producer and theatre director (*Arts Lives* for RTE, a theatre director for Field Day).

For Colm, broadcasting was a vocation, a way of life, television the medium to bring art and culture to the widest possible audience. He had enormous intellectual energy. By nature idealistic and totally committed to public service, he found the outlet for his vision for Ireland in various institutions.

You have only to name some of the positions he held to get the measure of this cultured patriotic man:

— Television producer
— Founder of Project '67, the origins of the Project Arts Centre
— Director of the Arts Council
— Director of the National College of Art and Design
— A term as General Secretary of the Labour Party
— Special Adviser to Michael D. Higgins as Minister for Arts, Culture and the Gaeltacht

— A key person in the drafting of the country's first plan for the arts with financial incentives for a native film industry.

Blessed with courage, confidence and determination, he undertook personal missions of innovation in pursuit of change in institutions that resisted any form of challenge to their authority and tradition.

A highlight of his varied career was undoubtedly his time as Director of the Arts Council (1975–1983). The position of head of the Arts Council is the most thankless job in Irish public life. Under-funded and never supported or appreciated by governments, the Council was forever under pressure to deliver and realise the vision and dreams of artists and art institutions.

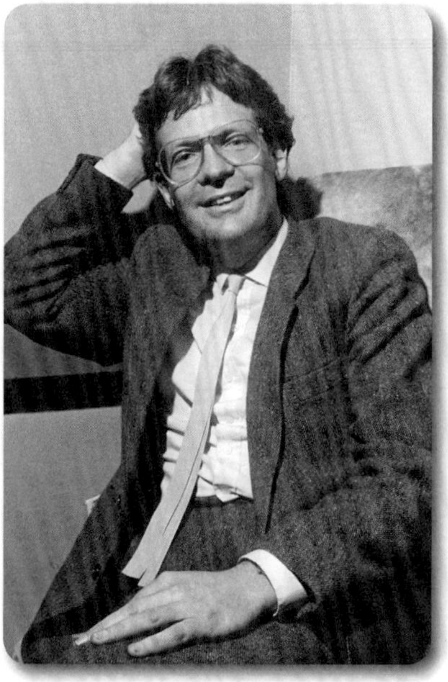

Colm Ó Briain, producer of the RTÉ arts magazine programme *Slants* 1986. Note the elegant tweed suit. (RTÉ)

I served on the Arts Council for a term. I had a note of congratulations and advice from Brian Friel: 'I'm glad you are on the Council. Sit with your back to the large window—nobody can see your face.' Colm never hid his face or avoided a public row or private dispute and there were many. His presence, his honesty, integrity and commitment to the arts in Ireland were never in question. Colm Ó Briain was the outstanding arts administrator of his generation.

Ard-fhear Colm. Bhí tú go híontach.

An Interesting Interruption

Garry Hynes

Sometime in the spring of 1975 I directed a production of a play *Elizabeth One* by American writer, Paul Foster, with—as I think we were then calling ourselves—the UCG Players. It would perform in the Jesuit Hall in Galway and then compete at some of the festivals on the amateur drama circuit.

On this particular day, RTÉ were filming a piece about the production. It would be broadcast on a weekly television arts programme called *Over the Barricades*. I can't remember how we managed to score such a significant piece of publicity but we were all very excited by it.

Then, right in the middle of filming, the producer, a man called Colm Ó Briain, got called away for an important phone call. I later learnt that he had just been appointed the first full-time Director of the Arts Council. Little did he, or indeed I, know then that less than a year later, as he was developing the first Arts Council strategic policy for the regions, a bunch of people, grandly calling themselves 'Druid the repertory theatre of Galway,' would apply for a grant.

And just to add: *Elizabeth One* won the Roscommon Festival (I still have the trophy). And Druid was successful in getting its first grant from the Arts Council.

I looked up to Colm, and I continued to admire him through his long and successful life. In his service to the arts and the culture of the Ireland that I live in he was peerless.

Memories that Counted

Peter Sheridan

I first met Colm when he adjudicated at the Roundwood Drama Festival in 1970. I was there with the Saint Laurence O'Toole's Musical and Dramatic Society—better and more familiarly known as Slot Players—where we presented our production of Samuel Beckett's *Waiting for Godot*.

The first thing that struck me was Colm's shirt. It didn't have a regular collar or regular buttons. It looked more like a kaftan. It was Asian and it was flamboyant. And he was comfortable in it, I could tell. I would love to have worn something like it but I didn't have the courage or the confidence. I was at an age where I still dressed to please my mother.

Waiting for Godot was not a play that was seen on the amateur circuit and it didn't go down well with the Roundwood audience. Some of them left with a clatter during the first act, making no secret of their displeasure. Others waited until after the show was over to vent their anger and their fury. Colm stepped on stage and delivered an adjudication that defended the play and the production. He acknowledged that Beckett was difficult and he commended Slot Players for 'their bravery in putting it on'. More than once he reminded the audience that good theatre and good art didn't exist without controversy.

My brother Jim—only ever known to the family as Shea—received the trophy for Best Director at Roundwood. I picked up the award for Best Supporting Actor for my portrayal of Vladimir. Colm was working as a television producer in RTÉ at this time and a few months later we got a message to the house that he was developing a children's programme called *Motley*. There were to be two presenters and he wanted Jim to audition for the male role. I was disgusted. He hadn't even seen Jim act. I was the better actor of the two of us and Colm was making a terrible mistake. I hid my disappointment as best I could and got on with studying for my exams. Da took me aside and told me that as I didn't have my Leaving Certificate, I wasn't eligible to work for RTÉ, it was against the law. So Jim became a television star—everyone in Sheriff Street called him Motley—and I lived on in obscurity and regret.

I was surprised when I got a call from Colm asking me to meet him in the Project Arts Centre which was situated at that time in the basement of the YMCA in Lower Abbey Street, directly across from the Peacock Theatre. It was the first time I had ever been inside an arts centre. There were paintings on the wall with numbers beside them and some of them had red dots, too. There was a receptionist sitting behind an office desk and she was typing but the thing that caught my attention was her mauve lipstick. I'd never seen that colour lipstick before. Her name was Rachel Doyne and while she looked flamboyant, she spoke in a clear, working-class Dublin accent. Colm was running late, she explained.

'He's a busy, busy man, but you probably know that.'

'Yeah, my brother Jim works with him out in RTÉ.'

'He's a clever man, too. The cleverest man I know.'

I asked her about the red dots and she explained that meant the work was sold. There were wooden and stone sculptures sitting on plinths, dotted around the floor, but very few of them displayed red dots. They were very expensive, so I wasn't surprised. Eventually Colm arrived, apologised and got straight down to business.

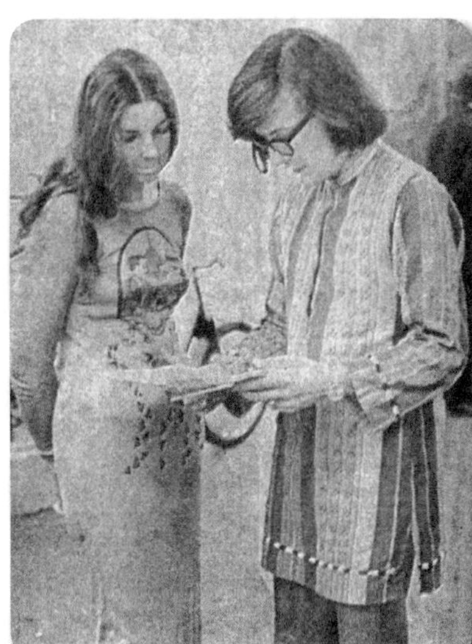

Rachel Doyne and Colm Ó Briain, Project Arts Centre 1970s.

'This is a gallery at the moment but I want it to be a theatre space as well. We've had one or two plays on here but I'm thinking about a season with lunchtime shows, evening shows and late-night shows at the weekend, Friday and Saturday. I'll need a stage manager and Shea says you're very practical.'

'Shea said that about me. That I was very practical.'

'No, that's a lie. He said you were a brilliant organiser. Are you surprised by that?'

'Yeah, I am, a bit.'

'Shea thinks the world of you but, sure, you know that, I'm sure. You're brothers, after all.'

Shea and me were forever in competition with one another. I'd gotten a pair of boxing gloves from Santy when I was ten and the routine was that we got one glove each, stood in the middle of the kitchen floor and went at one another full tilt. Da acted as a referee and there wasn't a bout between us that didn't end in a draw and a row. The truth is that the age difference tilted things in Shea's favour—he was three years older than me—and he hurt me more than I hurt him. But he was saying nice things about me to Colm Ó Briain so I forgave him for all the punches to the head.

My main job as stage manager of Project was to turn the venue into a theatre and back into a gallery when the performance had finished. Colm's mantra was simple—keep the artists happy and you'll have no problems. But that was easier said than done. You don't realise quite how heavy stone sculptures are until you try to move them. On your own. And paintings are easy to take down but not as easy to put back in exactly the same place. So I did my best after the first show ended—it was a poetry reading for about twenty patrons—only to realise that someone in the audience had moved the red dots. And the stone sculptures weren't on the same plinths and some of them looked ridiculous. I stood in the centre of the space and wondered what I could do. It was hopeless. I rang Rachel Doyne and apprised her of the situation.

'Stay where you are and don't panic. I'll send Jonathan down to you.'

The Jonathan in question was Jonathan Wade. An artist who had a painting in the exhibition. He arrived on his Honda 50 and parked it at the street level railings. I watched him as he came bounding down the steps and in through the door.

'So what's your problem, comrade?'

He was the first real painter I'd ever met and he was a breath of fresh air. Educated by the Christian Brothers, like myself, he wanted to know what my politics were and how much I was getting paid for stage managing the gig.

'Don't work for nothing,' he said to me.

'I'm not. Colm is paying me.'

'Of course he is. You won't go wrong there. He's a man with a conscience.'

Jonathan helped me put the exhibition back in place and then he gave me a lift home to Seville Place on the back of his Honda 50. He talked non-stop on the bike but I only picked up about a tenth of what he said. It was all political speak. The North. The Provos. The Stickies. Bank robberies. European terrorism. The Baader-Meinhof. Censorship. Project '67. Standing on the steps outside my home on Seville Place, it was Jonathan who explained the origins of Project and the infamous night at the Gate Theatre when Edna O'Brien and others challenged the Irish State by reading from their banned books.

'All art is political,' Jonathan informed me. 'You're either part of the process of changing society or you're part of keeping things the way they are. No one gets a free ride, my friend.'

Jonathan blew into my life in a whirlwind and just as quickly he blew out of it again. In January of 1973 he was tragically killed in a motor bike accident. He was thirty-one years old. Without him I never would have survived that Project baptism of fire.

The most controversial play in that first season at Project was *Journal of a Hole* which I was directing for Slot Players. Written by Jim Sheridan and Neil Jordan, the *Hole* of the title was Artane Industrial School, the prison for children out on the Malahide Road run by the Irish Christian Brothers. The play was based on the first-hand experiences of Robert Sheeran, a native of Sheriff Street who'd been sent there at the age of eight and released when he was fourteen. He now played guitar in a rock band with me.

I was anxious to get Colm's imprimatur on what we were doing. There were some graphic scenes in the play. One depicted a boy in a baby's nappy being made to stand by his bed all night because he was a 'bed-wetter'. Some people thought that Colm might defer the production until he had sought out a legal opinion. They thought we should keep him away from it. I was adamant that we let him see a run-through.

There was a scene in the school yard where the young Robert accidentally crosses the white line that separates the junior and senior boys. For this transgression, one of the Brothers punches him on the nose and it starts to bleed. He's told to clean up the mess. So he washes his nose under the yard tap. But he doesn't clean all of the blood. So the Brother punches him again and gives him the same instruction again. I had an actor dressed as a Christian Brother sitting in the audience—a plant—and at this scene he jumped up and started shouting.

'You ought to be ashamed of yourselves putting such lies on the stage,' the plant roared out, 'ashamed.' Then he stormed out of Project and up the stairs to the street.

Colm thought the play might provoke a response from the Christian Brothers. But that was only one side of the story.

'I think it's a welcome exposé of the industrial school system.'

'Do you think that's over the top, having someone interrupt the play like that,' I asked him.

'No. You just have to make sure he's believable, one hundred per cent believable.'

Colm had an issue with the collar. And he felt the brown shoes were not something a cleric would wear. Clerics only ever wore black. Colm had been educated by the Jesuits in Belvedere College. He didn't make mistakes when it came to clerical dress code. His reaction to the run-through and his positive words to us afterwards, filled everyone with renewed confidence.

Kane Archer, the theatre critic who reviewed it for *The Irish Times*, gave over two paragraphs of his notice to the 'enraged Cleric' who stood up and tried to shout down the play.

Nobody in Slot Players got paid for their services. I got paid for my stage management work but I kept that to myself. Almost. The only other person I told was Sheila O'Donoghue. She helped out with the coffee and occasionally operated the lights as well. Fran Roe, her college friend—she was Shea's girlfriend—had introduced us.

We became inseparable. I helped her with her college essays and she helped me with Project. In no time at all, Sheila was expecting a baby. We wanted to get married. My father tried to talk me out of it and her father tried to talk her out of it, too. But we were determined. I was supposed to be starting in college but I didn't care about college. I only cared about being with Sheila and our new baby. I didn't mind if I had to work. I loved stage management. Loved the theatre. Loved the Project. I went to see Colm. I asked him was he happy with my work.

'You've done really well. You're an excellent stage manager.'

I asked him about job opportunities in television, particularly in front of camera.

'There are no openings for presenters out in RTÉ I'm afraid.'

'I could do floor manager. I'd even say I could be a camera operator.'

'You need to go to college. You need to read. Join the drama society. Broaden your horizons.'

'I could stay on in Project if there was enough work for me. I love the place.'

'Project will still be here when you come out of college. Trust me. You need to get your degree above all else.'

Sheila and I got married in 1971 on Oscar Wilde's birthday, 16 October. I spent the next three years in Belfield, where I studied for six months of the year and worked for the other six months. I got involved in Dramsoc in first year and then I dropped out to become a bus conductor. Our son, Rossa, was born in the middle of my first-year exams—12 May 1972. Two years later I graduated with an honours degree in English and Philosophy. The Project Arts Centre was still alive but it had moved from Lower Abbey Street to South King Street beside the Dandelion Market.

A group of us from UCD had set up a company to tour children's theatre to schools. We rehearsed occasionally in Project but then word came down the line that the lease was up and Project would have to find a new premises. I decided to write my first proper play. I bought a manual typewriter, covered the keys with paper and learned how to type.

Project found a new home in East Essex Street. A large, two-storey building previously occupied by Dollard Printers. Shea thought it was a perfect space for my play which I had entitled *It's a Fair Squat but Don't Get Caught*. The place was a building site when I first visited there. Groups of people were beavering away trying to make it habitable. There were no seats. The roof leaked. There were toilets but no cubicles. Urinals but no pipes. Someone was building banked seating—Alan Stanford, I think, but he'd run out of foam. A man was building a projection room for a cinema that didn't yet exist. Two women were mixing cement. Alan Devlin offered to help them but they turned him down. An actor was sitting on the ground trying to learn lines from a play. Where's Colm, I thought. Where the fuck is Colm?

Colm was in Merrion Square. Number 70. Headquarters of the Arts Council of Ireland. An Comhairle Ealaíon. He was the new director of it. Holy shit. What did that mean? Was it good news or bad news? Should I leg it up to Merrion Square and tell him what was going on? Did he even know that I had graduated from college with my honours degree? The thing was that Colm and Muireann had lived at the bottom of Rutland Street, adjacent to Seán MacDermott Street, and I sometimes knocked on their door when I was passing. But Sheila and I had moved

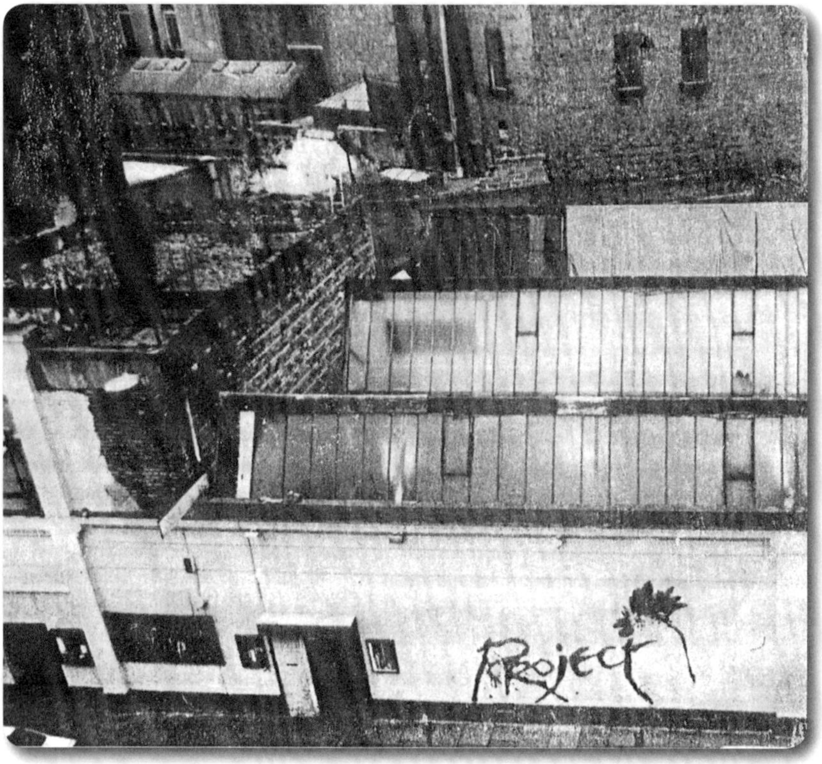

The Project Arts Centre moved a number of times before purchasing and renovating this semi-derelict printing works in Essex Street in Temple Bar. The Centre was subsequently rebuilt. (*Irish Stage and Screen* '25 Years of the Project Arts Centre')

out to a mobile home in Crumlin after we were married. I wasn't often in the area of the north inner city after that.

The Arts Council made a small renovation grant available to Project and Shea wanted to know if any of it could be put towards the play. The answer was a definite but emphatic No. In the circumstances, we did what we always did. We borrowed and we stole. John Olohan, one of the actors in the show, took responsibility for the set. In the laneway next to Project, John spotted a discarded No Entry sign that he thought would be great for the play. It was the perfect metaphor. I immediately changed the play title to *No Entry*. There were houses being knocked down on Dorset Street. We rescued a hall door and a window and made Robert Nolan's flat in Seán MacDermott Street with them.

No Entry opened to positive reviews and good houses. There just seemed to be an energy about Project. And not just the theatre but the gallery and the cinema, too. And the music end of things was taking shape. We were getting invitations from around the country—Clifden, Listowel, Cork, Belfast and Edinburgh. We were making a mark and so too was Colm up in Merrion Square. Out of the blue, he announced a cut of twenty thousand pounds in the Arts Council's grant to the Dublin Theatre Festival. Nothing like this had ever happened in the arts world before. It was a nuclear bomb. The Festival's director, Brendan Smith, went on the attack. He seemed to have some powerful supporters in his corner, chief amongst them Charlie Haughey. The Smith and Haughey families were close and that was largely down to the friendship between Beryl Fagan, Brendan Smith's wife, and Maureen Haughey, who was wife to Charlie and daughter to Seán Lemass.

It wasn't lost on some commentators that the Project Arts Centre might have been the beneficiary of the loss suffered by the Dublin Theatre Festival (DTF). In the year of this debacle, 1977, Project received a substantial increase in its annual funding. However, as its base funding was low, it wasn't a huge amount of money. It wasn't a difficult increase to defend. Shea and I, as joint artistic directors of the Centre, for example, both worked full time but we split a salary between us. Indeed, at the time when this row was brewing, we were talking to the DTF about producing a play with them that was too big for Project Arts Centre. The play in question was *The Liberty Suit*.

Set in Saint Patrick's Institution and with a cast of sixteen, it told the story of Gerard Mannix Flynn and how he had been abandoned and abused by the State from infancy to adulthood. I had written the play with his collaboration and not alone that, but Shea had cast him in the leading role. Colm was one hundred per cent behind the play. For him it was very much in tune with the social realism of *Journal of a Hole*, holding up a mirror to Irish society and forcing our audience to look at the uglier side of who and what we purported to be.

The Liberty Suit became a major hit and the DTF got a whole new lease of life. The Project Arts Centre, ironically, had saved the day. Brendan Smith was beaming when he announced that the DTF grant would be restored to its former level. The artistic programme for Project was expanding in all directions and so too was our ambition. But we had a fundamental problem and that was uncertainty of tenure. We could be turfed out of our premises at any time. So we floated the idea of buying the building with Colm. He embraced it from the get-go. He knew this would be transformational. But there were difficult waters to navigate, political and artistic. He steered the ship. He was our Arts Council champion and we couldn't have done it without his support and ingenuity.

Jim and I were at the helm for five years and I was exhausted by the time we quit. It was 1981 and I didn't want to see the inside of a theatre for another five years. Well, that's an exaggeration. But five months would have done me some good. In the North of Ireland the IRA had started a hunger strike and across the water Margaret Thatcher was digging trenches and preparing her people for war. In Dublin, Colm Ó Briain was busy working with Tony Cronin and others on an aspiration of Charlie Haughey's to establish an academy of artists and writers. It was to be called Aosdána. The important news was that its members would be entitled to a stipend so that they could concentrate full time on their artistic output. This seemed perfect for me. We had added two girls and a boy to our family and that meant six mouths to feed. A stipend was just what I needed.

I could not believe that I didn't meet the age requirement for Aosdána membership. I rang Colm thinking that there had to be a way around this.

'I'm sorry but you'll have to wait. The age requirement is non-negotiable.'

'So if Mozart applied you'd turn him down, is that what you're telling me.'

'Yes. There's no place for Mozart until he turns thirty.'

'That's stupid, really stupid. I can't believe you're enforcing that rule. Sounds like you're setting up a club for old-age pensioners.'

We argued the toss and always ended up back at the same place. Colm was above everything else a brilliant debater and he had answers for every argument I put forward. In the end, I just threw in the towel.

I applied for an Arts Council bursary and was successful. Being shut out of Aosdána wasn't as financially painful as it might otherwise have been. Sheila was still keen for me to be in Aosdána but I'd taken a stand and felt I couldn't go back on my decision. It took me thirty-two years to change my mind. The year was 2014 and I was performing a one-man show at the Civic Theatre in Tallaght. It was based on my theatre memoir, *Break a Leg*, and in it I told the story of how Jim and I met Colm Ó Briain at the Roundwood Drama Festival and how that encounter shaped both of our lives.

On the Friday night of the run there was a message at the stage door that Colm and Muireann were in the house and would love to see me for a drink afterwards. We met in the bar beside the restaurant. Colm did not look well. I asked him how we was and, forthright as ever, he told me he was suffering with diabetes, Type 2. He returned the question to me and I told him briefly about my throat cancer and how I seemed to have come out the other side of it. Having exchanged war stories, we smiled at one another.

They were both very complimentary about the show.

'Colm is sorry he gave up directing for the theatre,' Muireann said. 'He's jealous that you're still doing it. Aren't you, love?'

'There is nothing that compares to good theatre,' Colm said.

'I'd love you to direct my next show,' I said. 'But I don't know that I could afford you.'

'I don't know that I'll be available. I'll have to check my medical diary, I'm afraid!'

We had a wonderful chat, mainly about the early days of Project and some of the great characters that were no longer with us. I walked them out to the car park and it turned out they'd parked right in front of me. I sat in my car and watched them pull away. Colm had touched my life so deeply and he had left such a legacy to all those who worked in the arts sector in Ireland. So I made a decision. I got home and announced it to Sheila.

'Sheila, I'm going to do what I said I'd never do. I'm going to get someone to propose me for Aosdána.' I did and six months later, at the age of sixty-two, they let me in. Thank you, Colm. I got there in the end.

Lá breithe shona duit

Seóna Ní Bhriain

The time is now. The days are short;
the dark by five and chilly sort.
The hero of our earlier tales
is trudging now as he exhales
his steamy breath in the cold air.
He sees it linger briefly there,
so fragile and ephermal,
like all of life in general.
Such bitter cold, but he has learned
that seasons can be overturned.
And though the years add, still he
can claim them retroactively . . .
. . . when he retires.
He turns to FM104.
(Today he's driving door to door.)
The classic rock does not subject
his overburdened intellect
to further heady thoughts, which he
engages in too readily.
The tunes are bad but catchy too;
they'll help him see the winter through.
As Johnny Logan made it clear,
truly, 'What's another year?'
'I will survive' and 'Set me free'
he sings along, anthemically.

Renaissance

Ita Daly

When I was growing up in the fifties I thought that all writers were dead and, though I came from what might be called a bookish background, this seems to me to have been a reasonable enough view for a ten-year-old.

Writers were toiling away then as now but their endeavours and successes made hardly a ripple on our cultural surfaces. A book review in *The Irish Times*, if you were lucky, was as much as you could hope for. I don't know what the royalty cheques were like but I imagine that they were modest too.

We were a poor country in those days with low self-esteem and little time for the arts. If you were foolhardy enough to try to make a career for yourself as a painter or a writer then go ahead and starve in your garret.

And James Joyce: who he?

There was nothing unique about our attitude—throughout history the arts have been viewed by societies as something ephemeral, not necessary but, also, harmless enough, a source of pleasure, even, for some. So they, and more particularly, their practitioners, were allowed to get on with it—write, compose, paint—you are not as useful as a plumber but if that is how you want to spend your life, get on with it.

And, for the most part, artists tried to get on with it but many gave up because they couldn't make a living, or they made a bit of a living and then fashions changed, or they changed in what they wanted to do with their canvas or pen.

I do believe that full many a flower is better off being left to blush unseen but I also believe that in order for the arts to flourish, the arts must have patrons. Think of the court of Louis XIV, think of the Renaissance, think of Spain's Golden Age and the court of Philip IV: kings, popes, great merchant families like the Medici, have all been part of the support system that gave us Michaelangelo, Velazquez, the extraordinary beauty of Versailles.

And they in turn (the patrons) have rested on societies that were stable and wealthy with an educated élite who could and did enjoy a rhyming couplet or an aria or the rounded thigh of a marble nymph.

Artists and, therefore, the arts need money to flourish—even as important a figure as Vincent Van Gogh, could not, despite his genius, have left us those canvases without the support of his brother (patron) Theo.

Before you paint or write a novel or compose a concerto or choreograph a ballet, you need to eat and you need to have somewhere to sleep and to work.

And when you do finish your work, over which you have laboured, maybe for years, it may make your reputation or turn out to be a dud. And then, that dud may later be re-assessed and judged a work of genius—possibly when you are dead—and your friend who wrote a book that made serious money finds that his next one sells less than a thousand copies and his publisher is beginning to re-assess his worth.

Life is precarious but life as an artist is more precarious still. Hard work, perseverance, even talent, do not guarantee success and success itself does not guarantee a decent income.

This is an important point. Some artists have more commercial appeal than others—this does not make them better or worse, just different. Success does not equate with mediocrity but success does come to the mediocre as does comparative obscurity.

How many poets can make a living from their poetry or composers from their music?

I come back to my premise: in order to flourish, the arts need patronage.

And in 1981 the Irish government initiated a unique form of patronage with the establishment of Aosdána.

Occasionally an idea becomes current and seems to float around for a while before manifesting itself in more than one consciousness simultaneously. This can give rise to rows and accusations of plagiarism but when it happened in Ireland in 1981 there was a much happier outcome.

Colm Ó Briain was the director of the Arts Council and he had become concerned about the real poverty in which many artists were living having witnessed this poverty at first hand while working in the

Project Arts Centre. The Arts Council had initiated Ciste Cholmcille in the mid-1960s to help older artists and more recently Colm and the Council had begun to think in terms of an organisation to honour artists, somewhat on the lines of the Académie Française, but which would also support those artists who needed help by paying them a stipend.

At the very same time, Charles Haughey, Taoiseach and recognised patrons of the arts, was having the very same idea. The writer, Anthony Cronin, was Haughey's adviser on arts and culture and he let it be known that money could be made available to support working artists. This encouraged the Arts Council and Colm who set about putting flesh on the bones of the idea and Aosdána (meaning 'people of the arts') was born.

The members of Aosdána would be elected by their peers and the stipend, or cnuas,would be means tested, a modest sum but one which would allow the artist to work full time at their art.

Aosdána, from the beginning, has had many detractors who saw the organisation as élitist and cliquish and there is some truth in this. The membership is capped at 250 (originally 150), thus excluding a large number of those practising in the arts and it has never been clear how the original 89 artists were chosen. But I think the main reason why people found fault with Aosdána was because it was viewed by the public as something that Charles Haughey had brought about. The idea had, in fact, been discussed by the Arts Council for some years.

Haughey was always a controversial figure and his interest in and patronage of the arts was seen as an example of his self-aggrandisement—one comment being that it allowed him to see himself as a Medici prince. The establishment of Aosdána was just something else to add lustre to the Haughey brand is how some critics viewed the whole enterprise.

But Charles Haughey has been dead for many years, and I see the existence of Aosdána as something which adds lustre to the State rather than any individual, telling the world that as a civilised society we value and cherish our artists.

Well, 250 of them, anyway, I hear you murmur.

Yes, but one can't simply include every artist, one has to have some criterion to join any formal organisation and I think that selection by one's peers is the fairest one can come up with. An artist does not propose him or herself but is proposed and seconded by a member of Aosdána. This proposal is put to every member who then votes to admit or reject.

And some are rejected.

On the occasion when I proposed someone I was very struck by the attention with which my proposal was listened to by the members. I felt that it was something that they considered seriously and even though I might have been trying to give a leg-up to a friend (I wasn't!) each member was weighing up what I had to say with care and attention. Any nepotism on my part would not have got past them.

To be elected to Aosdána by one's peers is an honour—I certainly felt that when I was elected. I think even Groucho Marx might have been pleased by it for it is very different from some august personage or body—a committee of the cultured or a contemporary Lorenzo the Magnificent—deciding that one can join their club.

And, anyway, Aosdána is not a club, it is a gathering of people who earn their living practising the arts. They meet once a year in a general assembly when new members are elected and artistic matters discussed. For the rest of the year they just get on with their work.

To be elected to Aosdána is a recognition and public acknowledgement of your worth as an artist. This is particularly valuable for artists who have always been aware that it is cold outside and who, paradoxically, are outside anyway.

Because it is means-tested not every member of Aosdána receives the Cnuas and some years, if a work sells spectacularly well, a member may relinquish the money for a period. Some years ago when I became a full-time carer I stopped drawing down the Cnuas until I started to write full time again. The Cnuas is not abused or taken for granted by those of us who receive it, rather it is a huge encouragement to us to work and produce.

It differs from a bursary which is directly in the gift of the Arts Council and is awarded in order to allow an artist to pursue a particular project. The Cnuas recognises that which is unique about artistic work, the unpredictability of its quality. The artist cannot will this quality into being and all artists know what it is to abandon a novel, a picture, a concerto, after months, even years of endeavour and admit that this just isn't going to work. So you start again and now you have nothing to show for (maybe) a year of your life. And the thinking behind the Cnuas accepts that this happens and allows for it.

Unlike the world in which I grew up, the arts are flourishing in Ireland today: composers are having their works played in concert halls, every second person seems not only to be writing a book but getting it published, our architects are the talk of many towns.

I don't say that this flourishing has come about because of Aosdána but I am certain that Aosdána created an awareness of the importance of the arts to a society. It legitimises artistic endeavour whether that endeavour is carried out by its members or not. I do not think that this is too large a claim to make and I do strongly believe that at that serendipitous moment, when the vision and dedication of Colm Ó Briain, the vision and funding of Charles Haughey, and the general skills and work of *consigliere* Anthony Cronin, aligned, a rebirth of the arts came into being.

A Renaissance.

Dadó (Ar ócáid a 70ú lá breithe)

Seóna Ní Bhriain

An aithníonn tú an pictiúr seo?
Cathaoir leathan, mór go leor le spás do thriúr,
Tusa, mise, is mo dheirfiúr
Ag léamh scéil, ag dul ar thuras
An triúr againn agus C. S. Lewis
Go háiteanna nua, tíortha thar lear . . .
Ní raibh aon rud níos fearr ar domhan ná sin.
Smaoiním air seo is m'iníonacha
In aice le Daideo
An bheirt acu taobh leis, eisean sa lár
Tada sa saol ach an scéal os a gcomhair
Ag teacht an gheimhridh agus deireadh an fhómhair.
Nach orainn atá an t-ádh an-mhór?
Tá go leor le ceiliúradh againn anocht.
Ach go háirithe, grá agus samhlaíocht.

The Tyrone Guthrie Centre at Annaghmakerrig

Christopher Fitz-Simon

On 10 October 1981, ten years after Sir Tyrone Guthrie's death, the Tyrone Guthrie Centre at Annaghmakerrig was formally opened by the playwright Brian Friel in the presence of An Taoiseach, Garret FitzGerald, and two former taoisigh: Jack Lynch—during whose premiership Guthrie's bequest had been officially received—and Charles J.Haughey who was the first head of government to take any particular notice of the proposal for a writers' and artists' workplace. The presence of *trí Taoisigh* nudging for position on the front steps of the big house in remote Monaghan was a sight never witnessed before, nor likely to be seen again.

The Centre was an instantaneous success, so much so that in 1999 the ruinous stables and barns were converted for use as studios and self-catering accommodation. Had it not been for the patience and perseverance of the recently appointed director of An Chomhairle Ealaíon (the Arts Council of Ireland), Colm Ó Briain, the Centre would not have opened at all—for the proposal had lain comparatively dormant in the Council's files for fourteen years, surfacing from time to time to trickle between successive ministers, departments and civil servants, few of whom understood its potential—or, if they did, were defeated by the thought of the amount of money that would be required annually to maintain the envisaged institution.

The background to the Tyrone Guthrie Centre may be traced through the story of the house and the people who lived in it or were associated with it over almost two centuries. In 1820 a modest country residence, then known as Leesborough, looking out over Leesborough Lough, was purchased by an enterprising local man, John Moorehead of Newbliss. He probably moved into the house with his family in the same year. Mr Moorehead had business interests in the United States, acquiring properties in Pennsylvania and Ohio: history would name him as a member of the Ulster entrepreneurial diaspora. It happened that a young army officer named William Tyrone Power found himself on famine-relief duties in County Monaghan in the early 1850s, in charge of a platoon of redcoats who were hoking out the bogs of Corduff and Doohat in a drainage scheme the benefits of which are enjoyed to this day. (The scene, if not the stance, with its attendant redcoats, is similar to that portrayed in Brian Friel's masterpiece *Translations*.) Evidently William Tyrone's eye lit upon Miss Martha Moorehead; it is not fanciful to suppose that the Mooreheads took pity on this smart young officer and invited him into their home. William Tyrone Power and Martha Moorehead were married a decade later, he having risen spectacularly in the ranks and the match having been approved by Mr Moorehead, by now almost permanently resident in the United States.

This William Tyrone Power turned out to be the eldest son of the Irish actor and playwright, Tyrone Power (1797–1841) who wrote, directed and performed in major theatres all over the British Isles, the United States, Canada and Australia with his highly popular ensemble of artistes in his own distinctive comedies (great-grandfather of the Hollywood star Tyrone Power). He perished at the age of forty-four in the wreck of the steamship *President* off Cape Cod when returning from a business trip to the US having purchased lands in New York and Texas from the proceeds of several sold-out tours. In a curious way these two very different Irishmen—the showy theatrical Power and the solid businessman Moorehead, led parallel lives with their commercial undertakings in the New World.

The actor's widow, the former Annie Gilbert, had been left sufficiently well-off to see their children educated and well placed—none more so than their eldest who rose to become Commissary General-in-Chief of the British Army and Agent for New Zealand. Major-General William Tyrone Power was subsequently knighted by Queen Victoria in recognition of his prowess that contributed significantly to the advancement of her Empire, upon which, it had been said, the sun never set. When war between the United States and Canada became a distinct possibility Major-General William Tyrone Power was dispatched to Ottawa to take control of the military situation; had war broken out he would have found himself fighting against his wife's people in Pennsylvania and Ohio.

When his father-in-law John Moorehead died in the US leaving a considerable fortune, William Tyrone and Martha immediately made good use of it by extending Leesborough to the aspect and dimensions of the mansion we see today, also creating the handsome farmyard and the estate workers' dwellings in cottage-*ornée* style—and not forgetting the complete rebuilding of the picturesque church atop its drumlin at Aghabog. These building projects were undertaken by Messrs Henderson & Murray of Dublin who were contemporaneously employed in constructing an impressive range of sheds, signal-boxes and station houses for the Great Northern Railway in the county, including those at Newbliss. Martha and William decided their fine property should revert to its attractively rustic name, Annaghmakerrig—'McKerrig's Bog' to those who possessed an appreciation of the Irish language, which they did not.

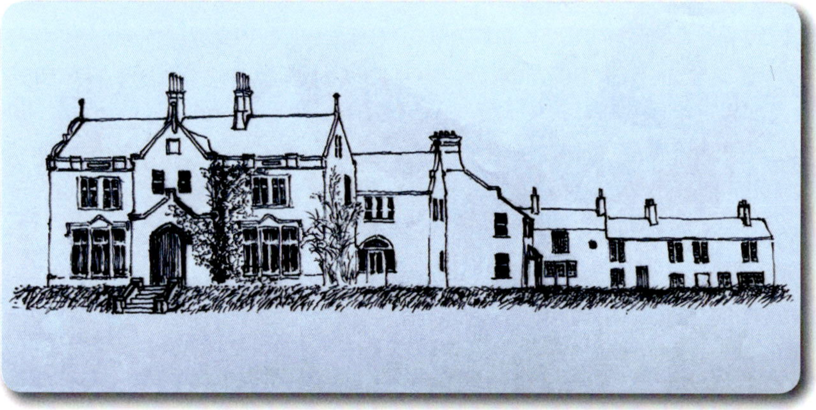

Pen and ink drawing of Annaghmakerrig by Christopher Fitz-Simon from his 2007 memoir *Eleven Houses*.

Sir William Tyrone and Dame Martha Power—these names are inscribed on commemorative brass plaques in Aghabog church—bequeathed Annaghmakerrig to their daughter Norah. Norah married Dr Thomas Guthrie of Edinburgh who became senior surgeon at Tunbridge Wells Hospital, Kent. Tunbridge Wells was—and still is—the epitome of classy English provinciality; as teenagers, both the Guthrie children, Tony (Tyrone) and Peggy (Susan Margaret), reacted strongly against its ethos, relishing the school holidays when they migrated with the entire household staff to Annaghmakerrig. When Dr Guthrie died prematurely of cancer Norah moved back permanently to the Power family base in Ireland. Tony went to Oxford University where he dallied seriously with the musical and dramatic societies. In St John's College he became friendly with another Irish ex-pat, Hubert Butler, who was to become a distinguished essayist and broadcaster on top of his activities as a market gardener in Kilkenny. He would later marry Tony's sister Peggy.

Tony's first job after graduation (with a very poor degree) was as assistant stage manager and bit-part-player with the Irish producer J. B. Fagan's Oxford Repertory Company. He applied for an advertised post with the BBC as a 'studio assistant'; allowed the choice of a number of cities where the Corporation was setting up regional broadcasting centres he opted for Belfast, where his voice was the first heard when the station opened on 15 September 1924. He made many friends in Belfast, returning time and again to direct plays in a social atmosphere that he greatly preferred over Dublin's 'self-satisfied parochialism'; much later he was elected Chancellor of Queen's University. This early encounter, however, lasted but two years, for he accepted an offer to move to Glasgow as producer with the young Scottish National Players, an engagement that led on to the Cambridge Festival Theatre where his innovative staging of contemporary European and American plays, as well as established international classics, placed him in the way of alluring and, on occasion, inspirational engagements in the West End and on Broadway. In 1931 he married his sister's childhood friend Judith Bretherton of Tunbridge Wells in Aghabog church and a celebratory bonfire was lighted on Mullaghmore hill. Many years later he wrote to Peggy recalling how their parents had expected him to proceed to the Military College at Sandhurst—or at least to join the Diplomatic Corps; while she was expected to be a grown-up tennis girl in the manner of John Betjeman's Miss Joan Hunter Dunne.

In 1933 Tyrone Guthrie became Producer—we would now use the term 'Artistic Director'—at the Old Vic, then the nearest there was to an English national dramatic ensemble. His tenure coincided with that

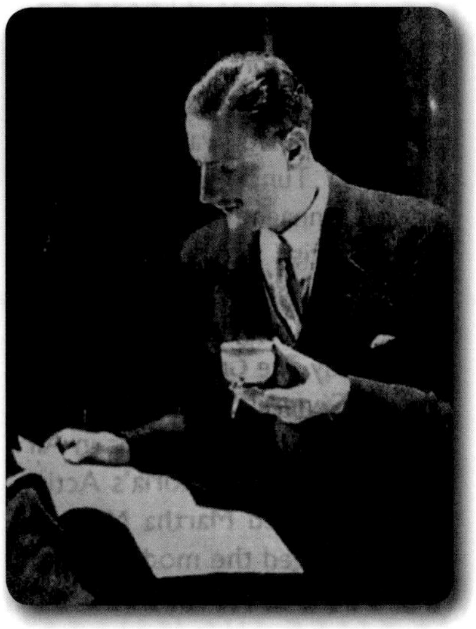

Tyrone Guthrie at a London press reception, probably at the Old Vic Theatre in the 1940s. He gifted his family home, Annaghmakerrig, Co. Monaghan, to the State for use as an artists' retreat. (Courtesy of the Tyrone Guthrie Centre)

of Peggy Ashcroft, Vivien Leigh, Sybil Thorndike, John Gielgud, Alec Guinness, Robert Helpmann, Laurence Olivier, Ralph Richardson and others. His principal mission was to remove from the English repertoire, and in particular Shakespeare, the residue of centuries of bombastic acting and 'naturalistic' stage design. His other important mission was to find a way of presenting 'period' plays in the way they were originally performed—the arena for Greek and Roman, the intimate thrust stage of the Tudor playhouse—thus eradicating the tyranny of the proscenium or picture-frame that had entirely dominated the western stage for almost three centuries.

A chance event at Elsinore, when an outdoor production of *Hamlet* had to be cancelled due to the weather, inspired Guthrie to make use of the castle ballroom on the spur of the moment; he proceeded to arrange chairs in a circle, advising the cast to 'get on with it' and try to make sure their faces were seen by all sections of the audience as much as possible as they moved around the intimate space. This resulted in a fairly shambolic presentation, well taken by the audience, that proved to Guthrie how well the play responded to being so close to the spectators. This influenced him to reject the proscenium theatre offered for his production of an obscure mediaeval Scottish play, *The Thrie Estaites*, at the first Edinburgh Festival in 1948, and make use of the floor of the Presbyterian Assembly Hall where he staged the unwieldy piece 'in the round' to enormous success and to the surprise of the local dignitaries.

Guthrie enjoyed three fairly tempestuous terms at the Old Vic, interspersed by engagements all over England and Scotland and also in Germany, Finland, Israel, Ireland—north and south—as well as in the United States and Canada where most of his work in his middle and later years was seen. It was at Stratford, Ontario, that his dream of creating the bricks-and-mortar of an open-stage theatre was first realised. This was followed by a similar building—known as The Guthrie—in Minneapolis. Its successor seats 1,200 persons, none of them more than fourteen rows from the stage.

When his mother Norah died in 1956, Tyrone Guthrie made Annaghmakerrig his home as well as his professional headquarters. Here he met authors whose work he was about to direct, representatives of managements who sought advice on programmes, actors who needed encouragement—Alec Guinness was one—composers, designers, broadcasters and journalists. He and his wife Judith had no children, so, inevitably, with the advancing years, the future of the country mansion in Monaghan became an anxiety, and later a burning family issue.

During his theatrical career Guthrie directed over 150 play productions, at least sixteen opera productions and an unaccountable number of radio drama productions. Many titles were repeats: those which come up most often are *Hamlet*, *Oedipus the King*, *A Midsummer Night's Dream*, *Carmen*, *Peter Grimes* and *The Cherry Orchard*—the latter in a translation which he commissioned from his brother-in-law, Hubert Butler. During World War II he was given responsibility for the combined forces of the Old Vic Theatre, the Sadlers Wells Opera and the Sadlers Wells Ballet—over 200 artistes—all of whom he evacuated to Burnley, Lancashire, where there was little likelihood of Luftwaffe bombs. The companies rehearsed in school gymnasiums and on factory floors, opening their productions in the Royal Victoria Theatre and then touring separately to cinemas and town halls throughout the more remote counties of England, to Scotland and to North Wales. He was universally observed as suave and unflappable—'but Burnley nearly put the kibosh on me', he later confessed.

He was honoured with doctorates from eleven universities from Aberdeen to Wartburg, Connecticut, and was knighted by Queen Elizabeth II in 1962 for 'services to the theatre'. One thinks of his grandfather Sir William Tyrone Power KCB, whom he greatly resembled in appearance—they were both Big Men—being knighted by Queen Victoria for 'services to the Empire'. Guthrie had little respect for the monarchy and his inclination was to refuse the offer from Buckingham Palace but his professional friends urged him to accept for the very practical reason that the word 'Sir' on playbills would 'be good for business'. He described the ceremony in a letter to his sister:

> ... a hideous great room with a tunnel-shaped roof; at one end in a gallery, against gold organ pipes, the Band of the Life Guards, resplendent in scarlet and gold [were] playing endlessly and very very poorly. They have to play softly enough not to be rowdy & interruptious, but loud enough to drown the creaking of royal stays, the snapping of elderly tendons, as Recipients fall to their knees ... There was Axminster on a daïs and Beefeaters, most of whom were in pince-nez that didn't accord too well with their ruffs and halberds and gave an air of Amateur Gilbert & Sullivan ...

Background material of this kind gradually disclosed itself to Colm Ó Briain when he took up the position of director of the reconstituted Arts Council of Ireland in 1975 and studied the documentation that had accrued in the Council's files and those of the Department of Finance since 1966 when Sir Tyrone Guthrie had initially offered his residence at Annaghmakerrig 'to be run as a hostel or hermitage in which artists seeking quiet in which to work, would receive free shelter and partial board.' Colm Ó Briain had never met Guthrie, who died in 1971, but was very much aware of his international standing. Guthrie's submission had received polite and grateful acknowledgement from time to time but little or no official action had been taken until the Council was reconstituted in 1973 with a new board, impressive headquarters in Merrion Square, Dublin, a hugely increased budget, an enlarged staff and, significantly, this new director, appointed two years later.

Previously the Arts Council had been a very small organisation indeed, with an office staff of four. Its secretary was the satiric novelist Mervyn Wall and its part-time director was a highly motivated Jesuit priest, Father Donal O'Sullivan, who possessed an extensive knowledge of the visual arts but had little interest in other art forms. It was not necessary that he should, for the Council, of its nature, did not support the professional theatre, the Abbey's annual subvention stemming directly from the Taoiseach's Department and no other theatres receiving any State funding whatsoever; classical music was almost entirely in the hands of Raidió Éireann with its two orchestras and its Singers, as well as the Music Schools in Dublin and Cork; the existence of Irish traditional or folk music was entirely disregarded. The original Council did administer a number of awards for literature and music.

Colm Ó Briain was much taken by the concept of a 'hostel or hermitage' for artists. He enquired how several in Italy and the United States were administered. He asked persons who had been close to Guthrie—among them his sister Peggy Butler and his Monaghan friend the writer Eugene McCabe—on the circumstances that had led Guthrie to make this extraordinarily philanthropic bequest. He may have been surprised to learn that the idea was not Guthrie's, and that there had been much inter-familial tension for a decade or more as to 'What will happen to Annaghmakerrig?'

Norah Guthrie had bequeathed the house and estate to both her children equally, with a clause stating that should Tony decide to sell the property he should recompense his sister by half of the sale price. Since he and Judith had no descendants he decided that he should leave the place to a representative of the people from whom his ancestors had (perhaps) wrested the land. He wrote his will, leaving Annaghmakerrig in its entirety to his farm steward, Seamus McGorman; by this means he was giving it away rather than selling it. He failed to inform his sister of his decision. When she and her husband eventually gleaned this intelligence they were intensely shocked—not so much at the decision as by the fact that he had kept it secret. A bitter correspondence ensued, Tony pointing out his legal rights, the Butlers suggesting that the mansion should be made useful to all the people of Ireland—as a Youth Hostel, for example—not just to one indigenous family who, they felt, would certainly dispose of the contents and sell the slates off the roof to avoid property tax. A meeting took place at the Butler home in Kilkenny in 1964 at which matters took such an emotional turn that Peggy, most uncharacteristically, cried 'Leave my house!'—which he did. It was a singularly unfortunate debâcle especially since brother and sister had always been so fond of one another, and Tony and Hubert Butler such long-standing friends since student times at Oxford.

Family disagreement continued through the middle 1960s, until it was tacitly agreed that although the bequest of the farmland to Seamus McGorman might stand, a much worthier purpose for the mansion must be found. At this point a friend of the Butlers, Pamela Travers—author of *Mary Poppins*—suggested that the house should become a residence for writers, musicians and visual artists on the lines of the Spencer Trask home at Yaddo in upstate New York, where the creative process was nurtured 'by providing an opportunity for artists to work without interruption'. A meeting was arranged in December 1965 at Radcliffe College, Massachusetts, where Miss Travers was Writer in Residence, at which she outlined to Tony and his niece Julia Crampton the widespread reciprocal benefits to be obtained from such an institution. 'It would be a wonderful way,' she remarked, 'to bring imaginative people together.' Julia conveyed the substance of the meeting to her parents, Hubert and Peggy Butler. The meeting was not immediately productive but paved the way for later plans, Julia and her husband Richard diligently researching other artists' colonies in the US. Guthrie informed a resentful McGorman family that they were not getting the house, only the land, a circumstance that caused residual local frictions over the following years.

Between theatre engagements in the United States and Britain, Guthrie set himself to consider the implications of running 'a residential workplace for artists' as outlined by Pamela Travers. He engaged an architect to draw up a plan of how the house might be adapted. A year after the meeting in Boston he submitted a proposal to the Arts Council of Ireland in which he stated that he envisaged the changes as happening while he and Lady Guthrie were still living, even suggesting themselves as the first residential wardens. The Council decided 'to approve the project in principle', showing its genuine interest by contributing to the cost of the architectural survey.

It is clear from surviving fragments of correspondence that Guthrie had a surprisingly Dickensian image of 'artists' as solitary poets, composers or painters for whom the lonely garret was the preferred stimulus for inspiration. He wrote that each inmate should have an electric ring in their room on which to cook their breakfast and lunch; but he also made it plain that all residents should meet for a daily meal provided by the house. What this meal might consist of can only be guessed at: the Canadian playwright Robertson Davies, who had stayed at Annaghmakerrig in 1960 as the Guthries' guest when planning the production of his comedy *Love and Libel*, wrote to his wife in Peterborough, Ontario, that the food was 'slimy and oniony'.

Guthrie revised his will in March 1971 leaving the house to the Minister for Finance with the barest of instructions as to how the artists' centre should be organised. What he could not have foreseen was his own demise, of heart failure, two months later, seated at his desk in Annaghmakerrig while planning a production of *The Devil on Show* by Constantine Fitzgibbon for the Abbey Theatre. The date was 15 May 1971. Thereafter the legal evidence of his gift to the nation lay comparatively dormant until Colm Ó Briain found it four years later, studying it with increasing interest mounting to excitement. Meanwhile, Judith Guthrie died and the empty house was looked after by two loyal retainers, Bob and Mary Burns, at a wage of £2 per week each, paid from the Guthrie estate with no allowances, not even for the price of a tin of wax polish.

When Colm Ó Briain came to involve himself deeply in the supervision of the project he dismissed the existing architectural plan and saw to the commissioning of another, much more comprehensive and also more sympathetic to the management of the proposed institution. An apparently insurmountable difficulty was that the residence stood in the midst of the McGorman farmland; those who desired access to this Victorian citadel would naturally have to obtain the McGormans' permission—which would probably be forthcoming but the daily comings and goings might become an understandable irritation to that family. There was the even more difficult matter of the residence owning none of its surroundings; for example, should an employee, or an artist, wish to sit out of doors to admire the view, permission would also have to be obtained from the McGormans. Clearly no artists' colony could even be considered for public funding with restrictions such as these hanging over it.

Making use of his legal training Colm sought discussion with the McGorman family and their lawyer. He must have added diplomacy to his bag of tricks because the McGormans readily agreed to sell the lawns on either side of the house to the proposed Tyrone Guthrie Centre (for a good price) and to allow free access as well as car-parking. Such measures as these were tentatively agreed before Colm could approach his Council with a viable plan to develop and maintain the envisaged institution.

What Colm Ó Briain must have found distinctly odd was that Guthrie did not appear to comprehend that the use he had himself made of Annaghmakerrig as a place for the initiation of creative endeavours should continue under the new dispensation. Colm viewed Annaghmakerrig as something greater than a haven for talented individuals: it could be a venue for Irish arts producers—who rarely, if ever, encountered one another—to meet in a convivial atmosphere and share objectives; it could be the scene of the dry-run of a dance enterprise, or a workshop on a new play, or a place from which nationwide art exhibitions could be planned. He immediately began to examine the advantages, constraints and costs of activities that would be of benefit both to the producing organisations and to the receiving public, suggesting that periods should be set aside to accommodate creative ensembles, quite distinct from the essential periods that must be devoted to private work, 'uninterrupted', as was the guiding principle set at Yaddo. He noted that Guthrie had declared in his will that 'should the Minister for Finance refuse the gift . . . it should be reassigned to Queen's University, Belfast.'

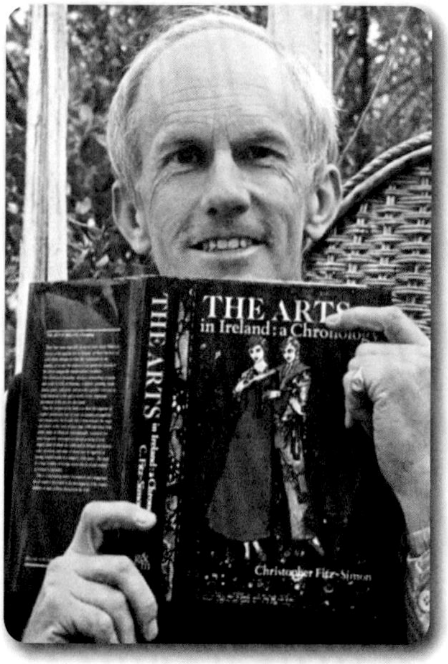

Christopher Fitz-Simon at the launch of his first book *The Arts in Ireland* in 1981, the year in which Colm Ó Briain invited him to join the board of the proposed Tyrone Guthrie Centre at Annaghmakerrig.

It was obvious to anyone who knew him that Guthrie had been more attuned to life in Northern Ireland than that in the 'Free State'. Colm Ó Briain, when producing current affairs programmes in Northern Ireland for RTÉ in the 1970s, had become very much aware of the human side of the 'Troubles'. At Annaghmakerrig, situated—somewhat confusingly to outsiders—in the province of Ulster, there might be a way of broadening the 'shared island' idea to include artistic endeavours from both sides of the border. He talked encouragingly on these lines to his Council, both at regular meetings and informally in a more personal way. The writer Eilís Dillon, who declared herself as totally behind the idea of a State-supported workplace for writers and artists, did express a doubt as to whether anyone would want to go to Monaghan. (Another member was said to have enquired, 'Where is Monaghan?', but that may be apocryphal.)

The first joint meeting of the two Arts Councils in Ireland took place in 1978 when Annaghmakerrig was on their shared agenda. There was much goodwill among members of both bodies, a distinct change from the somewhat cold reception that had been the case at earlier prospective meetings in Belfast. This may have been due to the warm relationship that developed between the new director of the Arts Council of Northern Ireland, Ken Jamison, and Colm Ó Briain.

The two Arts Councils accepted the bequest of what was to become the Tyrone Guthrie Centre in late 1978. The following year a board was formed, with each Council nominating four members, a ninth as chair to be nominated alternately by the Councils. The initial members from the south were Julia Crampton, Sir Tyrone's niece; Eugene McCabe, playwright; Joseph Hill, the Monaghan County education officer; and the present writer, then director of the Irish Theatre Company. The northern directors were Helen Hickey, curator of the Fermanagh Museum; Tom Mullarkey, architect; Terence Flanagan, painter; and George Thompson, director of the Ulster Folk Museum. The first chairman to be appointed was Patrick J. Rock, chief executive officer with the Irish Management Institute; he had previously served as chair of the Arts Council. The following year a capital grant was provided for renovations and an increasing annual administration grant to maintain the house and recruit employees prior to opening, after which it would be the responsibility of the board to apply annually to both Councils for administrative funding. The board appointed Bernard Loughlin as its first resident director and his wife Mary, a highly qualified caterer, to oversee domestic staff. The cuisine now provided was unrecognisable to those who had previously endured it.

As time went by the reputation of the Tyrone Guthrie Centre increased significantly while the agricultural ambitions of the McGorman family waned in parallel. The Centre was gradually able to 'buy back' the Annaghmakerrig land, greatly assisted by the two Arts Councils and a number of private donors. Over eleven thousand artists have made use of the residential facilities since 1981; about 60 per cent of these have been repeat or multiple visits; about 20 per cent of the total have come from overseas. Sir Tyrone Guthrie's head in bronze stands under the portrait of his grandfather Sir William Tyrone Power in the library. Other ancestral portraits hang in the same room and adorn the walls of hall and staircase. There is now an extensive collection of contemporary art, some of it donated by painters and sculptors who have spent time working as guests of the Centre. The 'Big End Room', designated by Dame Martha Power as a workplace, where children of the deserving poor were taught 'to cut and sew, be neat in everything', is now the music room where there are pianos, harpsichord and extensive electronic recording equipment. Studios in the former farmyard are dedicated to the visual arts, of various varieties as required, including printing. A new building at the top of the flower garden, close to the prehistoric circular enclosure on Mullenagarran hill, is a purpose-designed dance studio.

The Tyrone Guthrie Centre is open to qualified artists all the year round, except for Christmas and short periods for renovation. Following Sir Tyrone Guthrie's untimely death there was little impetus of the kind one might have expected and so his exceptional gift remained relatively undisclosed until Colm Ó Briain recovered it in the Arts Council's files, immediately recognising the potential for a uniquely creative undertaking.

Thanks to: Julia and Richard Crampton; An Chomhairle Ealaíon/The Arts Council; The Arts Council of Northern Ireland; The Public Records Office of Northern Ireland; The Tyrone Guthrie Centre at Annaghmakerrig.

Sources: Christopher Fitz-Simon (Ed.) *'Rise Above!'—Letters from Tyrone Guthrie* (Dublin 2017); James Forsyth *Tyrone Guthrie* (London 1976); Peg Guilfoyle *The Guthrie Theater* (Minneapolis 2006); Tyrone Guthrie *A Life in the Theatre (*London 1959), *A New Theatre* (New York 1964)

Friendship with Colm

Michael and Anne Gill

> We cannot tell the precise moment when friendship is formed. As in filling a vessel drop by drop, there is at last a drop that makes it run over.
>
> Boswell *Life of Johnson*

We think we both remember those first drops which eventually grew into a lifelong friendship with Colm for each of us. It began with Anne.

Anne: Sometime in the mid-1960s a group was formed to promote the availability of creative drama to young people. I was teaching English and Civics in a secondary school and had long been interested in drama. Colm was working, among other things, on Project '67 which became ultimately the Project Arts Centre. Among others involved were Grainne O'Flynn, Sr Eileen Sweeney and Nora Lever. We called ourselves, rather grandly, the National Association of Drama for Young People, NADYP for short. At the time, there was movement for change in various subject syllabi. For English there was demand for a modernisation of the syllabus which had been static for many years. NADYP paved the way for the introduction of drama into the curriculum and for the recognition of improvisation as a useful tool for learning in many other subjects. One distinction of NADYP was that it was formally wound up when the committee felt it had achieved its aims, rather than, like so many voluntary organisations, being allowed to wilt away.

Michael: I was first introduced to Colm by Anne. We soon found that we shared much in common. We were both northsiders: Colm was from Clontarf, and I grew up in Sutton. We had both been to Belvedere, although Colm was some years my junior. We had both experienced a school tour to Germany and Austria at a time when travel was overland and basic accommodation was arranged in a variety of hostels, monasteries and boarding schools. We both had appreciation of the same inspirational teachers at school. Each of us had rudimentary sailing skills, Colm's learned in Clontarf and mine in Howth. But the friendship was strengthened further when Colm married Muireann McHugh whom I had first met when a student at UCD.

Around 1973 we bought the *Argent Breach*, a fifty-year-old wooden cruiser on the Shannon in Athlone. It was to give us and our three daughters, Fionnuala, Marianne and Ruth, endless joy for the next eight years or so, accompanied by the inevitable frustrations recognised by all boat owners. Colm's family also had a boat on the Shannon, a distinctive Norfolk Broads cruiser called *Lady of Dublin*. The Gill and Ó Briain families met on numerous occasions on the river and enjoyed hospitality on one another's boats. The log of the *Argent Breach* survives and entries for June 1975 are as follows:

Friday 6 June: Arr. Dromod 18.30. Joined by Colm, Muireann, Aisling and Seóna Ó Briain at 20.00. A crowded night on board. Immense thunderstorm at 22.00. Does this mean a break in the weather? Very warm and humid.

Saturday 7 June: Away from Dromod at 10.45. Wind light SE. Sunny. Lunch and water at Carrick-on-Shannon. Stop at Cootehall to repair leaking fuel line. Arr. Rockingham 18.30.

Sunday 8 June: Rockingham. Very warm. Unbroken sunshine.

Monday 9 June: Dep. Rockingham 11.30. Again, perfect weather. Brief stop Carrick. Arr. Dromod 16.30. Dep. for Dublin 18.30. A good weekend, but eight on board renders boat something of a pressure cooker, effect of which is heightened by fractious infant.

(The fractious infant was almost certainly Seóna Ní Bhriain who is Anne's god-daughter, while Colm was an excellent godfather to our

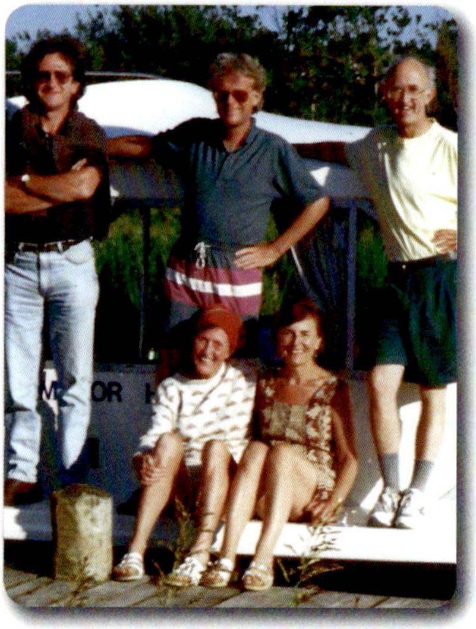

Unwritten Happy Days: a whole week of sunshine on the Shannon, through the restored Ballinamore Canal and on Lough Erne. (Back) Ciarán Benson, Colm Ó Briain, Michael Gill; (front) Muireann Ó Briain, Anne Gill.

daughter Ruth. The comments on the weather go to prove that the sun always shone when we were younger.)

The log for April 1976 reads:

Saturday 10 April: A new season begins. Colm Ó Briain and Michael take AB from Cloondara, en route Killaloe. Dep. Richmond Harbour 11.00. Arr. Athlone 14.00. Dep. Athlone 16.00. Overnight Banagher.

Sunday 11 April: Dep. Banagher 10.15. Starboard engine erratic. Airlocks? Raining and cold. Wind SE, 5/6. Arr. Portumna 14.00. Port engine running v. hot, 90°C. Decide not to risk Lough Derg and leave boat in charge of Arthur Kass.

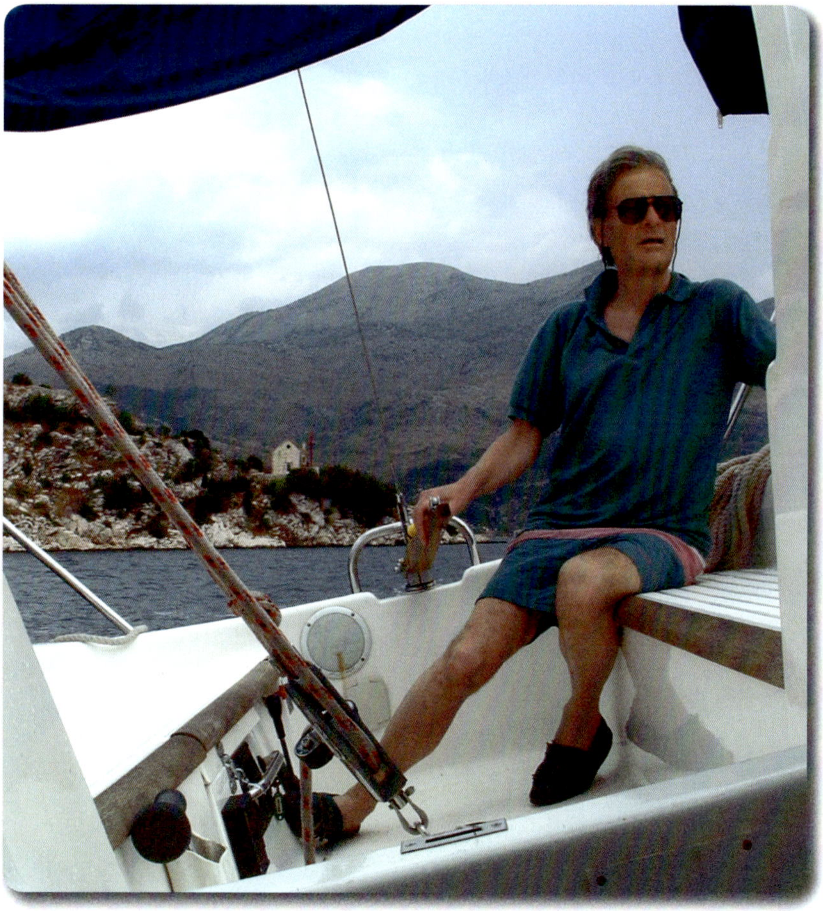

Colm Ó Briain sailing in Croatia. He was a keen sailor, from early family holidays in Skerries, Co. Dublin .

(Just as leaking roofs and rising damp are features of old houses, erratic engines and airlocks are well recognised by owners of old boats.)

Boats and sailing remained a permanent feature of our friendship with Colm and Muireann. In 1989 we spent a memorable two weeks sailing off the southern coast of Turkey. Some mutual friends expressed doubt about undertaking such a venture and wondered how four relatively strong-willed individuals could survive living in the confines of a sailing boat for two weeks. (We were joined by our daughter, Marianne, on the day she completed her Leaving Certificate exams.) But the experience was such that fifteen years later in 2004, the same quartet took to the seas off Croatia. The harmony among the crew was rarely broken except during occasional emergencies of an anchor dragging in a storm when voices were raised, and instructions disputed.

Not only was Colm a skilled sailor he was also an erudite companion with a wide knowledge of ancient Greek and Roman culture as we explored the remote archaeological sites on the Lycian shore. He also had remarkable recall of the various stages of the Balkan wars of the 1990s which informed many discussions as we sailed off the coast of the former Yugoslavia.

Indeed, Colm's frames of reference and the breadth of his interests seemed to know few limits. He was widely read. Anne recalls him introducing her to the writing of Elif Shafak, the Turkish novelist whose work was only beginning to be translated into English.

While he was always discreet in discussing his own working life, Colm had a genuine interest in the work of others. He interrogated Michael on many occasions about aspects of publishing as diverse as retail price maintenance and the impact of book awards on the industry. He often expressed curiosity about the multitude of literary awards in France and served for some years as a judge of the Irish Times Literary Awards. Later he was influential in the establishment of the IMPAC Dublin Literary Award in 1996 which is now known as the Dublin Literary Award and is sponsored solely by Dublin City Council. The jury of the prize is a panel of international librarians, a feature of which Colm was particularly proud. With a prize of €100,000 it is possibly the richest literary award in the world.

Drawing together the worlds of business and the arts for the mutual benefit of each was an abiding concern of Colm's which he promoted actively while lecturing on the Arts Administration course in UCD from the late 1980s.

Sometime in the early 1980s while director of the Arts Council, Colm asked Michael, in his role as publisher, to advise on a tax case arising from a refusal by the Revenue Commissioners to grant tax exemption to the writings of journalist John Healy, well-known at the time. Revenue frequently sought advice from the Arts Council in determining if a work met the formal criteria of being original, creative and of cultural or artistic merit. Revenue's refusal in this case was referred to an Appeal Commissioner and in addition to Michael, opinions were sought from Sean O'Faolain and Conor Cruise O'Brien.

Michael writes: I cannot remember contributing much to the discussion held in the tall Georgian room of the Appeal Commissioner on Stephen's Green, but the clash of opinion between O'Faolain and Cruise O'Brien was memorable. Their arguments on the meaning of the words 'original', 'creative', 'artistic' and 'cultural' reflected their strongly held and differing opinions of the appellant's case. It continued, without the Commissioner, through lunch in the Hibernian Hotel (accompanied by some delicious literary and political gossip), long into the afternoon and ended the following morning. The Commissioner admitted that he needed time to draw a conclusion on the case, hardly surprising given the complexity of the arguments and the force and passion with which they were expressed. But a determination of the case was never made. The Commissioner died sometime later and carried his opinion to the grave.

Many years later the criteria for the artists' tax exemption were carefully clarified and re-formulated. This was during the time that Colm served as special adviser to Michael D. Higgins when first Minister for Arts, Culture and the Gaeltacht between 1993 and 1997. Colm's influence was evident in the new policy document. He spoke to Michael often about the argument between O'Faolain and Cruise O'Brien, as Colm was convinced after the hearing in the Commissioner's office that the statement of the original criteria was insufficient to guarantee transparent decisions by Revenue.

Everyone who knew Colm recognised him as a man of principle, be it personal, social or political. His views were held strongly and expressed forcefully. When returning from our sailing holiday in Turkey, we had agreed among ourselves that there was no need to declare anything in our baggage as we were transit passengers through Gatwick airport *en route* to Dublin. However, Colm had a sudden change of mind, and declared to a customs officer that his sailing bag contained a *kilim,* or small Turkish carpet. Suspicions were raised and the bags of all his travelling companions were opened and examined to reveal a selection of cheap souvenirs and small bottles of mysterious alcoholic drinks. Colm's carpet was worth no more than £20 sterling or perhaps €50 in today's money. A receipt was demanded but it couldn't be found. Time passed. Our flight to Dublin was imminent. Anne, who had some knowledge of oriental carpets, explained to the customs officer that *kilims,* while attractive, would be valuable only if certified as antique and this clearly was not an antique. The customs officer relented. We ran for our Dublin flight and were the last passengers aboard. When we had recovered, Colm was challenged about his decision to declare his tiny carpet. It was a matter of principle, he said. Much of the flight home was spent in silence.

Among Colm's many gifts, there were two that we appreciated specially, his imagination and his flair—that instinct for choosing what was both unusual yet excellent. We saw this originally in the interior decoration of Colm and Muireann's first house in Lower Rutland Street, an outstanding feature of which was an entire wall decorated with posters from theatre events collected by Colm. We saw it again even more dramatically in the transformation of their house on Charleville Road in Rathmines. After it was bought and when we first saw it, our immediate instinct was dismay that such a potentially gracious space could have been allowed to deteriorate to a shabby tenement. We were also dubious about the wisdom of having purchased such a wreck. A year or so later it had become a spacious, interesting, colourful, welcoming home, resplendent with interesting art and imaginative furnishings.

When we had an opportunity ourselves to downsize and build our own home, we asked Colm to suggest an interior colour scheme. Working from architect's drawings he devised a scheme that was as imaginative as it was daring but we were not brave enough to carry it through. Perhaps in the future?

Colm's flair and imagination extended to his style of dress. Even on the most formal occasions his dress code was never traditional. It could have been described as 'smart bohemian'. We still recall Colm joining us for some days on a family holiday in Tuscany. He spent hours sunning himself meticulously on a wall, adopting poses reminiscent of sculptures by Auguste Rodin, followed by enlivening the evening with his inimitable gift of sparkling conversation and argument. (And how eloquently argumentative Colm could be!)

Colm's final years were difficult to witness, particularly for his family but also for his friends, as his lively intellect was extinguished slowly, and his life force faded away. But we have chosen to remember him from earlier days and will always cherish with gratitude his presence as a special friend in our lives.

From *Dreams and Responsibilities**

Brian P. Kennedy

Nineteen-seventy-five was a decisive year for the Arts Council. After an elaborate application process organised by the Council's chairman, Professor Geoffrey Hand, Colm Ó Briain was selected to be the new full-time director. Ó Briain had been a strong critic of previous policies and was regarded by many as a talented iconoclast. The Arts Council's decision to appoint him as director was a brave and enlightened choice. It surprised many art critics. Brian Fallon had predicted: 'The new Director is not likely to be a controversial figure, or a dominating one … most likely he will be a career administrator or civil servant, operating by the rules and by the consensus of the members, and more concerned with seeing that the machinery runs smoothly and the Arts Council's funds are fairly and discreetly apportioned, than with "educating" public taste.' (*Irish Times* 30, 31 Jan. 1974)

Fallon was proved wrong. Colm Ó Briain was controversial, dominant, and not a civil servant but a television producer and director. He interpreted rules and encouraged Council members to see things his way which they usually did. He was concerned that the Arts Council ran with its policies and proclaimed loudly how its funds were apportioned. Finally, he was preoccupied with educating public taste. Composer Brian Boydell attributed the Council's new vigour, commitment and enthusiasm after 1975 to Ó Briain: 'He was a natural human dynamo and used his socialist views to argue for arts for the masses, bringing art to all the people. Colm Ó Briain was the right man at the right time. He shook the Council out of its complacency and gave it a new image.' (Interview, 18 April 1987)

In November 1975, the Department of the Taoiseach sanctioned the

* Abridged excerpt (pages 182–207, 212) from *Dreams and Responsibilities: The State and the Arts in Independent Ireland* by Dr Brian P. Kennedy. Published by the Arts Council, Dublin 1990, 1998. See the 1990 edition for sources and complete references.

appointment of four new posts to the Arts Council: in literature, music, visual arts and administration. The new officers had to be committed to their tasks in order to keep up with the director, Colm Ó Briain. As he explained to a journalist: 'When I got this job I had the choice of sitting back and waiting for things to happen—or of jumping in. So I jumped in . . . I'm pushing myself. But it's rough on the staff because I'm pushing them too.' (*Sunday Independent* 18 Jan. 1976)

Ó Briain was an arch-propagandist for the Arts Council. He was a naturally gifted communicator who cultivated a high media profile. For example, on 21 September 1976 he gave a lunchtime lecture at the National Gallery. His subject was 'Performance Art' and instead of discussing it, he treated his startled audience to a performance. He placed two chairs with their backs to the audience. He sat on one of the chairs and used a television camera to show his face to the audience. He wore a motor-cycle helmet and visor, a pair of flippers, shorts and a t-shirt with the number 19 on it. The teddy bear he was holding had the number 76 written on it. Ó Briain's point was simple. Performance art could have visual and dramatic impact but if it failed to become more than a mere happening, it was not art. (Interview 9 Jan. 1988)

Soon after Ó Briain's appointment as director, Professor Hand was succeeded as chairman by Patrick Rock, who was appointed by Taoiseach Liam Cosgrave on 2 July 1975. Rock was a senior management consultant at the Irish Management Institute who admitted candidly to 'having no abiding dedication to any particular form of art.' *(Evening Herald* 4 July 1975) He was chairman of the Fine Gael constituency council in Dún Laoghaire/Rathdown, which was Liam Cosgrave's constituency. The Taoiseach was convinced that Rock's management expertise would be useful to the Arts Council. The appointment was an excellent one. Rock was a shrewd and effective chairman who, while he had great admiration for Colm Ó Briain and the Council staff, helped to keep their efforts compatible with the development of a disciplined organisation. He encouraged the use of better accounts presentation, planning and projections. He also introduced annual two-day meetings at which the Council and its staff discussed the development of new policies. In a strong public statement, he proclaimed a clear sense of purpose:

'We have an obligation to our artists to ensure that proper facilities exist for training, exhibition and performance; and we have an obligation to the public, both children and adults, to ensure that they are provided with a wider and deeper appreciation of the arts. Furthermore, we have an obligation to both artists and public to see that adequate facilities exist, especially at regional level, to enable all to participate meaningfully in the arts.' (*Annual Report* 1975)

The Arts Council received a vital boost to its aims when, on 19 December 1975, the Minister for Finance, Richie Ryan, announced that the Government had decided to transfer responsibility for the funding of the Abbey Theatre, the Gate Theatre, the Irish Theatre Company, the Irish Ballet Company and the Dublin Theatre Festival, from the Department of Finance to the Arts Council. The decision was consistent with the Taoiseach's view that the Arts Council was 'the vehicle of State patronage' of the arts. The effect on the scale of the Council's finding was dramatic. The State grant-in-aid increased from £200,000 in 1975 to £990,000 the following year. The Taoiseach further distanced the Council from the Department of Finance when he decided that, as from 1975, he would present the Council's estimate in Dáil Eireann and not the Minister for Finance.

The Department of Finance was delighted to rid itself of what were referred to as the 'Big 5'. Principal officer Bob Whitty called them his 'crown of thorns'. (Interview 11 Feb. 1987) The Irish Ballet Company, based in Cork, had won the patronage of the former Taoiseach, Jack Lynch. The Irish Theatre Company began its operations touring plays throughout Ireland in February 1975. The Dublin Theatre Festival waged a constant battle for survival and the Abbey and Gate Theatres had financial and personality troubles. But the Government's decision to transfer the 'Big 5' to the Arts Council represented important official recognition of its role as the national body responsible for fostering all the arts.

There were other signs that official attitudes to the arts were improving with the development of the National Concert Hall and an extension to the Chester Beatty Library in Dublin, financed from public funds. There were indications of a progressive attitude to the arts by local authorities also.

The development of the Arts Council's policies was helped considerably by the publication in January 1976 of the so-called 'Richards Report' produced by a consultative committee of Irish arts experts chaired by Sir James Richards (editor of *The Architectural Review* 1937–1971). The report, titled *Provision for the Arts,* sought to clarify how Irish arts organisations were organised and financed, and to make recommendations to help the Arts Council to structure its future programmes to achieve maximum effectiveness from its resources.

The Richards Report provided a vital independent assessment of the state of the arts in Ireland. It was supportive of the Arts Council's role: 'The Arts Council should be regarded as the body responsible to the nation for the welfare of all the arts, and it should be in a position to take action accordingly'.

The Arts Council under the chairmanship of Patrick Rock and the directorship of Colm Ó Briain studied the Richards Report carefully and acted on its recommendations with a stream of innovative programmes. The Council developed two key policy aims and spelt them out in the *Annual Report* for 1976. The first line of that report said: 'Provision for the individual writer, artist and musician was identified as a major priority for the Council'. A scheme of bursaries for creative writers which began in 1975 was extended quickly to include a programme of scholarships and awards in music and the visual arts.

The second key policy aim was stated self-critically: 'Previous reports from the Council have given an indication of some bias in favour of arts activities in Dublin as opposed to the rest of the country. The Council has undertaken to correct this imbalance and to encourage regional development of the arts as a matter of urgency.'

The Richards Report's recommendation that the Arts Council should establish schemes in liaison with the existing regional development organisations throughout the country was implemented.

The growth of artistic activity throughout the country created ever-increasing demands by client organisations for funding from the Arts Council. This led inevitably to demands by the Council itself for increased funding from the Government. The Council adopted a vigorous approach. Although the Government had increased the Council's grant by 22 per cent to £1,565,000 in 1976, the Council decided to run the risk of seeming ungrateful for the significant increase in its funding by declaring that 'a proper level of funding has never been provided for arts activities' and 'inflation in the arts negated the value of most of the increased allocations'. Patrick Rock said: 'The State as a patron of the arts reflects the general indifference of the people to the arts in general'. The Council argued that the State had a duty to support the arts. There was, of course, a role for private funding of the arts. But the Council argued that private funding could not be asked to make up for under-financing by Government.

The Council identified 'a desperate need for new buildings to house the arts, particularly at local level'. There was a limit to what local festivals and touring companies could achieve without adequate premises. Colm Ó Briain had personal experience of the Project Arts Centre and was anxious to see the spread of regional arts centres. In 1977 the Arts Council grant-aided four arts centres (Project and Grapevine in Dublin, Gorey and Wexford) and five arts festivals (Dublin, Dún Laoghaire, Inishbofin, Kilkenny and Listowel). The Council began to lobby the Government for a capital allocation to finance the building of one arts centre in each of the twenty-six counties.

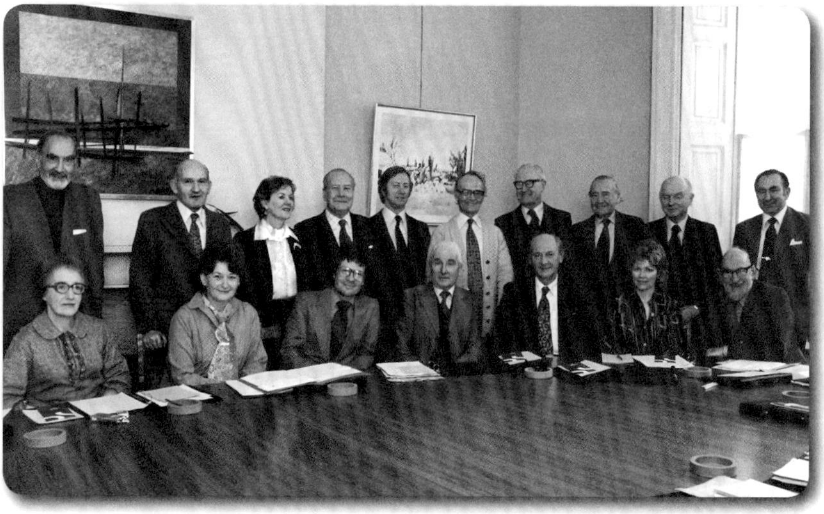

The first meeting of the Arts Council of 1978. (Front, left to right) Bridget Doolan, Nora Relihan, Colm Ó Briain (Director), James White (Chair), Jack Lynch (Taoiseach), Kathleen Barrington, Brian Boydell. (Back, left to right) Andy Devane, Seán Ó Tuama, Máire de Paor, James Warwick, Richard Stokes, Hugh Maguire, Dr T. J. Walsh, Michael Scott, J. B. Kearney, Donie Potter. (Lensmen, courtesy of the Arts Council)

In developing a regional policy, the Arts Council benefited from the experience of its counterpart organisations in Great Britain and Northern Ireland. There had been many informal contacts over the years between the Councils, the two oldest such organisations in the world, but it was useful to have a formal discussion of policies and activities. In 1977 meetings were held between the so-called 'Celtic Quartet' of Arts Councils (An Chomhairle Ealaíon and the Arts Councils of Northern Ireland, Scotland and Wales). In January 1978, the Arts Council of Northern Ireland invited An Chomhairle Ealaíon to a one-day joint meeting in Belfast to discuss future co-operation between the two Councils. The invitation was accepted enthusiastically and the meeting took place on 20 April 1978. One of the topics discussed was the final arrangement for the financing and structuring of the Tyrone Guthrie Centre at Annaghmakerrig, County Monaghan. Patrick Rock hailed the meeting as 'a historic milestone in the cultural development of Ireland as a whole' and Colm Ó Briain said 'as far as the arts are concerned, we're going to operate as if the Border didn't exist'. (*Irish Press* 21 April 1978) On 13 October 1978, the second joint meeting of the two Arts Councils took place in Dublin.

The post-1973 Arts Council bore little resemblance to the mild-mannered and cautious institution headed by Fr Donal O'Sullivan SJ from 1960 to 1973. This was most obvious from the way in which the Council, spearheaded by Colm Ó Briain, used its position as a prescribed body under the Local Government (Planning and Development) Act 1963, to campaign against the destruction of Dublin's architectural heritage. The Council took a leading role in successfully resisting the efforts of Bord na Móna to demolish Georgian buildings at 28–32 Upper Pembroke Street, Dublin, and to construct, in replacement, a new office block with reproduction façade.

The Arts Council's campaign against Bord na Móna was significant for a number of reasons. It firmly established the Council's independence because it proved that neither Government ministers nor State-sponsored bodies were considered to be above public criticism. The Council increased its credibility among its client arts organisations by showing that it was committed to action not words. Finally, as Colm Ó Briain's personal popularity increased, the Arts Council won vital media attention. Journalists were sympathetic to Ó Briain and afforded him every opportunity to defend State funding of the arts. In September 1976, Ó Briain set the publicity machine in motion to counter a member of the European Parliament's attack on the tax-free exemption scheme for artists resident in Ireland.

Ó Briain defended the scheme: 'The legislation is concerned with creative Irish artists. It was brought in to stop the brain drain, to keep Irish people and talent at home. Just because American and other writers are coming to Ireland and also benefiting from it, is no reason to repeal the legislation. Does one do away with a good thing just because there are a few people abusing it?' (*Evening Press* 2 September 1976) The controversy evaporated when the European Commission stated that it had no power to prevent the Irish Government from implementing the measure.

The term of the Sixth Arts Council came to an end on December 1978. Colm Ó Briain assessed its achievements and concluded: 'The Council was trying to do too much too quickly ... The transfer to the Council in 1976 of the five national [theatre] companies caused huge problems but also brought the Council face to face with some of the real issues facing the future of the arts in Ireland. There was an accelerated movement of the Arts Council to the centre of the stage.' (*Irish Press* 2 November 76) Patrick Rock made a final public statement (1 Nov. 1978) that the arts were still not being taken seriously enough by politicians and civil servants. He credited the Government for increasing the level of arts funding but claimed that it was still inadequate. The Arts Council, he said, was being hampered by having aid to the arts channelled through other sources like An Bord Fáilte, the Tourist Board: 'we maintain that as the national body with a responsibility for all the arts, direct government support should be administered through the Arts Council.'

There was some criticism of the Arts Council for seeking to control all State arts funding. 'The Arts Council is becoming power-mad and dictator-like', wrote one critic (*Sunday Press* 12 Nov. 1978) while another commented: 'The Council's excellent record of initiative was directed at proving the Council's worth whereas it should focus on developing a strong economic and political case for the arts ... The ultimate irony that the outgoing Council faces is that all the brilliant achievements of the past few years have generated a momentum which they cannot service and an appetite which they cannot satisfy. The real and final test of its term of office will be the Oireachtas grant to the new Council.' (*Hibernia* 30 Nov. 1978)

The new Arts Council was nominated by Jack Lynch who had replaced Liam Cosgrave as Taoiseach when Fianna Fáil won a general election in July 1977. James White, the highly regarded Director of the National Gallery of Ireland, was appointed as chairman of the Arts Council. His five years as chairman were marked by political resistance to some of the Council's policies. The basic problem was that the Council, having established its absolute independence under Patrick Rock, attempted to push the Government into further acknowledging the arts as a legitimate and essential part of public expenditure. This policy coincided with the rapid expansion of arts activity in Ireland and it became necessary for the Council to cease or reduce funding of some arts organisations in order to live within its grant-in-aid from the Government. These arts organisations began to put political pressure on the Government to increase the Council's grant-in-aid. Relations with the Taoiseach became strained, especially following the accession of Charles Haughey to the post in December 1979. Haughey was acknowledged to be a most impressive politician and he did not appreciate what appeared to him to be the Arts Council's concerted efforts to erode his credibility as a patron of the arts.

In its *Annual Report* for 1978, the Arts Council again stressed the need for the Government to provide funds for housing the arts. Priorities for the new Council would be to secure capital funding, to demand a government policy on the arts in the education system, to develop community arts and to increase support to the individual artist. The Government responded to the appeal for capital funding in 1979 when a total of £273,000 was distributed to nine Irish theatres. It was also decided that arts organisations, such as Comhaltas Ceoltóirí Éireann, which had previously been funded by An Bord Fáilte, should in future be the responsibility of the Arts Council. The result of these two decisions, plus additional funding to compensate for inflation, was an increase in the Council's grant-in-aid from £1,565,000 in 1978 to £2,340,000 in 1979. The Council's staff was expanded to seventeen although Colm Ó Briain observed: 'every new post created and every grant-in-aid increase had to be fought for'. Nevertheless, the Department of the Taoiseach was being generous to the Arts Council and it is fair to say that it received little thanks from the Council. The Council's strategy of arguing that, despite any increases, the level of arts funding was too low, was bound to irritate the Taoiseach and his civil servants. It was only a matter of time before the Council entered into conflict with the Government.

Increased funding gave the Council self-confidence and a sense-of-purpose. Brian Boydell commented: 'The Council members had tremendous integrity and drive to see good things done. Michael Scott, who was reappointed to the Council in 1978, was very surprised at the new regime. At times it was quite clear that he thought things were still done on the "nod" system where everything was fixed beforehand. Quite the opposite was true—things were thrashed out over the Council table in discussion which became quite heated and passionate.' (Interview, 18 April 1987)

The Arts Council decided to set the agenda for the Government regarding the arts in Irish education by establishing a working party to examine and report on the matter. Ciarán Benson was employed by the Arts Council to coordinate the project. In February 1979, *The Place of the Arts in Irish Education* was published. It provided 119 recommendations for improving the position of the arts within the Irish education system. These ranged from encouraging the Arts Council to build up a specialist educational arts service to proposing that the Minister for Education should establish a consultative committee to monitor progress made to develop the arts in education. The Arts Council fully endorsed the 'Benson Report' and called on the Department of Education to respond to it. The Department did so in a brief chapter on 'The Arts' in the *White Paper on Educational Development* published in December 1980. The Department felt that some evidence of the increasing popularity of the arts was found in the statistics that between 1970 and 1980 the numbers taking art at Intermediate Certificate examinations rose from 11,700 to 18,600 and at Leaving Certificate from 1,750 to 6,200.

The White Paper made one proposal only, taken from the Benson Report, that a committee would 'be established to examine the extent to which artistic and creative activities are being catered for in second-level schools.' As if to explain why so little action was planned, the Department offered in the White Paper the following explanation for the general low place of the arts in Irish education: 'Public demands on the school system are less urgent in art-related subjects. Indeed schools have daily experience of pressure for examination results in the traditional subject-areas and an education system must maintain a dynamic interaction with the society it serves.'

The Arts Council reacted strongly to this dependence on demand factors: 'The Department seems to be surprisingly reluctant to give sustained or serious consideration to the state of the arts in our education system . . . The White Paper's emphasis on the lack of popular support for the arts in Irish schools can only be interpreted as an attempt to shirk the real issue. It is clearly the case that as the arts have never been adequately taught in our schools they are hardly likely to command the wide attention of parents.' (*Annual Report* 1980)

There were some promising developments introduced by the Department of Education. The Department asked teacher training colleges to consider giving a points weighting to applicants who had good results in arts subjects. Courses for school teachers were organised to promote visual education. Colm Ó Briain congratulated the Department for agreeing to establish posts of Arts Education Organiser in three Vocational Education Committees—Kilkenny, Sligo and Westmeath. These posts were designed to complement the work being done by Regional Arts Officers. For its part, the Arts Council launched two new schemes in 1980 along the lines of the successful 'Writers in Schools' programme. The first scheme, 'Prints in Schools' comprised four exhibitions of modern art prints and accompanying catalogues prepared by the Arts Council. It was open to schools to apply to borrow one of the exhibitions for up to three weeks at a time. The second scheme, 'Murals in Schools', later known as 'Paint on the Wall' allowed schools to select artists from lists provided by the Arts Council and to have them design a mural for a wall of the school. The idea was that the artist would design the mural and the schoolchildren would help to paint it. The artist's fee and expenses were paid by the Arts Council. This imaginative scheme led to the creation of murals in several hundred schools throughout the country.

A spirit of participation also characterised the Arts Council's policy to stimulate community arts. The Council defined community arts as those which have the objective of 'community participation in the arts'. Community arts could be seen as 'the process of creation in concert with one's audience as opposed to the traditional view that the work of art is an end in itself, divorced from the social context of its making'. Groups like the Pintsize Puppet Theatre, Moving Theatre and Alternative Entertainments, encouraged participation by audiences in the creation of artistic entertainment. They were determined to bring art to the people as part of an educative and creative process. The Arts Council encouraged the breaking down of barriers to art by promoting its own schemes of art in public places. The Council joined with An Bord Fáilte and the National Tidy Towns Competition to launch a major sculpture commission scheme. The winning town was given the finance to commission a work of environmental sculpture from an Irish artist, subject to the work being erected in a public place in the town.

The Arts Council policy of seeking to give direct assistance to individual artists by way of commissions, bursaries and scholarship schemes was strengthened in 1980 when the amount allocated to such activities was raised to £150,000, a 100 per cent increase on the previous year. The Arts Council was concerned, however, that the reality of life for artists in Ireland was such that grant schemes and awards were of minor assistance only. The Council decided to seek a detailed survey which would attempt to provide accurate information on the living and working conditions of artists in Ireland. The findings of the survey, conducted by Irish Marketing Surveys, were published in April 1980. They were described by the Council as 'very worrying, though not unexpected'. The survey found that the average artist was someone who was not a full-time artist, had no pension entitlements, earned a small and irregular income from artistic activity, and favoured increased Government and Arts Council support for the individual artist. The majority of artists qualifying for income tax exemption under Section 2 of the Finance Act, 1969, earned less than £1,000 per year. The politician who had introduced that enlightened legislative measure, Charles Haughey, was impressed by the strength of the report's findings and began, in consultation with his Arts Adviser, Anthony Cronin, to consider what measures could be introduced to improve the situation for individual artists.

The first measure was suggested by the Arts Council. This was the extension of the fund known as Ciste Cholmcille which had been established in 1966. On 3 September 1980, the Taoiseach, Charles Haughey, signed an Additional Function Order under the Arts Act 1951, allowing grants as well as annuities to be paid to individual artists or their dependants who were in poor financial circumstances. The Arts Council was authorised, if it so wished, to apply part of its annual grant-in-aid from the Oireachtas for the purpose of financing the fund. This allowed the Council to develop Ciste Cholmcille into a more effective and practical source of assistance for deserving artists, writers and their dependants.

A more dramatic measure was formulated by the Arts Council following a suggestion made by Charles Haughey and Anthony Cronin. The Taoiseach informed the Arts Council that he wished to see the system of bursary schemes and scholarships extended in such a way that established artists would not have to go through the demeaning procedure of constantly filling in application forms for State assistance.

Colm Ó Briain considered this suggestion carefully and proposed that 100 creative artists should be selected to receive an annual grant from the State. He was inspired to name the scheme An Torc after seeing a gold torc on the cover of his child's Irish history school book. Ó Briain spoke to Anthony Cronin about the idea. Cronin was enthusiastic and suggested that it would be better to allow for 150 creative artists. This would also follow the reference to 150 poets in the novel *At Swim-Two-Birds* by Flann O'Brien (Brian O'Nolan).

The Arts Council staff discussed and developed the proposal. It was envisaged that 'an affiliation of artists' would be established 'to honour those artists whose work had made an outstanding contribution to the arts in Ireland, and to encourage and assist members in devoting their energies fully to their art'. The State would fund the organisation through the Arts Council which would handle the financial and administrative arrangements. The organisation would be self-regulating through a supervisory board of ten members, known as Toscairí, elected by the membership which would meet annually in general assembly 'to discuss issues relevant to the status of the artist and the arts in society, and to review the affairs of the organisation'. To be considered for membership, an artist must have been born in Ireland, or resident in the country for five years, could not be less than thirty years of age and must have produced 'original and creative works of distinction in one or more of the following forms: literature (poetry, fiction, drama), visual art (painting, sculpture, printmaking, photography, film or video) and music'. Certain distinguished members, up to a maximum of five, could be selected as Saoi (wise men) in recognition of their outstanding contributions to the arts in Ireland. Finally, members engaged full-time on artistic work would be eligible to apply for an annuity or Cnuas from the Arts Council for a period of five years. Eligibility for the Cnuas was means-tested, the threshold to be established by the Arts Council from time to time. Members in receipt of the Cnuas were obliged to join a contributory pension scheme and other members could volunteer to join it if they wished (the Arts Council paid one-half of the annual contribution and the artist paid the other half).

The proposal was considered by the Arts Council at a two-day policy meeting in September 1980. The Council gave its full support to the scheme. Máire de Paor, a Council member since 1973, suggested that Aosdána was a more appropriate title than An Torc. In ancient Ireland, the 'aes dána' (poets of the tribe) were men of art whose skill gave them a status beyond that due to them at birth. It was decided that a gold torc should be a symbol of Aosdána and one would be presented to those members selected as Saoi.

Aosdána was launched by Charles Haughey on 5 March 1981 and the first 89 members were named the following December. The scheme received widespread acclaim and was described by Bernard Levin in *The Times* (18 March 1981) as 'the nicest bandwagon you ever saw'. For Colm Ó Briain, Aosdána represented 'the culmination of six years' work by the Arts Council'. (*Irish Times* 6 November 1982) The emphasis of the Arts Council's policies had now been shifted firmly from aid to arts organisations to assistance for individual artists.

The Arts Council's *Annual Report* for 1980 stated that 'the year was marked by a new confidence in the arts.' The mood of Irish arts organisations was one of expectation that the 1980s would see the continuation of increased government funding. Colm Ó Briain argued that although the arts were now on the political agenda, they were still under-financed:

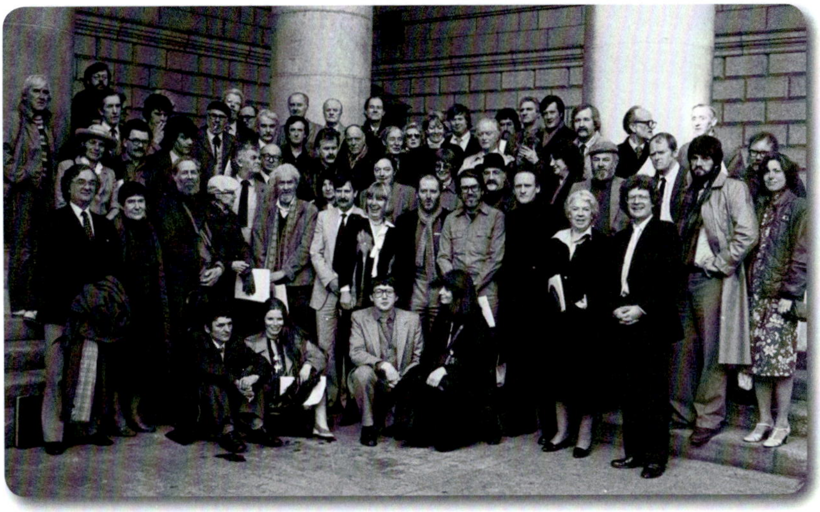

First meeting of Aosdána 1983. Colm Ó Briain is pictured in front (right) beside Mary Lavin. Micheál O'Siadhail is immediately behind Colm. (Pat Langan, The Irish Times)

'When times are good, development projects other than the arts are more "urgent"; when times are bad, there are more "important" problems to be dealt with than the arts. It would seem that there never has been an appropriate time to give a realistic level of support to the arts ... The result is that we have the lowest per capita expenditure on the arts in these islands.' (*Irish Press* 27 Jan. 1981)

Funding was not the only issue to worry the Arts Council. Proposals by Fianna Fáil to establish a National Heritage Council, by Fine Gael to establish a Department of Arts and Culture, and by civil servants to establish a Department of the Gaeltacht and National Culture, pointed to increased direct government involvement in the arts. The Arts Council had strong views about these proposals, stated in the *Annual Report* for 1981: 'Centralising all cultural activities in one department is clearly a rational approach which would give the arts and culture a specific voice at Government level. Centralisation, of course, also has its problems. A single centralised fund for the arts might be more vulnerable to cuts during a period of restrictions in public expenditure.'

But the Council's main concern was that its independence would be compromised and its influence in artistic matters diminished: 'Since it was established in 1951 the Council has regarded its independence as one of its great strengths. To be able to act as a buffer between Government and the arts community is in fact one of the principal reasons why the Council was established. The Council believes that it should jealously guard this independence while, of course, welcoming the increased interest in the arts shown by elected representatives of all parties in recent years.'

Fianna Fáil's proposed National Heritage Council was intended to be a State-sponsored body to carry out State functions in relation to archaeology, museum development, historic monuments, national parks, heritage houses and gardens, and forest parks. There was no obvious indication that the Arts Council's role would be changed in relation to the living arts. Nevertheless, the Arts Council noted with dismay the Government's decision to subvent the National Concert Hall by way of grant from the Department of the Taoiseach. The Council expected that it would be given responsibility for the Concert Hall but, instead, it was to be managed by a twelve-member board appointed by the Taoiseach. The Council wondered whether this was an indication of future government policy to limit its role and influence. The Council was also nervous of the policy behind the formation of the Irish Film Board. It was established in 1981 to offer assistance to the film industry based on commercial criteria. It was the Council's view 'that the funding of film-making by the state should be primarily undertaken for cultural reasons and that return on investment should remain a secondary, though desirable aim'. (*Annual Report* 1981)

As an alternative to the National Heritage Council, the Department of the Public Service proposed that time and expense would be saved by enlarging the Department of the Gaeltacht to avoid having to set up a new organisation. This was effectively a revival of the proposal made in the 'Devlin Report'. As in 1969, the Government rejected it.

In March 1982, Fianna Fáil was returned to power. Although Fianna Fáil only remained in office until December 1982, the months of this government proved to be very difficult for the Arts Council. The reason was that the Council had too many worthy applicants for grants and had not enough funds to assist all of them. The Council's grant-in-aid was increased from £3,750,000 in 1981 to £4,082,000 in 1982 but, set against high inflation, this represented an eight per cent cut in real terms. The Arts Council's solution to the crisis of funding was to cut back on the grants to some large arts bodies so that it could grant aid the activities of a large number of small, young and promising arts groups.

The Arts Council's priorities were laudable and the Council members and staff maintained that if the government refused to increase the annual grant-in-aid, they would have to use their independent discretion as to which arts organisations best deserved continued support. The Council had to conduct a balancing act between the maintenance of established institutions and the development of the conditions for the creation of art by providing new facilities like arts centres and theatres.

The area of funding which absorbed the greatest part of the Council's grant-in-aid was drama. The Council had successfully reduced the percentage of its grant spent on drama from 66 per cent in 1976 to 49 per cent in 1980. Faced with a shortage of funds, the Council decided to make some brave decisions. A strong line was adopted towards the Gate Theatre which had serious financial difficulties. The grant to the Dublin Theatre Festival was curtailed. Finally, the Council decided to cease funding the Irish Theatre Company which folded up as a result. The savings were used by the Council to fund the development of theatres outside Dublin including Druid Theatre, Galway; Cork Opera House and the Everyman Theatre, Cork; Siamsa Tíre (the National Folk Theatre), Tralee; the Hawkswell Theatre, Sligo; and the Belltable Arts Centre, Limerick. The Council also expanded an Independent Theatre Management's scheme launched in August 1979. Cuts were made by the Arts Council to other areas beside drama. Funding was withdrawn from the Douglas Hyde Gallery (at Trinity College, Dublin), the Dublin Contemporary Dance group, and the Cork Film Festival.

The effect of all these decisions was to cause a predictable public outcry. Unfortunately for the Arts Council, its actions were seen as aggressive and insensitive. The Taoiseach, Charles Haughey, was infuriated by the Council's approach to the shortage of funds. From a political angle, the Council was exercising undue pressure in attempting to force a crisis situation in order to win extra funding. The Taoiseach had a personal interest in the work of the Gate Theatre, the Dublin Theatre Festival and the Irish Theatre Company. The Council's harsh treatment of them was not calculated to win the Taoiseach's favour.

In Colm Ó Briain's opinion: 'The Irish Theatre Company saga was the breakpoint with the Taoiseach. The decision to abolish it represented a watershed in the Council's history. The Council was asserting its independence. It would not be a postman for the Taoiseach. It would decide policy and not just implement it.' (Interview 9 Jan. 1988)

The Arts Council described the decision to withdraw its support for the Irish Theatre Company as 'an unpleasant necessity'. But in March and April 1982, newspaper articles began to appear which suggested that the Taoiseach was seeking the removal of Colm Ó Briain as Director of the Arts Council. One article alleged: 'There is a general feeling among the artistic community that Colm Ó Briain and his officers decide who gets funded and to what extent; the Arts Council merely assent to what has already been decided. There is increasing resentment among artists that their work is not being judged by their peers.' (*In Dublin* 31 March 1982)

Another article alleged that the Taoiseach was coming under increasing pressure from the artistic community to reorganise the Arts Council and replace it 'with something more democratic and attuned to the times.' (*Sunday Press* 18 April 1982)Although these articles overdramatised the situation, the Taoiseach's arts adviser, Anthony Cronin, did contact the Arts Council Chairman, James White, to convey the Taoiseach's wish that Colm Ó Briain should be asked to resign as Director. (Interview 23 Feb. 1988) James White refused and, instead, stated that the Arts Council had complete confidence in the Director.

The Arts Council decided to respond publicly to the suggestion that its officials were in control of policy and that it should be replaced by a Ministry of Arts and Culture. The Council supported its staff fully and accepted responsibility for all policy decisions. The Council claimed that it was incorrect to suggest that the Director and the staff were out of control. The staff deserved public appreciation and not reprobation for their enthusiasm and commitment. James White, Máire de Paor and Brian Boydell made trenchant speeches in defence of the Arts Council.

Máire de Paor argued: 'The only effective approach to State patronage of the arts is the one embodied in the principle of the Arts Council—an independent body which guarantees the freedom of the artist from political interference while managing State funds efficiently. The Arts

Council concept has its problems and the Council can make mistakes but the suggestion seems to be that the arts should be administered by civil servants from some new Ministry of Culture. This is a ridiculous concept. The arts are not like some drainage scheme which can be handled by a set of bureaucratic forms.' (*Sunday Press* 2 May 1982)

On 4 May 1982, Anthony Cronin telephoned James White to say that both he and the Taoiseach 'were very disturbed at the concerted attack on the Taoiseach and the Government.' He said that the Council members were challenging the Government and this was unacceptable. He then clarified the Taoiseach's position as confirmed by James White in a letter written the next day:

'I have been reflecting carefully on our telephone conversation of last evening and I would like to thank you for your assurance that the Taoiseach has confirmed that he has no intention of altering the autonomy of the Arts Council or of setting up a Ministry of the Arts. This is most consoling since the Council members feel a sense almost of siege, following the continual barrage of criticism it has received and then, after the change of Government the snide references in the Press that he intended to take various actions derogatory of the Council and staff. I am delighted to have your confirmation that this is unfounded. For my part I can confirm that the Council's staff will take no part in Press criticism of the Government.' (Arts Council, CE file A18)

Anthony Cronin replied to say that there was no basis to 'unfounded journalistic reports' that the Government planned to 'take control' of the arts and he hoped that his telephone conversation with James White had 'cleared the air'.

The confrontation between the Arts Council and the Taoiseach resulted in a re-affirmation of the Council's independence. It also led to a marked improvement in the Council's funding from £4,082,000 in 1982 to £4,954,000 in 1983, a 10.6 per cent increase in real terms. It did not dissuade the Fine Gael-Labour Coalition Government which assumed office in December 1982 from appointing a Minister of State for Arts and Culture. The new Minister of State, Ted Nealon, assured the Arts Council that the statutory autonomy of the Council would not be infringed, that the promotion of all the arts as defined by the Arts Act would remain the function of the Council, and that the Council would continue to be appointed by the Taoiseach. These assurances were accepted by the Arts Council which, in a gesture of pragmatism and hope, welcomed the Minister of State's appointment as a signal of 'a commitment by the Government to the greater development of the artistic and cultural life of the nation'.

*****

On 6 May 1983, three weeks after the inauguration of Aosdána, Colm Ó Briain resigned as Director of the Arts Council. James White issued a press statement to inform the public that the resignation had been 'reluctantly accepted'.

'Members of the Council expressed in the strongest possible terms their feelings of regret at the loss of a Director who has proved to be so dynamic and resourceful in the development of the Council's work over the eight years during which he has directed its activities.'

Colm Ó Briain's aim had been to change the emphasis of State assistance to the arts from organisations to individual artists. Aosdána was the final element in securing this change and, having seen it into existence, Ó Briain decided that he had made his contribution to the Arts Council. (Interview 9 Jan. 1988)

A selection of the many messages to Colm Ó Briain following his resignation

Mary Lavin Oh Colm, my first sense was one of such sadness and loss for the arts and for artists. Believe me I felt some strange personal bereavement. But as time went on and I moved around the house you were continually on my mind, and remembering that I have known you since you were a student—a very young man, and that all the decisions you had made were *right*, I felt much better. I also saw there was a selfishness in my own feelings about your decisions. I had always been aware of security—someone I could call on in a difficulty regarding my work. Now, getting a moment to write, I want to tell you that I feel nothing but happiness for you in your integrity, intelligence and courage to make decisions.

Eilís Dillon I know you never wanted to stay forever and leave your bones in the back garden, but you'll be sadly missed. We all knew you were responsible for putting so much life into everything, for having big ideas and putting them into action at once, for making the lives of all our artists, God help them, forward-looking and active instead of morose and complaining. God knows they had plenty to complain of but things will never be the same again since your time.

Paul Durcan You have done such an outstanding job in the last eight years that the prospect of your departure is rather frightening. . . . In my lifetime I have seen two revolutions in Ireland: television in the 1960s and, in the 1970s, the new Arts Council, embodied by yourself.

Brendan Kennelly Listening to you on the radio this morning, I was struck by your reluctant integrity and a quality I can only describe as far-seeingness. It is always easy to write to someone who is leaving a position, but I would like to say that your peculiar contribution over the past few years—basically a gift of youthfulness, a shifting of dust, a healthy creation of enemies and friends, a gift for innovation (I cite the writers-in-prisons as a modest example, from my own point of view)—will be seen, and quite soon, to be far-reaching and deep, I suppose we never talked together really (and when we did we were very much on opposite sides!)—but I want to say that your refusal to settle into a position of Artistic Authority or Symbolic Significance is a work of genuine intelligence, and more than that, trust in your own future. I know that same future will be full of brightness.

Jim O'Callaghan, Office of the Revenue Commissioners Bad news it was as far as the Taxes Branch and myself are concerned. I have admired over the years the artistic skills you have displayed in dealing with your thespian brethren and sisterhood. It was a tremendous task and the public tributes you have received were richly deserved. We will miss your assistance and cooperation here.

'A National Cultural Bank'*

Sean O'Faolain

21 June 1983

Dear Colm,

Ever since I heard you are about to come to the rescue of that antique body, the Irish Labour Party, I have been, in my old gentleman's lazy, procrastinating way, wanting to express my delight at the prospect of some injection of light and life into Irish Socialism—"nay" (as they used to cry)—into Socialism tout court. The main, if not the overriding impulse up to our immediate time behind Irish Labour has been egalitarianism in cash terms. This is, of course, a universal impulse, but elsewhere (the U.S. especially) social structures go far to leave the road open to other, larger, more basic ambitions. See, two easy examples, Senator Daniel Patrick Moynahan, (East Side, poor Irish) and the present Mayor of Chicago. The part of the social structures here that interests me most is education—a word of use in the widest sense of Culture, which again I use in its all-embracing sense of a way of living. In the Arts Council you were obliged to use the word in a limited connotation. Henceforth you have the job (if you want to take it on) of making it basic to the outlook and ambitions of the Party—to include, that is, Housing, town-planning, living conditions, Health, technical training, cooking (Oh! Lots of THAT!), hygiene (ditto), schooling from bottom to top, sport, scientific sophistication—and so on until all adds up to A Way of Life (of, i.e., living and planning for living) —to a pattern of life NOT FOR THIS GENERATION, not for the so-called worker of today (we are all workers) but for our/his progeny, for the generations ahead of him—which means the putting of increased wages way down the line of Labour's priorities in favour of a ten to twenty to thirty year PLAN (government plan) for the workers' families' education. Otherwise the

---

* Letter to Colm Ó Briain on his appointment as General Secretary of the Labour Party.

present utterly wasteful war to the knife situation—profiting nobody in the long-term—between employers and employees will go on forever.

Furthermore, and this I barely mentioned to you when you were out here with Paddy Lynch, this 20 year educational scheme for workers' families must be in the field of technics, which within your lifetime certainly will have dominated the way of life of every country in the world.

Only a man of your calibre can hope to fire a body like the I.L.P. with this realism of the pre-eminence of A Way of Life over a WAR of Wages, and wish the truth of the fact that only by a modernised educational system can A Way of Life—priority over-wages 20 Year plan liberate those future generations which, by their expertise, will continue the task of what I call Creative Labour Government.

I enclose an article which you may have read not to support my points but to mark the importance of clearly defining the central idea that liberation comes only from education. This article is wrongly weighted. The poor remain the poor only because their parents are under-educated, have low standards AND ABOVE ALL ARE SLAVISHLY MONEY CONSCIOUS, i.e. cannot see beyond the pay-packet. They live meanwhile in (often) appalling and disheartening circumstances, have no cultural (in the large sense, e.g. food) standards, in short they live unambitious, low-level 19th century lives. Naturally their kids follow their example.

In brief: no more "More Cash". Henceforth A National Cultural Bank and More Cash to be paid into it by the employers—all in the interest of the future emancipation through technical development of the common country of the workers and the employers.

How would you work it? Strike if you must, but never (by present values) for, say, more than 5%, on condition

That the employer puts an equivalent sum into the National Cultural Bank, and

That the Government likewise puts an equivalent sum into a super-modernised technical Cultural system of education for the strikers children's children, and secula seculorum.

Am I balmy?

With Best wishes in all your future careers.

Ever

Sean

Growing Up

Aisling Ní Bhriain

A parent's task is to equip his or her offspring with the innate skills to thrive whatever weather life might present. Looking back on the phases of my own growth, I think of my father like he was in the garden: initially simply positioning me with sufficient exposure to light and water (stimulus and inspiration); later applying more focus, like his ceaseless patience in trying to get a wayward climbing-rose to grow over a trellis.

Like many children, my relationship with my parents grew over a number of broad phases. As a pre-teen: complete and happy dependence on this glamorous, G&T-drinking couple with great taste in music, who brought me on exciting holidays, and held the only views and opinions worth holding on any given topic. As a teen: complete and *un*happy dependence on these guys, who still had great taste in music, but no idea who *I* really was and an intensely frustrating absence of empathy for the woes which burdened *my* life. Small wonder that I was provoked, on numerous occasions, to exit exasperating discussions, flouncing off with a flourishing slam of my door, followed by a cascade of tears into my pillow accompanied by muffled mutterings: 'I hate them, I hate them, I hate them, I HATE them!'

In my twenties: gleeful independence. Admittedly this was fully achieved only by my *late* twenties. And even then, I welcomed the occasional windfall from BOMAD (the Bank of Mam and Dad). At that stage, as I pursued my career abroad, it was easy to see that whereas my many qualities were due to the strength of my own winning personality, my inconvenient weaknesses (those inevitable wobbles in confidence and hard-to-shake feelings of inadequacy) could be traced right back to my parents and their parenting flaws and failures.

In my thirties: my own experiment with parenthood returned me to dependence on them. Their visits to the UK or to the Netherlands were meticulously planned around my need for child-care, while I zoomed off to business meetings around the globe. As I wrestled with the demands of work and family, I became acutely aware of the effort it must have taken my parents to make my childhood so effortless. Whilst I felt worthy of an Olympic gold medal for simply being able to hold down a job and get my children clothed and fed before they left for school in the morning, my parents had accomplished this while also enjoying the most prolific and colourful set of extra-curricular activities. And their expansive world had created the exhilarating environment in which I and my sister grew up.

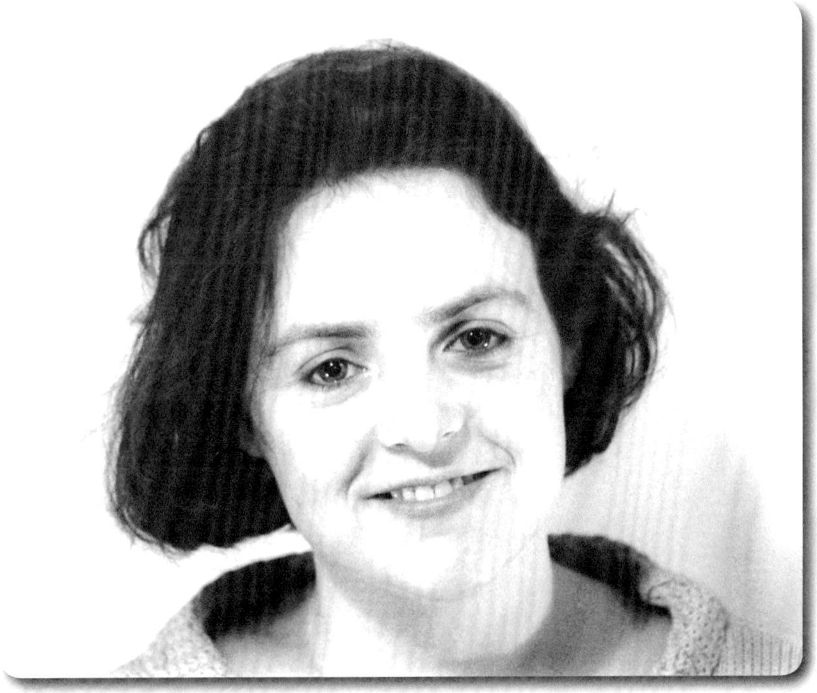

Aisling Ní Bhriain, Colm Ó Briain's second daughter: President of the Student Union, UCD, 1994.

Our home constantly welcomed people not in our immediate family. Au pairs became life-long friends. We had visits from people fleeing torture, imprisonment or death in the Philippines, as well as Dutch and German activists who formed part of the Philippines solidarity movement. We frequently entertained and accommodated politicians, human rights lawyers, Hollywood film directors, artists, poets, writers, journalists and actors. We thought it was normal to have a constant stream of the exotic and eclectic arrive for dinner parties to debate matters of national and international importance, whilst gobbling gourmet home-made dinners. My parents were the ultimate entertaining double-act: Mam would produce incredible food—such as home-baked bread rolls, home-cured *gravadlax*, and stunning desserts like choux pastry profiteroles—while Dad would conduct the dinner table through a series of fascinating topics of conversation, ranging from geo-politics to Anglo-Irish relations, to the role of the Church in Irish society, to whatever was the burning issue of the day. These meals might be capped by a *digestif* of homemade fig wine, made from fruit hand-carried from Bulgaria by Mam herself, following a client consultation with the Bulgarian government suspected of being behind the plot to kill the Pope.

There were a few inconveniences: no homemade flapjacks in my lunchbox for a few weeks while my Mam was off in the Philippine mountains advising the communists on a potential peace treaty with the regime of Cory Aquino. (My friends at school were very understanding.) Parts of the weekend would occasionally have to be sacrificed to distributing leaflets for Ruairí Quinn at election time, or supporting divorce at referendum time. Now and again, placards would be needed for demonstrations at the American Embassy against Reagan, the bomb, or US policy in Nicaragua. (Luckily our attendance at these demonstrations was not raised with Seóna during her interview to become a US citizen.) Mam and Dad's interpretation of 'keeping your children active' was, well, keeping them 'politically' active.

We were culturally active too: we were brought to the theatre, to art galleries, to concerts where we would often meet the live performer, the artist, the playwright, the composer, or the manager of the venue. The arts were not just something to be enjoyed for entertainment purposes, but something to which my father was deeply connected on many levels—personal, administrative, and political. We also of course saw the plays Dad himself had directed: these were the ones I would attend feeling I was the famous 'daughter of the director'. Never quite as famous—inevitably—as my sister, who landed the part of a small boy in his production of *Antigone* at the Peacock.

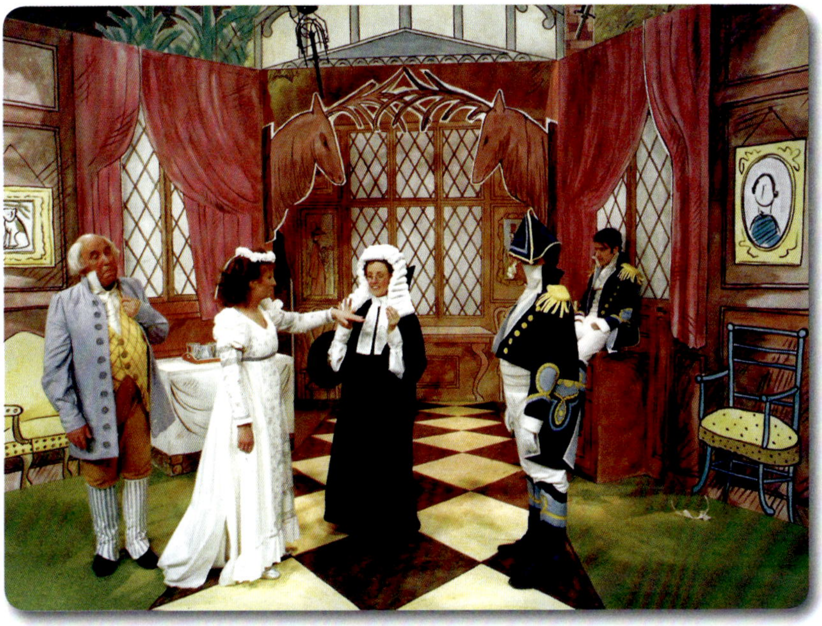

'Ham it up'—a scene from Opera Ireland's production of Haydn's opera *L'infedeltà Delusa*. Colm Ó Briain, as director, renamed it *Country Matters* 'to dispel any notions of grandeur—God forbid—just because it's opera!' (RTÉ)

The stage embodied the culmination of ideas I'd first hear casually discussed in our living room. He didn't talk to us about his work, but Dad would often sit in his dressing-gown on our red sofa, outlining—on our ahead-of-its-time push-button red and black telephone—his ideas to his theatre colleagues. I recall being struck by his artistic courage, flair and sense of humour in his discussions concerning the Opera Ireland commission to direct Haydn's *L'infedeltà Delusa*, an opera (in his words) with a wafer-thin plot and superficial characterisation, set in the dreary provinces. Why not take advantage of the opera's weaknesses? Ham it up with self-parody and slap-stick acting? Make the set design look like cardboard cut-outs, a fitting backdrop to the cardboard characters? And call the production 'Country Matters' to dispel any notions of grandeur—God forbid—just because it's opera!

Opera had a prominent place on the soundtrack of Charleville Road. It was not unusual to wake on a Sunday morning to the dulcet sounds of *La Traviata* or *Carmen* wafting under my bedroom door, carried in on the tantalising aroma of freshly baked scones, mingling with an Irish breakfast fry-up. Bach, Beethoven, Mahler, Wagner, Philip Glass, Jean-Michel Jarre, Paul Simon, Leonard Cohen, *Rondo Veneziano* all featured too.

My dad's penchant for great dinner-party conversation was matched by his interest in exploring at our breakfast or weekday dinner table the current affairs playing out in our teenage lives. The more seemingly intractable the issue, the more he would relish the process of getting to the nub of it, and strategising approaches to tackle it. He was adept at discovering the essence of a quandary, identifying the fundamental principle at its heart, from which the correct course of action would become clear, however inconvenient or painful.

How best to deal with the teacher who made a racist comment? Raise it with the teacher, raise it with the school principal, involve or not involve the person about whom the comment was made? In the end, the strategy was to write an article in the school magazine about the need to 'Teach the Teachers'. That led to another evening spent with Dad deciding how to deal with the principal, who objected to and ultimately censored the article. And more time with Dad preparing for the discussion I would have with her when I was summoned. Anchored as I was by then in the fundamental principle of equality, and the role of the teacher in a learning environment, I had nothing to fear from that meeting.

Dad handled a short shop-lifting phase of mine as an eleven-year-old, not only by pointing out the moral wrongs of my behaviour, but by bringing me back to the wronged establishments to confess my misdeeds in person and shamefacedly return the items. He taught me not only the difference between right and wrong, but how to own my mistakes and to deal with them bravely. He accompanied me on this walk of shame, not to ensure I would go through with it, but to support me as I did so. He had his arm around me the whole time.

During my sabbatical year as president of my university's student union, when I also held a seat on the governing body of the university, my father was brilliant in helping me to tease out a particularly difficult situation involving issues of freedom of the press, freedom of speech, and the responsibilities of governance in public office. Unlike the instance of the errant teacher, simple resort to the media was not an appropriate response in this situation. The process of discussing the issues with Dad helped me not only to identify the right decision to make, but also gave me the moral clarity from which flowed the required resilience and courage to weather the painful storm which followed, when that decision was upended by a disaffected colleague.

A discussion with Colm wasn't just about getting advice. His warmth and wisdom would gently expose the relevant principles, values and responsibilities, so that you could be rooted in yourself and who you wanted to be, whether weathering life's gales or flourishing in the sunshine. I feel truly blessed to have had that thoughtful, caring arm around me through so many dilemmas as I grew up. And blessed too to have the muscle memory within my own arm, though it will never completely replace my Dad's, now that he is gone.

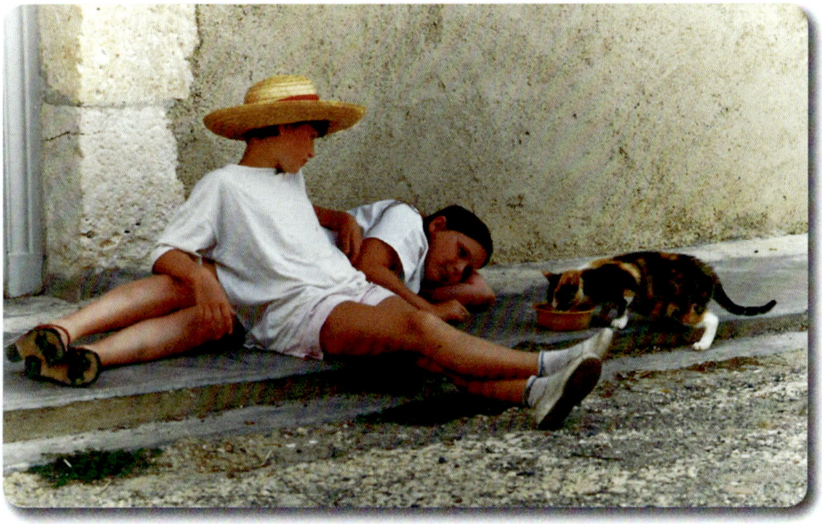

Aisling and Seóna, on holiday in France.

Friday Nights in Pubs

Seóna Ní Bhriain

Older friends are bolder friends
Among whom you're too young to be.
They may be nice
You may be wise
But don't react with such surprise
When we express our discontent;
It is not meant to target you
But just the places you frequent.

Older friends have moulded trends
Of rolling joints and crushing stubs
Of cigarettes in smokey pubs;
Where men get drunk and drugs are passed
And passes made, and you are there.
We disapprove.

Please know it is not you we doubt,
Nor even those you hang about.
It's just the world that is let out
On Friday nights in pubs.

An Exciting Election

Eithne FitzGerald

A great theatre director takes diverse characters, talents and egos, and through vision, encouragement, brutal honesty and a lot of sheer hard work, brings them to perform as a successful ensemble. In some ways, directing an election campaign is not so different, harnessing the energy of volunteers, party members, and the candidate to deliver a co-ordinated and effective electoral performance. An election campaign will often have more prima donnas than a grand opera. Unlike a conventional play, however, there is no clear script, and a lot of improv. Alongside the candidate and canvassers who perform on thousands of doorsteps, sets and props are provided by posters and election leaflets.

In the 1989 election, the Labour Party in Dublin South had a near miss. A few hundred votes in the difference might have seen Green transfers elect the Labour candidate rather than my transfers electing Roger Garland as Ireland's first Green TD.

To try and clinch success in Dublin South in the following general election, Ruairí Quinn generously proposed seconding Colm Ó Briain from his own constituency organisation in neighbouring Dublin South East to turn the Dublin South organisation into a more effective fighting force. A renowned theatre director, former head of the Arts Council, and former General Secretary of the Labour Party Colm brought his sharp political brain, his organising skills, and his capacity to draw excellent performances from a diverse bunch of people. Working hand in glove with the super-efficient Fionnuala Richardson of the People's College, this duo of producer and director brought success beyond what we had ever imagined—not only winning a Dáil seat, but topping the national poll with 17,256 votes. Colm had many successes on the stage, but always looked on the 1992 General Election result in Dublin South as one of his most successful productions.

Coming in to our organisation as a relative outsider, Colm got us to take a good hard look at ourselves, acknowledge our mistakes and weaknesses, and identify what we could do better. It's always easier for any organisation to blame outside forces for its lack of success, rather than take a searching look at its own performance and what's within its own control. This was the brutal honesty bit, which needed to be a starting point for change and growth.

Colm organised a two-day workshop in a modest hotel in Donabate over a winter weekend, an unheard-of innovation for our constituency organisation. He made us take an honest look at our failings. The brutal honesty piece extended to my appearance and dress sense, as the presumptive candidate. The comrades all agreed my slightly hippy look and Mick Wallace-type wild hair needed to be replaced by a more tailored, professional style. The sessions were tough and challenging, and Colm drove us hard. But we also had great fun role-playing encounters with voters, and discovered Jim Butler's marvellous thespian talents in doing a doorstep crank. We brainstormed and we strategised, and emerged with a clear plan to build our organisation and profile, and meet with and persuade voters. Most importantly, it built a real sense of team and common purpose.

Fionnuala Richardson is a genius at project management, and she turned the different plans and strategies into concrete action points and time lines, assigning responsibility for different streams of the long campaign.

John Horgan always said, you don't win votes at election time, you harvest them. So the years following the 1989 defeat involved a campaign to try and reach out to and meet as many as possible of the 80,000 voters living in the 40,000 houses across the constituency. This meant appearances at gathering points like shopping centres, after-school pick-ups, or Sunday churches. We prepared a series of 'A-boards' with my poster and name on them, so people would know their candidate was there. This was literally standing for election—taking up a fixed spot at a chilly shopping centre over many hours. I invested in special fleece-lined trousers to stay warm. There was the round of summer fêtes, where I indulged my weakness for buying plants, and my young family appreciated the home-made cakes, Taney and Kilternan tying for the honour of the most delicious of the home-made fare.

Then there was door-to-door canvassing—this bit was running for election, trying to cover as many houses as possible in the time. Morning

FITZGERALD, Eithne The Labour Party	1

LABOUR

I want to offer you a new vision for Ireland of the 1990s, based on values of mutual support, partnership and co-operation.

Let us reject the culture of conflict, individual greed and exclusion, and build together a society founded on community solidarity, which has always been a unique feature of Irish life. All citizens must be given the opportunities to realise their full potential – men and women, our young people and our senior citizens, both inside and outside the workplace.

As your representative I will work to re-establish values of equality, justice and integrity in public life. I will emphasise community and worker participation, together with radical change in the role and structures of public administration. Empowerment is the key.

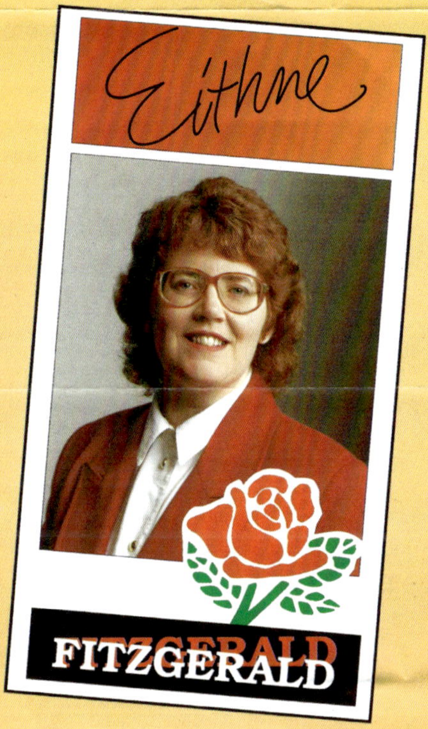

PUT JUSTICE INTO THE ECONOMY
To address the critical issue of unemployment I believe in an active role for public enterprise in leading the creation of sustainable jobs. Targetted action is needed to break the cycle of long term unemployment and loss of hope in families and communities. A new social partnership is essential to ensure that the long term unemployed can take up a quarter of new job opportunities.

A MATTER OF INTEREST
There is limited scope to change interest rates which are set by international factors; Labour however calls for support during the interest rate crisis for those most under pressure – first time home buyers and small businesses.

PROMOTING HEALTH AND WELLBEING
Labour is committed to equal access to quality healthcare and a positive approach to health through education and information. The rights of people with mental handicap and their families to essential services must be guaranteed.

CHERISHING THE NATION'S CHILDREN?
Resources must be allocated to make the **Child Care Act 1991** a reality. Major expansion of child care and pre-school facilities is needed and tax relief should be given for child care expenses.

LEARNING TO GET IT RIGHT
In the debate on the **Education Green Paper**, I support the creation of Local Education Authorities to make education policies and priorities publicly accountable.

THE STRUGGLE FOR EQUALITY
Labour's **Equal Status Bill** remains the most comprehensive piece of equality legislation ever produced in this country. The grounds on which the Bill prohibits discrimination includes sex, religion, disability and sexual orientation. The objective of the Bill is to make discrimination unlawful not only in the workplace, but also in education, the provision of goods, facilities and services. The Fianna Fáil and P.D. parties were united in opposing this Bill.

LET'S MAKE IRELAND WORK!

Published by Frank Buckley, 4 Highfield Drive, Dublin 16. Agent for the Candidate. *Printed on paper made from recycled sugarcane pulp.*

Labour candidate Eithne FitzGerald topped the poll in the Dublin South constituency in the 1992 general election. Colm Ó Briain directed her campaign and brought 'brutal honesty' to the task.

times mainly meant pensioners, an afternoon canvass would find some mothers at home after school with their kids, and once the days began to stretch, a larger number of evening canvasses were added to the programme. I became best friends with the shoemaker in Dundrum, as my footwear needed resoling almost weekly. We had a map of the different pubs across the constituency, and systematically each would be visited by half a dozen of us in red scarves, taking well-earned refreshment after a night of knocking on doors.

A further day-long workshop, 'Donabate 2', this time in a back room of a pub in the constituency, further refined our election preparations.

The 1990 election of Mary Robinson was a highlight. There was huge energy and momentum behind the campaign, and for the first time in my canvassing career, a majority of voters we met were backing our woman. At her election count in the RDS, I met people in tears, old leftists who had never previously voted for a candidate who had actually won. Many people who joined the Robinson campaign in our patch joined the party or stayed on as volunteer canvassers. Colm had contacts, through the arts world and elsewhere, who also came on board to help.

This was the time of the emerging planning scandals that were later explored by the Flood and Mahon Tribunals, and Frank Buckley and myself were busy on Dublin County Council fighting to oppose and expose what was going on. We had a surge of support in the 1991 local elections, greatly strengthening the Labour team on the county council with the arrival of people like Joan Burton and Niamh Bhreathnach. In June 1992, I was elected as Chair of Dublin County Council. Woman is born free but was everywhere in chains, as I clanked my way through a series of official engagements weighed down by this symbol of office.

The murky politics of the corrupt rezonings taking place at local level were mirrored in a series of high profile scandals at national level. Dick Spring played a leading role in exposing insider deals to a golden circle, and beef industry scandals that culminated in the Beef Tribunal. So when the General Election of 1992 was called for November, Labour's manifesto calling for legislation on ethics in public office, freedom of information, and action to curb political donations struck a chord with the public. In Dublin South, thanks to Colm and Fionnuala, we were also supremely well-prepared, with a detailed plan for the three weeks of the campaign, a solid foundation of pre-election canvassing, and an enthusiastic team on board.

An unexpected stroke of luck was the last minute decision of Fine Gael TD Nuala Fennell to retire. As a committed feminist with a solid track record, she had attracted many otherwise natural Labour voters. We thought we were now in with a shout for the fifth seat.

As Director of Elections, Fionnuala managed the canvass programme and assigned the growing volume of volunteers to their tasks. I got my first mobile phone, rented—it was a large brick—to keep in touch with HQ and the canvass team. Colm focused more on the media and publicity side. This was a pre-email, pre-social media campaign with traditional publicity through posters, canvass cards, the election address posted to households, newspapers and TV. Large posters, with the 'Elect Eithne' slogan, were pasted on to big sheets of hardboard and erected. Colm organised for a video to be shot, and production of a mini-newspaper. He prepped me for Irish language and other TV debates. This duo ran the nightly meetings of the core Election Committee, from which I was kept away—the candidate was to concentrate on meeting voters, and getting enough sleep, and not to get caught up in the administrative minutiae of an election. So as a surge of support was being felt from the doorsteps, as the Spring Tide began to roll, I missed the fierce internal debate in the election team about whether to add Frank Buckley to the ticket and try for two seats—an impossible thought at the start of the campaign.

In the event, I ran solo, and notched up a 29 per cent vote share, which with tight vote management could have brought two seats. On the morning of the count, I had a long-standing arrangement to give a lecture in the IPA at 9, and by the time I arrived at the count centre at 10.30 it was clear I would top the local poll and get in on the first count. As the votes poured in, the euphoria was tempered by the realisation that we should probably have run two candidates, giving Frank Buckley a fighting chance of taking a second seat. Instead my surplus ultimately went to elect the PD's Liz O'Donnell for the first time. It was only after lunch that day that it began to dawn that not only would I top the poll in Dublin South, I would also top it nationwide. On my fifth run for the Dáil I had finally made it, but Colm and Fionnuala deserved Tony Awards for Best Directors.

Labour had won a record 33 seats, there was a record 20 women in the Dáil of which I was one. Fianna Fáil offered a deal that was effectively the Labour Party manifesto with a couple of minor omissions—like commitment to enact Freedom of Information—and the Reynolds –Spring Government was formed. Michael D. became Minister for Arts, Culture and the Gaeltacht, where one of his best decisions was to take on Colm as his adviser. I was made Minister of State at the Office of the Tánaiste, with responsibility for enacting ethics legislation, and 'considering' Freedom of Information. I was also made Minister of State for Finance, with responsibility, under Bertie Ahern as senior Minister, for EU structural funds, and the National Development Plan.

Preparing the Ethics in Public Office legislation from scratch was tough. It was the first update in over three quarters of a century of the 1889–1916 Prevention of Corruption Acts. It seemed to touch a raw nerve—this was before the extent of Haughey's venality as shown by the Moriarty Tribunal, was known. It was bitterly fought on the floor of the Dáil.

A breakdown in trust between Dick Spring and Albert Reynolds led to the collapse of the 1993–4 FF–Labour Government, and the formation of the Rainbow Coalition with FG and Democratic Left. I was again assigned to the office of the Tánaiste as Minister of State, and also appointed to Labour Affairs, serving with Richard Bruton as the senior Minister. Michael D. continued in Arts, Culture and the Gaeltacht, again ably supported by Colm as his adviser.

A legacy of the Beef Tribunal findings was a political commitment in the new Government programme to actually enact Freedom of Information legislation. We had already begun work on this in the Office of the Tánaiste, and the pace of work accelerated. Unlike the Ethics in Public Office Act, this was pure joy, with a particularly useful and constructive debate in the Seanad, where I was happy to accept many amendments. It hit stickier ground in the Dáil, with what appeared like a filibuster. However, that was eventually paused, enabling the Freedom of Information Act to be passed just before the 1997 General Election was called.

Sadly, my Dáil career proved a one-term wonder, not a long-running show like *The Mousetrap*. But a lot was achieved in those four and a half years.

I got to pass laws on ethics and on freedom of information, and to chair the Task Force on Violence against Women. Mervyn Taylor introduced far-reaching equality legislation, and a successful referendum on divorce. Michael D., with Colm at his side, invigorated the arts, set up a network of theatres around the country, and established TG4. Niamh Bhreathnach abolished third level fees. Dick Spring and Albert Reynolds negotiated the Downing Street Declaration, and paved the way for the Good Friday Agreement of 1998.

In total, I ran for the Dáil seven times, and got elected once. However, the spectacular fashion of that election, and what it enabled me and my colleagues to achieve, owes a huge debt to the genius and commitment of Colm Ó Briain, and to the Dublin South team he helped professionalise. We miss him. May he rest in peace.

Gaia: The Failed Opportunity

Tony Boland

The Gaia Atlas of Planet Management set my imagination alight. This wonderful book had been gifted to me in the mid-1980s. At the time I was the casting director for the Entertainment Department in RTÉ. My job was to identify and manage the groups or individuals who would be part of our television programmes. A large part of our entertainment schedule was *The Late Late Show*.

Reading the *Gaia Atlas*, I not only understood the danger and the immensity of the climate change that was upon us, but how all the changes that were coming intersected and affected each other. I realised what a marvellous television series it would make.

In 1986 RTÉ was offering a redundancy package to try and reduce the size of its staff. I decided to take the leap and to set up my own independent production company. Planet Pictures Limited was born. Using my redundancy fund I bought the rights to the *Gaia Atlas* for one year.

Bob Geldof was the obvious choice as a presenter of the series I envisaged. Colm Ó Briain was the obvious person to help me to bring the series to life.

I had previously helped Bob with the organisation of the Live Aid concert in 1985. Whereas he had originally envisaged a broadcast where money would be raised from the broadcasting fees, I suggested a Telethon where the money would be raised from the public. We got sponsorship from AIB for the cost of the broadcast. The Telethon was hugely successful in Ireland, raising more money per capita than in any other country where it was broadcast.

I suppose it was that experience of raising awareness of our globalised world and the devastating effects of drought on whole peoples that convinced me of the importance of bringing the *Gaia Atlas* to life in a visual form. Colm loved the book as well, and shared the vision. While I sought to raise the money for the production, he worked on a plan for how the series would look and work.

These were the very early days of independent television production in Ireland. RTÉ had no money, and we needed a lot. I manged to get agreement from the BBC to fund the initial development of the series, but the support just wasn't enough. I found myself more and more in London trying to drum up business for Planet, with some success – but not for Gaia. Eventually the company was only producing the *Big Breakfast Show* for Channel 4, and of course that kept me in London and extremely busy. After renewing the rights to Gaia over several years, I had to abandon my vision for it. Colm did manage to do a small series on the environment for RTÉ, focusing on awareness-raising in schools, and otherwise continued as a freelancer in theatre and television for the following few years. It is only now, some thirty years later, that environmental programmes are being appreciated by mass audiences. But, according to the Gaia timetable, it is already too late to save the planet.

Television is a powerful medium, and working in it can give one a great sense of opportunity and achievement. But the complexities of doing that work can also reduce us to constant compromising of values and standards, and even to the loss of our own self-worth. At the same time, the creativity and energy that I shared with people like Colm from the world of broadcasting provide wonderful memories, and new ones are emerging as I watch my son Murray Boland in that world of opportunity and achievement today.

High Standards in Arts Management

Pat Cooke

The UCD-based programme in Arts Management and Cultural Policy, which I directed from 2006 until my retirement in 2020, had its origins in an initiative of the Irish Museums Trust (IMT) in the 1980s. In 1982 Seán Popplewell, then executive secretary to the Trust, which had been established in 1978 as a fund-raising body dedicated to supporting the Irish museum sector, spearheaded an initiative with the Industrial Training Authority (AnCO) to set up a training course to provide career opportunities in museums and arts organisations for unemployed arts graduates. This objective aligned with what had been one of Colm Ó Briain's main goals as director of the Arts Council from 1975 to 1982: to enhance the administrative skills, management capacities and overall professionalism of those working in the arts sector.

The course was modelled on a diploma programme then being run at City University, London, and was first run over the months August–December 1982. It sought to cover all the practical aspects of managing a museum or arts venue: finance, marketing, public relations, conservation, human resources, graphics, display, insurance, programming, and so on. Jenni Rogers, then director of TCD's Douglas Hyde Gallery (and a graduate of the London course) was appointed director for the first year. One of the distinctive features of the initial programme—and which has remained one of its main attractions ever since—was a work placement in a cultural institution.

With the support of Alistair Rowan, Professor of Art History, lectures were held at Ardmore House in UCD, thus establishing a link that would prove vital to the course's long-term viability. It proved so popular in its first year (with over one hundred applicants) that it was offered again in 1983 and 1984, with Paula McCarthy (who had been the Arts Council's visual arts officer from 1975 to 1980) as director. Though AnCO funding ceased in 1985, it proved possible to run the course again in 1985 with support from the European Social Fund. Art curator

Siubhan Barry was director that year. But in 1986 the IMT concluded an agreement with UCD to host the course for three years. Following interviews held in August 1986, Colm Ó Briain was appointed director of the now fully UCD-based programme.

There can be little doubt that Colm's reputation and standing as the former director of the Arts Council added enormous credibility to the whole process of embedding the diploma as a university-based academic programme. The class of 1986–7 was the first group of students to experience the full force of Colm's qualities as teacher and mentor. Among them was Garrett Phelan, now one of the country's most prominent visual artists. He remembers being impressed by Colm's insistence on the importance of record-keeping, the need to 'take what we do seriously, even with respect to the minutiae of administration'. This left him with an enduring sense of the importance of professionalism in the overall development of the arts. Clíodhna Shaffrey (the director of Temple Bar Studios), recalls a teacher of extraordinary energy, determined that his students would learn primarily by 'going to the theatre or gallery, getting behind the scenes, speaking to the organisers, directors, and curators'. She has the impression that 'we must have visited every single gallery, arts centre and theatre, on several "mind-blowing' trips"'. She offers this vivid picture of his pedagogic qualities in the round:

'Colm loved debate. He was extremely articulate, passionate, full blown. He had this "voice" a way of speaking, arms gesticulating, but clear, sharp, fluent, intelligent. He believed in the public good, investment in services, equality of access. There was an urgency to his thinking, the necessity of breaking old orders, being open to new ideas, risk-taking and whatever was needed to build a broader arts community and make the arts accessible, turning tables on their heads, resisting elitism and wanting art to be challenging.'

Vincent O'Shea, who has maintained an unbroken career as a freelance consultant in the arts and heritage, was class representative that year. He took readily to Colm's argumentative style of teaching and engagement. 'Colm could happily argue with you, mostly at length, over something as trivial as the gravitational pull of two flies on a wall, or the intricacies of some obscure government policy,' he recalls. He sums up the essence of his qualities as a teacher in a quote adapted from

Beckett: 'I must go on, I can't go on, I'll go on . . .'. He, like Clíodhna, has abiding memories of those field trips. In characteristic sleeves-up, hands-on activist mode, it was Colm who rented and drove the minibus. Vincent recalls, 'I usually rode shotgun, as there wasn't always a rush for the front passenger seat beside him, with his tendency to argufy in his unique Socratic manner. On those journeys, there wasn't a constituency in the country where he couldn't regale you with a story of some political intrigue.' The latter knowledge, no doubt, deriving from his standing as a Labour Party supporter and more particularly from his experience as the party's general secretary from 1983 to 1985. Overall, the challenging intensity of Colm's teaching style left him with the sense of having had a kind of 'special forces type training', which has helped him (much like his mentor) to fend for himself as a life-long freelancer in the arts.

Colm stepped down as director in 1988 and was succeeded by Anne Kelly, who held the post for eighteen years, until her retirement in 2006. But that was not the end of his involvement with the programme. Over the following years, he gave lectures, assisted with internships and sat on interview boards for admissions. These contributions only ended when he became director of the National College of Art and Design in 2005.

A sociologist by profession, Anne was driven by a strong commitment to cultural democracy. She sought to reframe the role of the arts within a wider and more socially inclusive understanding of cultural values. Thus, under her guidance, the programme achieved a more balanced relationship between the broader and more theoretical goals of cultural policy and the specific and practical skills required for arts management. She first met Colm in 1985. The following year, he invited her to deliver a module on Irish cultural policy during his first year as director. One of the principles established by Colm was the need to take special care over the recruitment of students for such a vocationally oriented course. He therefore devoted a great deal of time to interviewing candidates in person. Echoing the observations made above by some of his first students, Anne observes that 'he admired passion and commitment above everything and many of his teaching methods emphasised developing the ability to argue a case.' She also highlights his leadership, during his time as Arts Council director, in a drive to persuade local authorities to appoint arts officers. As a result, many of the graduates of the programme were subsequently appointed as arts officers around the country.*

Given that UCD's commitment was only for three years, Anne began her tenure fully conscious of the programme's tenuous standing within the academy—in particular, the absence of 'strong support links with the faculty power structure, academic opportunities and funding'. She fought successfully to secure those links over the following years. In 2002 she oversaw the transformation of the Diploma in Arts Administration Studies into the MA in Cultural Policy and Arts Management, a move that helped to consolidate the programme's prestige and academic standing within the university, as well as attracting greater interest from international candidates.

Following Anne Kelly's retirement in 2006, I became director, having spent two-thirds of my career as a heritage professional in the Office of Public Works as director of the Pearse Museum and Kilmainham Gaol. Over the following years, the programme was progressively internationalised, with the number of foreign students each year ranging between a third and over half. Over the past decade or so, the programme has also attracted a succession of doctoral students, whose work provides a body of independent, critical research that can contribute to the formulation of arts and cultural policies over the years to come.

Annette Clancy, herself an experienced arts practitioner and consultant of many years standing, took over as director in the autumn of 2020. It is now the longest running and most prestigious programme of its kind in the country. Some of the hallmarks that make it so can be traced to Colm Ó Briain's innovations during his short but inspirational reign as director between 1986 and 1988.

I am grateful to Seán Popplewell, Dr Anne Kelly, Garrett Phelan, Vincent O'Shea and Clíodhna Shaffrey for their generous assistance with this article.

* According to the Association of Local Authority Arts Officers website, there are currently 34 arts officers in City and County Local Authorities across Ireland. https://www.artsandhealth.ie/directory/association-of-local-authority-arts-officers

Cothú and the Business Community

Gerry Watson

It was 1988, and Mairtín McCullough was chairman of the Arts Council. For his day job he was chairman of the Irish National/New Ireland group of companies, and he also ran the much-loved and long-established family business, McCullough Piggot, retailers of musical instruments and sheet music. Alongside his business interests, he was and remains, passionate about the arts.

From his chair on the Arts Council, Mairtín had an overview of the financial foundations underpinning the arts in Ireland and indeed, in much of Europe. He noted that in a number of other countries, notably the UK and France, business-funded organisations had been established with the express purpose of encouraging business sponsorship of the arts, and asked himself why not in Ireland too?

He shrewdly decided to pitch his ideas to Dermot Egan, second in command at AIB Group, a patrician figure in business and the arts, and a man with a reputation for getting things done. AIB had built an important representative collection of Irish art, and was an active sponsor across the arts in general. Dermot promptly hosted a dinner to which he invited a number of prominent business people, seeking their support in establishing an organisation to encourage business sponsorship of the arts in Ireland.

The outcome was the formation of an enthusiastic working group, determined to set up an Irish organisation modelled along the lines of the successful business sponsorship association which had been operating in the UK for a number of years. At Mairtín's suggestion, Colm Ó Briain became a member of the group from the very beginning. Given his background as a former director of the Arts Council, together with his significant achievements, high standing and reputation in the arts, Colm certainly knew his way around the block. He was perfectly suited to give guidance and direction to the working group.

With Colm's help and advice, clear policy objectives and a modus

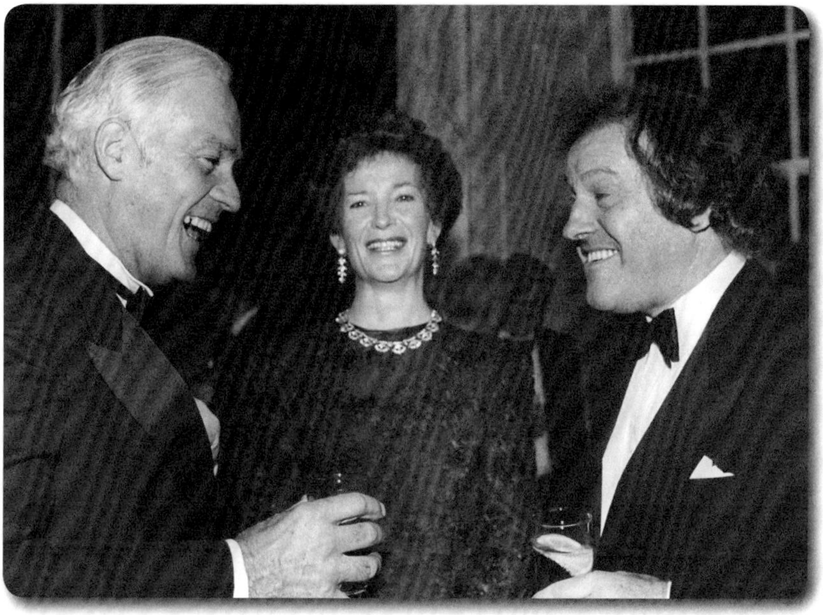

The Arts Sponsor of the Year Awards 1993. (Left) Dermot Egan (Chair) with President Mary Robinson and Gerry Watson (Chief Executive Cothú).

operandi for the new organisation were formulated, its likely funding requirements were assessed, a business membership funding model was drawn up, and the decision was taken to formally establish the new association as a company limited by guarantee.

As might be expected, this decision led to lively discussions regarding a name for the new body. The ensuing somewhat circuitous debate was finally brought to an abrupt end at one meeting, when Colm made a presentation proposing a name and including graphic designs and a logo. His proposal was that the new body should have an Irish name, and that the name should be Cothú (meaning 'sustenance' or 'fosterage'). Colm was seeking to enshrine within the new association the image of a supportive partnership between Irish business and the arts in Ireland. To be charitable, one could describe the working group's response as underwhelming. But they had not bargained on Colm's quietly persuasive and compelling debating style, and as the meeting broke up, we were all congratulating ourselves on being such clever fellows and having made such a good decision.

And what a good decision it was—the name turned out to be a winner: one word; easy to say; easy to remember; a word which swiftly became synonymous with the link between business and the arts—an invaluable asset for a small emerging organisation.

Shortly afterwards, Cothú Teoranta was duly incorporated. Its first directors were Dermot Egan (chairman), Charles Kenny, Denis Magee, Neil Monahan, Robert Myerscough, Malachy Smith and the writer. Mairtín joined shortly afterwards when his term as chairman of the Arts Council ended. The company secretary was Michael Feehan. Collectively, the group represented the banking, engineering, information technology, insurance, property development and retail business sectors.

From this point onwards, Colm became the public face of Cothú. He was a freelancer at that time, engaged in a variety of arts activities, and it was agreed that he would give a day and a half per week to Cothú, to get the organisation up and running. And he got down to business straight away. First off, at a formal reception held at the National Gallery, before a large audience from the business and arts communities, the good ship Cothú was launched with appropriate pomp and ceremony by the Taoiseach, Charles J. Haughey.

Colm then focused his attention on introducing Cothú to the arts community, and developing initial relationships between Cothú and arts organisations across the country. Eithne Healy, who later became chair of the Abbey Theatre, volunteered her services and was active in spreading the gospel within the business community. At the same time, an enthusiastic board was working to develop a corporate membership base to provide the necessary ongoing funding to allow Cothú to develop and operate.

All this work yielded fruit. It soon became clear that the organisation needed to be run on a full-time basis, and I became Cothú's first full-time employee. In 1998, Cothú was able to report that in the ten years since its incorporation, annual business sponsorship of the arts in Ireland, expressed in euro, had grown from €600,000 to €13 million, at which point it equated to one-third of total Arts Council annual funding. As a percentage of GDP, business sponsorship of the arts in Ireland ranked higher than in eight other EU countries, and was also higher than in the US.

I left Cothú in 1998 and I am therefore unable to provide first-hand information as to its progress since then. However, I can say that it is now thirty-four years since Cothú was founded, and that during all that time, the organisation—now called Business to Arts—has worked energetically, not only to fulfil its primary objective, namely the development of business sponsorship of the arts, but has also successfully developed a comprehensive programme of innovative and bespoke services, designed to reach beyond sponsorship, to facilitate the development of a wider range of ongoing creative partnerships between business and the arts.

It is fair to say that this committed organisation has lived up to, and even surpassed, the vision and commitment of its true founders Mairtín McCullough and Colm Ó Briain.

A Transformative Impact*

Paul Shovlin
Chairperson of the National Library of Ireland 2015–20

The National Library of Ireland (NLI) is particularly indebted to Colm for his role as special adviser to the then Minister for Arts, Culture and the Gaeltacht, Michael D. Higgins, who introduced the National Cultural Institutions Act, 1997 and Section 1003 of the Taxes Consolidation Act, 1997. The former legislation fundamentally changed the status of the NLI. Although known as a national institution by name, the NLI up to this point had no separate legal existence of its own and effectively operated as an agency under the auspices of whichever Government department had responsibility for it from time to time. With the commencement of the National Cultural Institutions Act in 2005, a Board of the National Library of Ireland was established and the institution became a corporate entity, independent in its form and function, and autonomous in the discharge of its responsibilities.

As significant a transformation as this legislation had on the NLI's status and governance, the Section 1003 of the Taxes Consolidation Act, 1997 had an equally far-reaching and positive impact on the Library's collections. Without this legislation, the NLI would not have been able to acquire collections of national heritage importance such as the archives of W. B. Yeats, Brian Friel, Sean O'Casey, James Joyce, Seamus Heaney and Sáirséal agus Dill to name just a few.

Without the above mentioned constitutional framework it is unlikely that the NLI would have been in a position to establish such ground-breaking initiatives as the 'Seamus Heaney: Listen Now Again' exhibition at the Bank of Ireland Cultural and Heritage Centre or the Museum of Literature Ireland (MoLI) at Newman House.

We are profoundly grateful for Colm's contribution to Ireland's arts, culture and heritage, and the transformative impact his contribution had in particular on the National Library of Ireland.

---

* Extract from letter of condolence on the death of Colm Ó Briain

L'Imaginaire Irlandais

Doireann Ní Bhriain

By the time I left UCD and the joys of Dramsoc and the Cumann Drámaíochta, I had one objective in life, and that was to be an actor. I had won a few university drama awards and was still convinced I was destined for a life on the stage. My mother and one of my uncles were actors, and I had been a child radio actor myself, so I got the bug early. And so, when I got the call from Gael Linn to take part in a drama workshop they had organised, prior to casting for a production for the Dublin Theatre Festival, I jumped at the opportunity. The workshops were to be conducted by Colm Ó Briain, and they were run over a series of Saturdays in the Damer Hall. Even with the sun beating down outside, I wasn't one bit reluctant to spend my Saturdays in the gloom with a bunch of other Irish-language actors and this remarkable director, whose reputation I was already aware of.

I just loved those sessions: Colm was, as he would continue to be in the other contexts in which I worked with him, demanding, creative, encouraging and firm. You just knew you had to give him your best. Out of that process came a production called *Cúis Gáire Chugainn*, a translation by Tomás Tóibín (Niall Tóibín's father) of *Histoire de Rire* by Armand Salacrou which ran for a week in Amharclann an Damer in October 1970. It was a frothy French piece, and we had great fun performing it. There had been talk—not for the first time—of setting up an Irish-language repertory company, but lack of funding put paid to that.

By then, I had decided to spend another year at UCD doing a H.Dip., to satisfy my anxious father that I would have a backup plan to work as a teacher, if my artistic dreams came to nothing. In fact I ended up with a 'real', if temporary job, as a researcher on a sociolinguistic research project about the use of the Irish language, though I kept doing my part-time radio announcing and whatever bits of performance work came my way.

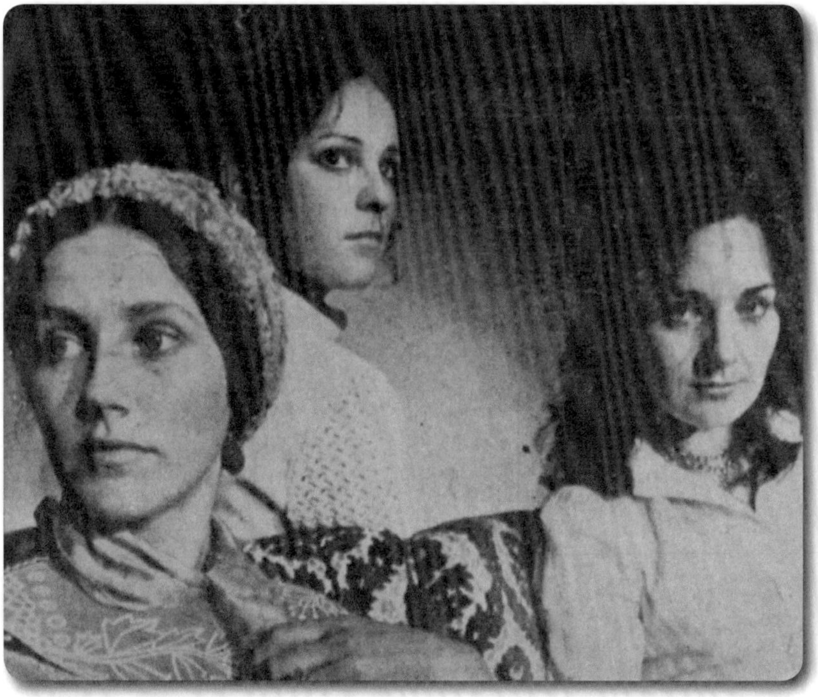

Dara de Brí, Doireann Ní Bhriain and Mary Finan in *Cúis Gháire Chugainn*, directed by Colm Ó Briain, Damer Theatre 1970. (The Irish Times)

In the summer of 1972, I was on holidays in Corca Dhuibhne, staying with friends in a small house at the foot of Mount Brandon. One night, when we went to Tigh Chatháin in Baile an Fheirtéaraigh, about ten miles from where I was staying, Donal Ó Catháin, the owner, called me aside and said 'there was a fella in here the other day looking for you'. He had left his number and asked me to call him. The fella turned out to be Colm, who had recently joined RTÉ television and was starting up a new five nights a week magazine programme to be called *Tangents*. Would I be interested in taking on a role as co-presenter with Cathal O'Shannon and John O'Donoghue, two very experienced and well-known TV personalities? Would I what! The details of whether I auditioned for the role, or whether Colm just took a chance on me and issued a contract, I can't remember, but I do remember not having a moment's hesitation in throwing up the job I had at the time and accepting the offer.

Back in Dublin, I took a call from Peter Kennerly, one of the programme's producers, who had been told by Colm, who was the overall editor, to bring me with him to the Blasket Islands where, with Cathal O'Shannon as reporter, they were to film an insert for one of the forthcoming *Tangents* programmes. Colm thought I, as an Irish speaker, could do an interview with some of the former inhabitants of An Blascaod Mór about what life had been like on the island, and do a reading to camera of an excerpt from Peig Sayers' autobiography about Christmas on the Blaskets, the latter for transmission at Christmas. There followed an eventful few days on the island. Peter was like a Hollywood director, and we flew there in great style by helicopter from Dingle to film an American who had bought all or maybe just part of the island, and was planning to renovate some of the houses. My own interview with the islanders still pops up on RTÉ and TG4 archive programmes—I think it's also in Ionad an Bhlascaoid in Dún Chaoin, and it makes me cringe every time I see it. I had had some TV experience—storytelling for children, for example, but I had no proper interviewing skills, spoke too fast and was terrified of leaving a gap in the conversation, leaving no time for the interviewees to speak at their own thoughtful, slow pace. It was a hectic beginning to my television career, and I had Colm to thank for throwing me in, as he usually did, at the deep end.

I remember not long after that being assigned by him to go and interview someone who was being deported from Ireland, and I said I didn't think I was the best person to do it as I knew nothing about the story. 'Well, go and find out,', he barked, and of course I did what I was told, terrified all the time of being rumbled as a complete fraud. There was no formal training for TV journalism at the time, so I had to learn on the job, and did. Between Colm, the other producers and Cathal and John as colleagues and mentors in the first year, I relished my steep learning curve and emerged with a confidence that went on to serve me very well throughout my career. And it was Colm who gave me that. Thinking back on it from his perspective, he was taking a big risk by throwing a young woman with no experience into a highly exposed role on a popular nightly TV programme. But he seemed to believe I could do it, so I had to as well.

Colm left RTÉ after a year of *Tangents*—I think he had a falling out with management about funding for the programme, and our paths didn't cross professionally for many years after that. I went on to have a very satisfying career as a TV and radio presenter and producer. By the way, I discovered many years later that because Colm and I had the same surname, many people believed I was a relation of his, whom he had brought in by the back door. I was very cross to discover that!

In 1976 I was getting itchy feet, and went off to live and work in Kenya for a year. I came back to RTÉ in 1977 but the itchy feet started twitching again in the early '80s, when I applied for and was granted a scholarship to spend a year in Paris with an organisation called *Journalistes en Europe*. I went from being something of a celebrity in Ireland, having presented the Eurovision Song contest in 1981, to living like a poor student on a small stipend in Paris, which was why, when Colm found himself in Paris during that year, and was invited to dinner in the Irish Embassy, he invited me along. He probably realised how little posh living I was doing and sure enough, I relished the wonderful dinner that evening.

It turned out I was to repay the favour by helping him out with the task that had brought him to Paris. By then, Colm was director of the Arts Council. Aosdána had recently been set up and Colm and the writers involved wanted to nominate Samuel Beckett as its first Saoi. I can't remember now whether they had had any correspondence on the matter—they must have had—but Colm needed to send word to Beckett that he was in Paris and would like to meet him. He could not be contacted by telephone, or at least, Colm hadn't managed to locate him that way. However, Paris at the time had the extraordinary message-delivering system known as the *pneumatique*. This was a series of underground pipes all over Paris into which written messages could be placed from a post-office and delivered by air-pressure to some other part of the city, then delivered to one's door by a postman, all within a two-hour window. Colm, whose French was limited, didn't feel he had the linguistic skills to engage with the counter staff at the central post office to organise a *pneu*, as they were called, so he asked me to come with him and do the necessary. A few hours later, he phoned me to say Beckett had responded, and he was to meet him the following day in the Hotel St Jacques, Beckett's 'local'. I plucked up the courage to ask

Colm if I could tag along, not for the meeting, of course, but just to see the great man from a distance. So, the next day, I met Colm in the hotel foyer and kept my distance when the tall, enigmatic man walked in to meet him. I watched them shake hands and move off to a little table, and I, knowing my place, made myself scarce, as agreed. It can hardly be described as an encounter with Samuel Beckett, but I do cherish the memory. Beckett did in the end consent to becoming a Saoi, and I always feel I played a tiny part in making that happen.

On my return from Paris, I became a TV presenter again, married, had children and moved to radio production. I ran into Colm on and off, usually at the theatre. He and Muireann kindly invited me and my husband, Andy Pollak, to their lovely house for parties and dinners from time to time, and we got to know their impressive daughters, Seóna and Aisling, both of whom babysat my own children, Sorcha and Gráinne.

In the spring of 1990, that year's Celtic Film Festival was to be held in Gaoth Dóbhair in the Donegal Gaeltacht. Colm was appointed director of the week-long event, where jurors spent several days viewing the material in competition. This was followed by seminars, workshops and a big awards ceremony. In those days, everything was presented in English, French and Irish, so Colm offered me the job of being the presenter/translator for the week. The day before I was due to leave, our younger daughter, Gráinne, then nine months old, broke her leg and ended up in hospital. My distress at this shocking event, and the pain of being away from my suffering baby for five days were over-ridden by my loyalty to Colm and the knowledge that finding a replacement for me at that late stage would be almost impossible for him. And so I went, and cried down the phone to Andy every night as he took to his camp bed by Gráinne's side in the hospital. I only tell the story to show that I could not have countenanced letting Colm down, despite the abject misery I was suffering. That was the nature of our relationship of trust.

Our next professional encounter was in 1993, after the election which gave Ireland its first Minister for Culture, Michael D. Higgins. I was a radio producer on the nightly *Arts Show*, presented by Mike Murphy. When Michael D. was appointed, we devoted a full programme to an interview with him and I was the producer. I can't remember whether Colm, who had been appointed the Minister's adviser, came into studio with him or not, but I would certainly have been in contact with him in order to prepare the brief for the presenter. Some weeks later, on a Saturday afternoon, there was a knock on my door and there was Colm standing on the doorstep. He wasn't in the habit of dropping in (although he did live quite close by) but I did what most Irish people would do and invited him in for a cup of tea. We chatted away, firstly about his new role and the great potential of the new government department, and then about my work on the *Arts Show*. I remember telling him I was a bit frustrated with the job, and that I felt I was a parasite on other people's creativity. By that I meant that I was reflecting others' creative achievements on the programme, but didn't feel I had enough opportunity to be creative myself. We talked about our respective daughters, and about the world in general and off he trotted.

Shortly after this encounter, I got a phone call from the Assistant Secretary of the Department of Arts, Culture and the Gaeltacht, as it was then called, asking whether I would like to come in and talk to him about the possibility of taking on the job of being Irish Commissioner of *l'Imaginaire Irlandais*, a festival of Irish culture to be held in France in 1996. It had arisen from a conversation between Ireland's President Mary Robinson and the then French president, François Mitterand, in the course of which he had remarked how interested French people were in Irish culture. It transpired that it was mainly the culture of the past they knew about, so President Robinson suggested we be given an opportunity to showcase our contemporary culture, to which he apparently assented. Nobody had worked out how it would be done, or what it would consist of, but both governments agreed to put some money in the pot to make it happen.

So that was why Colm had 'dropped in' on that Saturday afternoon! He was checking me out, and, on reflection, asking searching questions in order to confirm his belief that I was the best person for the job of Irish Commissioner. In my favour, apart from my production and arts experience, I had very good French, which was more of a pre-requisite than anyone could have imagined for getting things done in France. But I had never managed a large group of people, nor a large budget (one million punts from the Irish side, and at that stage a promise of a similar amount on the French side), and I had no diplomatic experience, apart from being a member of the Department of Foreign Affairs Cultural Relations Committee for a few years. Once again, Colm was pushing me way beyond my comfort zone—further, I think, than even he knew.

There followed a rollercoaster period of two and a half years, working between Paris and Dublin, with huge mountains to climb in order to deliver something approaching the hoped-for outcome. There was obdurate bureaucracy to overcome, enormous expectations from Irish artists, many misunderstandings on both sides about what was expected or could be delivered and many professional and personal difficulties to deal with. Colm sat on the advisory committee on the Irish side, and got regularly outraged by the slow development of the project. To be fair, he wasn't blaming me for this!

My diplomatic skills were increasing by the second, and I was learning very fast that things were done differently in France and how complex even in organisational terms French cultural bureaucracy was. I often found it hard to explain this back home. I would try and calm Colm down and explain that No, this was not the time to march to my defence and demand answers, and he would reluctantly step back. I vividly remember a phone conversation with him on one occasion where I shouted at him, 'Colm, if I took that attitude I wouldn't get out of bed in the morning!' I cannot now remember what the attitude was, but I know I felt quite proud of having got the better of him and having stood my ground.

Colm's was a very strong personality, and I could be pretty stubborn myself, but I was not in the habit of arguing so vehemently with him. I did know, though, that he had my back at all times, especially when it came to arguing about money. In my first week in that job, I was told by some civil servants that I should not hire any other people to run this project, the implication being that if I was any good, I could do it on my own. Colm advised me to hang in there and not lose my cool—which I was very tempted to do—and bit by bit I managed to employ a small staff to support the huge demands of the project. I developed a good relationship with the Department, and, probably because my father had been a civil servant, learned how to see things from their perspective as well as that of their fiery Minister and his adviser!

L'Imaginaire irlandais, although it turned out to be something very different from what had originally been envisaged, was deemed a great success, and I just about survived it. But of course, I learned a huge amount on the job, just like I had when Colm had hired me as a neophyte TV reporter. I emerged from *L'Imaginaire irlandais* as a competent cultural manager and went on to use the skills I had learned in many other ways in the coming years. I maintained a friendship with Colm and his family after that, and often suggested to him that he should write a memoir of his extraordinary career. I wasn't the only one pushing him in that direction, but Colm was not a man to be pushed.

I have rarely had the opportunity to give public thanks to people who were strong influences in my life, However, when the French government honoured me by naming me a *Chevalier* of the *Ordre National du Mérite* in 2016, I had to write a little speech for the occasion. Pulling together the professional strings of my life for that speech, I realised just how central Colm had been to my career. When as an aspiring actor I first met him, he had faith in my ability. His decision to take a risk by putting an unknown and inexperienced young woman on air as a TV presenter in a prime time slot was a crucial turning point in my professional life. Even more so his decision to suggest me for the *L'Imaginaire Irlandais* Commissioner job. As a result of that, I was able to marry my journalistic and production skills with my passion for the arts, and it led me on a path to so many satisfying areas of work thereafter. I have tried to follow his example by seeing potential in people, and supporting them as they develop.

Luckily, I got the chance to thank Colm in his presence at that occasion in the French Embassy in March 2016. He left us far too soon, but he achieved a remarkable amount during his impressive and productive life. I will always remember him with great fondness and with enormous gratitude.

Happy Days with Colm

Nuala Hayes

In January 1998 my father Micheál Ó hAodha died suddenly overnight, as a result of a massive heart attack. My mother was alone with him when he breathed his last. The shock to her and to our family was enormous. They had been married for over fifty years and although, like many marriages, it wasn't always sweetness and light, there had grown over many years a strong bond of mutual love and dependency.

My mother was bereft. Her life had revolved around her family and the care of my father. Without him she was like a bird with one wing. As time passed, she would talk about the 'Halcyon Days' of their marriage. She and I knew that this wasn't a permanent state, but was a time of ease and peace and relaxation between them; rare but memorable. A period of calm delight to which we all aspire in one way or another. Happy Days. It is the fantasy, or illusion which everyone buys into when we decide to commit to a lifelong relationship.

Almost a year later, on 4 January 1999, I was invited by Bríd Dukes to visit the new theatre in Tallaght which she had just taken over as manager. The Civic Theatre had been designed as a performance space to provide live theatre and travelling shows for the community in Tallaght. The policy to create theatre spaces which would be part of the infrastructure of the local council in towns, suburbs and counties across Ireland was an enlightened one, which had been developed when Michael D. Higgins was Minister for Arts, Culture and the Gaeltacht from 1993 to 1997.

My heart leapt when I walked into the venue. The intimacy, excellent acoustics and the warm atmosphere of the empty space impressed me. At that moment *Happy Days* by Beckett jumped into my mind. It was a play I had always loved and I had harboured a secret wish that I might one day play the part of Winnie, the main character, a woman in her 'middle years', just where I was at the time.

I was aware, however, that, given the small world of professional theatre in Ireland, which was then in the control of a number of powerful fiefdoms, it was unlikely I would ever be invited to do so.

I mentioned this to Bríd and suggested that perhaps Colm might be interested in becoming involved with a production in this fresh new venue.

Colm had been an adviser to Michael D. during his period in government, and I knew he was passionately committed to making the arts more democratic and accessible to all.

Colm's had been an eclectic career. An *enfant terrible* in the arts world, as founder of the Project Arts Centre, as producer and actor in Beckett plays going back to the 1960s, as television director, as administrator and as a creator of cultural policy in the state.

He had directed *I'll Go On*, an adaptation of Beckett's prose works by Gerry Dukes, with actor Barry McGovern at the Gate Theatre. The show later went on to tour the world. In my view, his interpretation of *Not I*, played by Adele King, better known as Twink, was a spot-on presentation of Beckett's fascination with a woman's ability to talk without hardly taking a breath. Only her mouth is visible on the stage, hilarious and horrifying at the same time. A woman talking herself almost to death in order to stay alive!

Bríd Dukes had also worked with Colm in the past and admired him greatly.

The one person I would have wished for, to play Willie, Winnie's recalcitrant husband in *Happy Days*, was Mick Lally, who at the time was a household name as Miley in *Glenroe*. I myself had done a stint in the first year of *Glenroe*, and performed with Mick, in the first production of *Translations* by Brian Friel in Derry in 1980. and in the two-hander *Yesterday's Lovers* by Hugh Carr, as part of the Dublin Theatre Festival. Mick had the face, the presence, and empathy which I thought would be perfect for the part of Willie, who says little, but whose presence is vital in the surreal situation the couple find themselves in.

Winnie reaches back through her memories and yearns each day for another 'happy day', despite the fact that they are stuck in the sands of time, unable to move beyond the mound they share as the heat of the sun beats mercilessly down and day follows night with monotonous regularity.

Colm was interested and Mick also agreeable to the idea, but the question was would we get the rights to perform the play in this new untried venue outside the established audience of Dublin theatre?

We devised a plan, which involved funding the play ourselves, with the support of the Civic Theatre as producer, and then touring it around the country, until we managed to recover the costs. We got permission to do this, on condition we didn't perform the play in Dublin city, where the rights for Beckett's work were held by the Gate Theatre.

I had known Colm reasonably well by this stage since I was married to his younger brother Art. However, the Colm I came to know during the preparation, rehearsals, and the production of the play in September 1999, was completely different to the person I saw in many different contexts.

Within the family, he was the least gregarious of the siblings, more often found quietly sipping his gin and tonic in the corner, than performing party pieces enthusiastically at the many parties which his parents threw in their house in Clontarf. Their's was a large, talented and lively family of four boys and two girls. I always had the feeling that Colm, as the eldest would just 'let them all at it' when it came to performing or reciting party pieces. One notable exception was on his sixtieth birthday when he sang the McGarrigles' famous song *First Born*, with great aplomb and identification, as the first born in the family.

'Some of them make it, some of them don't
Some of them can't, others won't grow up.'

I had also seen him in action at the large family dining table, where issues of a global nature, politics and power, would be discussed passionately after dinner, and disagreements were loud and often vitriolic. Colm could be single-minded in his views and a debate with him was not for the faint hearted.

At one time, he was given the role of director of training at the Abbey Theatre, whilst I was a member of that well-established company. His style appeared dictatorial to many of the permanent actors, who were resistant to the idea that after many years on stage, they should submit to any training at all.

However, working with him on *Happy Days*, from the summer of 1999 to May 2000, was an entirely different experience. It was then I met Colm the artist. I had a sense that theatre and the process of making it, was his

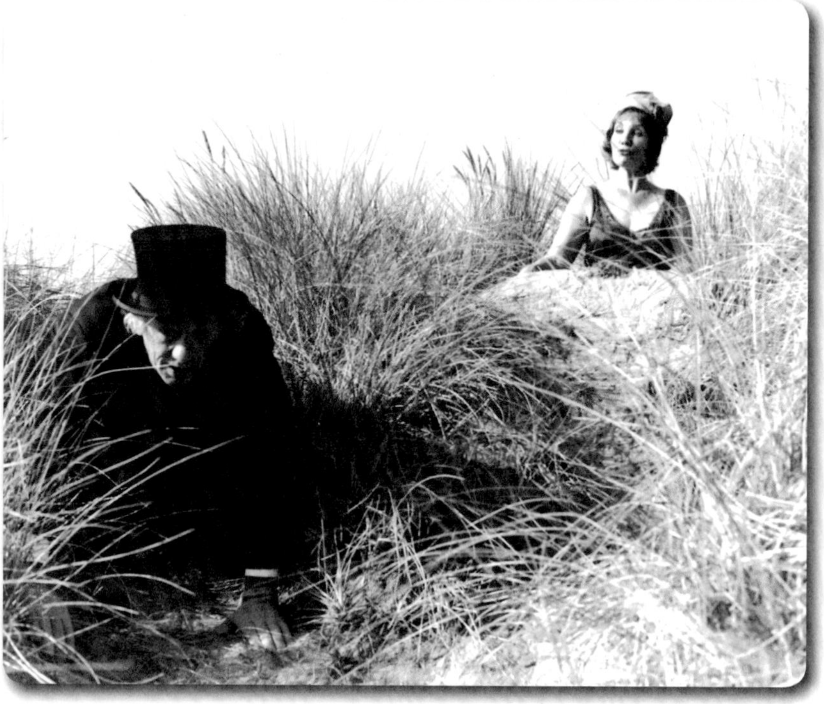

Publicity photo for Samuel Beckett's *Happy Days*: Mick Lally and Nuala Hayes in the sand dunes in Dollymount Strand. The play, directed by Colm Ó Briain, was performed in the Civic Theatre, Tallaght, in 1999/2000. (Louise Roden)

first love. He was open and curious, wanting only to explore and serve Beckett's text, which he considered perfectly composed and complete.

We rehearsed throughout the summer months of 1999 and were both prepared to give as much time to exploring the play as we felt necessary. Colm was rigorous and very knowledgeable, but he never imposed his views on me, as a performer. He allowed me to come to the text slowly and in my own way. I would position myself on a kneeling stool, which was used to support my back and we would slowly dissect each word and phrase, and allow Beckett's stage directions to guide us. Whenever we forced interpretation, the truth evaded us. I found that Winnie's favourite phrase 'just do it' was the key to finding the meaning.

'Just do it . . .' Follow the text and the meaning would reveal itself.

We would stop when we thought we had reached an understanding of one section, I would go home and spend time absorbing the words, by speaking them out loud, for a few days. The text is famously circular, as Winnie repeats the same lines, over and over, but slightly changing and diminishing as time passes and the light shifts and fades.

I have no memory of struggling to learn the lines. The rhythm and the patterns were seeping into my body and I would know when I had gone wrong by a sense that the rhythm had slipped.

Colm was infinitely patient and understanding. He never directed me, in the manner of other directors I had worked with. With Winnie stuck, first to her waist, and then to her neck, in the mound of rubbish, or whatever it was, there wasn't much to direct in terms of movement. Beckett had dealt with that.

Little by little Winnie grew under my skin. Her tone of voice, her remarks and her language were familiar to me. Dublin middle-class respectability in 'the old style', one of her favourite repeat phrases. I had grown up in suburban Dublin, in Highfield Park, Dundrum, with some very respectable Protestant neighbours with good manners and good jobs. Kindly ladies would sometimes invite children into their very tidy houses, for tea, muffins and cucumber sandwiches in the afternoon. A treat for us, more used to brown bread, butter and jam. Winnie's beloved paraphernalia, her bag, her mirror, her toothbrush, her umbrella, and her daily routine, kept chaos at bay, and were the survival tools of the middle-class lady she embodied. And the paradox of the ever-present gun was always there.

Colm paid attention to every syllable and detail in the production, and it was a total pleasure throughout. I was intrigued with Beckett's very precise stage directions, the notated pauses and dashes and the irregular direction pause: . . . do . . . Did that mean ditto . . . repeat ?

I decided that since all other bodily functions were impossible perhaps this was a moment for Winnie to relieve herself, politely. I suggested this to Colm, he agreed and we quietly included this in the subtext, as it were.

It worked for me, and I noted it in my script as no.1 or no. 2.

We rarely chatted about anything outside the context of the play. Sharing of personal experiences, which is often part and parcel of exploring drama in rehearsal, was kept to a minimum.

Nor was the play over-analysed for its meaning. Any understanding was intuitive. I was aware that the pain and loss which Colm had suffered in his life, and which I had recently been through, after the death of my father, was always there. The fragility of life was mentioned but not dwelt on.

I do remember one incident on a warm summer day in Rathmines. There had been much publicity about an eclipse of the sun, which was due that afternoon.

The Ó Briains' house where we rehearsed was across the road from the grassy grounds of St Louis Convent and I was aware of the crowd of people gathering there, wearing the protective orange plastic glasses so as not to damage their eyes. We had been warned not to look directly at the sun, for fear of this.

I was very keen to stop working and experience this phenomenon outside. I asked Colm to come but he refused. I went out and was astonished to experience how, while the moon covered the life-giving force of the sun, colour was sucked out of everything. Grass, flowers, gardens, houses, people, animals, the road, the cars, the convent—all were the same shade of watery grey.

A world without colour. Neither night nor day. Like Death.

When the moment passed and the sun emerged, and colour returned to the world, I returned to the house, elated. I asked Colm why he hadn't come out to experience this, and he answered 'I couldn't trust myself not to look at the sun.' I didn't understand the answer. A moment of fear or vulnerability perhaps.

Meanwhile ... The work on the set was ongoing. Geraldine O'Malley, with whom Colm had worked when he was a television producer, was the designer of the edifice which was the mound Winnie inhabits, and into which she is slowly sinking. Paul Keogan was the lighting designer and Davóg Rynne was the production manager for the run at the Civic Theatre in Tallaght and the subsequent national tour. Mick joined us in September, when rehearsals moved to the theatre space at the Civic.

Happy Days was the opening production at the brand new venue.

Colm's calm control of the production never faltered. Nor was he ever over effusive in his encouragement. He was no 'luvvie'! His comment after one of the last run throughs of the show to me was 'brimming with intelligence'.

I couldn't have asked for a greater compliment.

For what it's worth, the theatre was packed out for the run at the Civic. The reviews were excellent but better still our tour of venues all over the island, some of them one-night stands, did really well. In Cork, Portlaoise, Galway, Sligo, Limerick, Letterkenny, Mullingar, Waterford and back to Tallaght for a second time, people packed in. Perhaps it was the novelty of Beckett's work being seen beyond the urban centres of Dublin and Cork. Perhaps it was due to the popularity of Mick Lally, but for me thc experience of working on *Happy Days* was profound. Funny and heart-breaking at times, it's an extraordinary piece of live theatre and, thanks to Colm's openness and sensitivity to the work, it remains in my memory as a highlight in my life.

The play is a searing, honest reflection on the human condition. We watch as Winnie's life slowly diminishes until there is nothing left. No more words, no sounds, just a song and a breath. It's a play about love. Love of life, and the human desire to keep going until the inevitable end. Winnie is aware of her fate, but she never loses her positive optimism: her need to 'do' something despite the darkness which slowly envelopes her.

Colm had the wisdom, and the humility to let the play speak for itself, and it was an honour for me to be part of it.

I remember the production photo-shoot which Colm organised in the sand dunes of Dollymount Strand with photographer Louise Roden. He was very clear and specific about what he wanted, including the exact time of day and the particular spot in the dunes where Winnie and Willie might have been found in the sand and sedge grassy mound. It was at the end of summer and for some reason that morning, I had read a poem by Beckett, which still resonates with me. We included the poem in the programme for the production.

I like to remember Colm as he was that day on Dollymount: open minded, focused, thoughtful and very creative.

Mar thú

Seóna Ní Bhriain

Is mar thú, a labhraím.
Sin a chloisim ó na daoine mór thimpeall orm
Agus mar sin
Sa mhí thuiscint, tá tuiscint ann.
Éistim.
Guth cruthaithe le cruth m'athair air.
Míniú cruinn faoi cheilt 'sna focla
Níl baint aige le cad tá ráite
Ach fite fuaite sa fuaim
Tá fírinne.

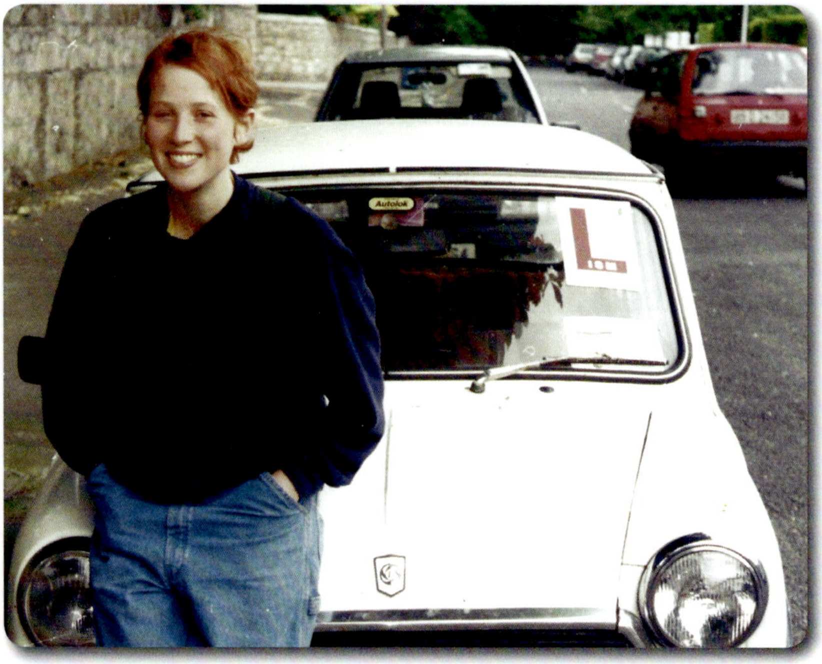

Seóna Ní Bhriain—new hair colour, new car.

Beckett's *Hommage* to Colm

Gerry Dukes

I cannot now recall when I first met Colm. It was Colm who introduced my wife Bríd and me to the pleasures of cooked mussels—he did the cooking—on an occasion when Muireann and he were staying with us in the Kerry Gaeltacht. He also introduced me to the snake serum in the fridge of an ancient farmhouse in Gascony when we were taking over house-minding duties from him and Muireann. But long before that, like many others, I knew Colm by reputation, particularly as one of the prime movers of the Project Arts group in Dublin and for his ground-breaking work in Irish television. His time as director of the Arts Council was, to say the least, legendary. Personally I have benefitted from one of Colm's most visionary arts initiatives—The Tyrone Guthrie Centre—where I spent two very productive residences. During the first of these I wrote my very first scholarly essay on the work of Samuel Beckett for presentation at an international conference in Holland. By an extraordinary coincidence it was Beckett's work which allowed me to work with Colm in the theatre.

In the spring of 1985 Bríd, who was a long-time friend of Colm's, attended the Patrick Kavanagh Weekend in Iniskeen with me. The weekend culminated in a reading by Abbey Theatre actors of Kavanagh's work. It was a wet and miserable Sunday morning and after the performance some of the audience and most of the cast repaired to a local public house. It was there I first met Barry McGovern. Over warming hot whiskeys we discovered that we shared an abiding enthusiam for the work of Beckett, not just for the plays but for the whole canon of his work. Barry had just been invited by Michael Colgan of the Gate Theatre to undertake a one-man show, to be directed for the Gate by Colm, based on Beckett's work, for that year's Dublin Theatre Festival and Barry asked me if I would be interested in being involved in assembling a script. Would I what!

Not much happened for a long while except we all read and re-read the entire published canon and eventually decided that the source for the script had to be the so-called Trilogy of novels, *Molloy, Malone Dies,* and *The Unnamable* which Beckett had written in French in the late forties. One of the constraints we had to work with was that the theatre wanted to feature the piece as a late-night show in two acts, the first of which could be no more than fifty minutes duration and the second no more than forty. By mid-June the script had been finalised except for the opening which we agreed needed something more arresting.

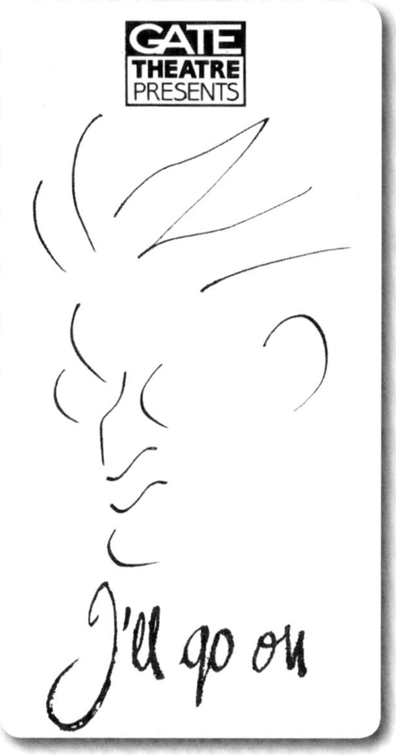

From the programme for the 1985 Gate Theatre production of *I'll Go On* based on the novels by Samuel Beckett, directed by Colm Ó Briain.

At this point I drove *en famille* to the south of France for holidays, bringing my working copy of the three novels with me so as to continue my search for an attention-grabbing opening. We had rented an apartment in Paris for a week after leaving the south and while there I found a passage late on in the third novel that struck me as particularly appropriate. I immediately set about collecting a satchel of small change to fund two calls from a phone box on a local street. I called Colm and gave him the page and line references and then called Barry with the same information. The first of those calls was to be my only moment of collaboration with the director of the show which premiered as *I'll Go On* at the Gate in September, 1985, with set design by the artist Robert Ballagh and lighting by the late, great Rupert Murray.

To call the show a success would be a considerable understatement. Barry McGovern has played it to great acclaim and stunning reviews all over the world. In the immediate aftermath of the show Michael Colgan asked me what I wanted for my work on the script. My answer was simple: a return air ticket to Paris and a meeting with Samuel Beckett.

The meeting took place in Paris the following April. There was lots of talk and laughter and inevitably, there was talk about the vicissitudes of touring theatre. Beckett spoke of Billie Whitelaw's recent problems touring his plays *Rockaby* and *Footfalls* in Australia where she found herself in direct aural competition with a Vietnam War epic that featured a raucous sound-track of Bruce Springsteen's music that all but drowned out his softly spoken words. He said that the space she had played in 'was insufficiently impermeable to sound'. Beckett noticed my reaction to his use of 'impermeable'. I explained that I had been listening intently while he spoke to hear if his long immersion in French and francophone culture had impacted on his use of his native tongue. 'And has it?' he asked with a slight grin. I pointed out that Billie's theatre space was insufficiently sound-proofed. Beckett quietly laughed and said that if 'impermeable' was good enough for the Master (meaning Joyce) in his fable of the Mookse and the Gripes it was good enough for him. When I got home I immediately consulted the Master's *Finnegans Wake* and realised I needed to apologise to Beckett. I did so by letter that day and received an acknowledgement from Beckett within the week. And so was established an epistolary connection which lasted until Beckett's death in the last days of 1989.

But it was Colm Ó Briain who inadvertently provided me with an opportunity to exculpate myself with Beckett some time later. While directing an exceptionally fine production of *Waiting for Godot* in Cork, Colm was persuaded by his actors that a fragment of dialogue early in the play could be misinterpreted by a Cork audience. This was the passage in question:

Vladimir: Tied?
Estragon: Ti-ed.
Vladimir: How do you mean tied?
Estragon: Down.
Vladimir: But to whom. By whom?
Estragon: To your man.
Vladimir: To Godot? Tied to Godot? What an idea!

Colm's actors convinced him that the phrase 'your man' would be heard in Cork as slightly derogatory. Colm and the cast agreed to change 'your man' to 'himself' which is neutral if not slightly respectful. Beckett was delighted with the change and praised the production's 'meticulous attention to detail'. He bemoaned the fact that not all directors of his plays took such care as Colm had.

A Mosaic of Life and Possibilities

Maureen Gilbert

In 1992 Colm Ó Briain directed the Jacob's Award-winning TV series In From the Margins. *It was his professional introduction to disability issues. He went on to chair the Arts and Culture Working Group of the Commission on the Status of People with Disabilities in 1995–6. Maureen Gilbert was part of both ground-breaking initiatives.*

In From the Margins started as one of those self-righteous 'somebody ought to do something' conversations. Donal Toolan, the charismatic, mellifluous-voiced, politically-minded, wheelchair-using presenter of RTÉ Radio 1's *Not So Different* series on disability issues had his eye on gaining a wider audience through television. As the series consultant, I could only agree. In time it became clear that unless we did it, a TV series looking at disability issues as experienced and interpreted by people with disabilities themselves would never happen.

Donal was a public figure, photogenic, articulate and an appointee to the Council of State; I was a public servant in the National Rehabilitation Board working on disability inclusion issues. Steeped as we were in disability rights and politics, neither of us knew the first thing about television. Luckily, Donal knew Ed Guiney, these days the genius behind the all-conquering Element Pictures, but in the early 1990s just starting out as an independent TV producer. Calm and practical when we were jumpy and all over the place, Ed agreed to be the producer, and steered us towards making an outline proposal to RTÉ. And in August 1991 he called to say that, subject to budget negotiations, the series was in the bag.

Now it all got real, and terrifying. RTÉ wouldn't be hail fellow-well-met for much longer unless we upped our game. That meant engaging a politically-minded director who could understand the nuances of what we wanted to achieve: the look and style of the series was going to be at least as important as the message. Since the rest of us were wet behind the ears, we needed someone with a decent track record. That we were going to be operating on a grant and a loan taken out against my new mortgage wasn't helpful.

Ed had a definite first choice; way ahead of the field, he said. So one morning in September 1991 I found myself in Bewley's on Grafton Street in Dublin, scanning the clientele for a man who might also be scanning the clientele. After ten minutes one man was still scanning, so that had to be this Colm Ó Briain person . . .

I'd been warned that he was intense, combative and frightening, as well as 'a sort of genius', as Lar Cassidy, of the Arts Council, put it. In fact, while half the time it seemed like it was he who was interviewing me, rather than the other way round (thus setting the tone for our working relationship for some considerable time), he was charming and warm and self-effacing as well. He thought we'd got the wrong man: he knew nothing about disability, surely we wanted his brother, Art, who did know about disability? No, we wanted him; he knew about the kind of television we wanted to make, we'd do the disability bit. Well, he had so many irons in the fire, we had a million more hoops to jump through before there would be a contract or money, this sounded interesting but there was no guarantee that he would be available . . .

By the start of October Donal and I had planned out the whole series: six half-hour programmes, anchored by Donal, dealing with education, employment, housing, the costs of disability, arts and culture, and relationships, as experienced by people with various kinds

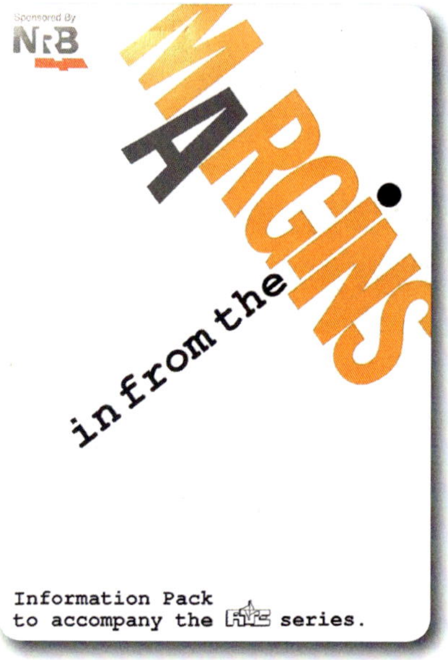

Cover of information pack to accompany the RTÉ series *In From the Margins*. 'When Irish Society at large fully recognises that people with disabilities have the same wants, same needs, same desires as everybody else, then we will truly have come in from the margins.'

of disabilities. No non-disabled 'experts', no commentators. It was new, it was bold and it was a big risk. Just Colm's style.

By late October I noted that Colm kept saying 'we' when discussing the series, now called *In From the Margins*, taken from Donal's assertion that 'when other people with disabilities can celebrate themselves as I do, then truly we will have come in from the margins'. By the middle of November the budget was agreed, Colm was in, RTÉ had announced it, everyone's anxiety levels were stratospheric and we were away.

As predicted, RTÉ's promises started to unspool in December. Colm began to school me in the dark arts of negotiating with RTÉ, how to pull rank and how never, ever, to give an inch. As a result, for the next year I fought with everyone in Montrose and got a reputation for being utterly uncompromising. They must have known well that Colm was the *éminence grise* but I took every bit of flak, sure in the knowledge (drilled by Colm) that we would win because they needed Donal on side. Looking back with thirty years of hindsight, I think a bit more graciousness from our side would have made life smoother, but at that stage I was unaware of just how epic was Colm's use of drama.

As the filming schedule approached and pressure ratcheted ever upwards, I soon learnt. When he accepted the contract, Colm warned me that he was going to push me hard, that we were going to clash frequently. He also said that, in the end, I was going to win because it was Donal and me who knew about disability (and were paying him, he might have added). I kept trying to remember that as, time after time, row after row, it felt like it was me who was on the carpet.

Lar Cassidy had told me that only tenacity would work with Colm—you couldn't possibly win with logic. Colm's clarity of purpose was laser-sharp and his total commitment to the project meant that he wouldn't give an inch if he thought it would compromise on quality or vision: the art of the possible never came into it. Colm chivvied and demanded and bullied and pulled rank and threatened to resign. Every phone call from Colm, purportedly made under the guise of easing the pressure, generally applied much more. Everything was a drama. The North Face of the Eiger had nothing on my learning curve.

Donal found the filming strenuous, and his unreliability, turning up late for shoots, not submitting scripts on time, if at all, drove Colm to

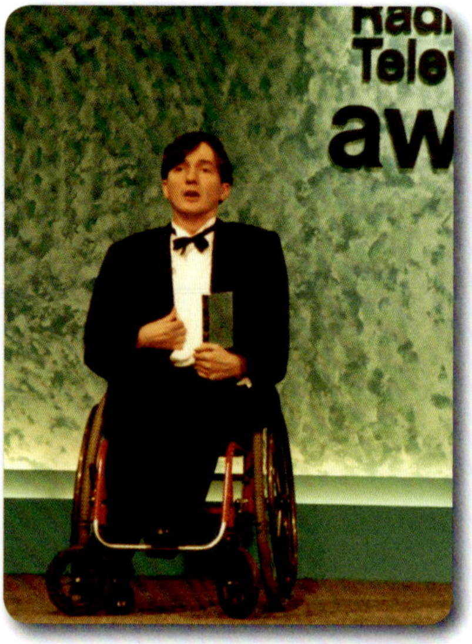

Donal Toolan, disability rights campaigner, accepting a Jacob's Award for his work on *In From the Margins,* 1993. (Dublin City Library and Archive)

distraction. It all came to a head one evening when Colm, acid in tone and precise as a stiletto blade, insisted that, if Donal wasn't going to deliver two essential scripts by tomorrow, I would have to. I couldn't see why, if Colm knew exactly what needed to be said and in how many seconds, he couldn't write it himself. He screamed, I wept. I went home in a fury, worked all night and produced some of my best-ever writing, punchy and direct, boiling with rage and indignation, somehow knowing he was right and that no-one else could possibly have got it out of me.

I tolerated it all because, as far as I could see, he knew everything about television. Colm's standards were astronomical, his style was devastating and exhausting but his instincts and vision were always spot on. He never quite accepted that the imperfect real world was as stubborn as he was, and thus would not agree to be moulded in his image. In the end, I came to see him as an unrepentant Nietzschean—his relentless hectoring didn't kill me and it did make the series stronger. He drove me to the brink, but I never doubted his integrity.

One day everything changed. Colm had phoned up in a fury about the edit of the fifth programme in the series, 'Something to Celebrate', about arts and culture from the perspective of people with disabilities. I'd always expected this would be a tricky one, since he knew so much about the arts. One of the people featured in the programme was a very talented visual artist called George McCutcheon, who showed and talked about his work. George had Down Syndrome. Colm said the material was incomprehensible and impossible and couldn't be used. He wouldn't be mollified, so I abandoned my day job for the millionth time and raced down to the editing suite in Windmill Lane, where I found Colm spitting tacks.

I watched the rough assembly. George was mumbling, all right, but he was also discussing his work in a profound and moving way which was humbling in its sincerity. I started to explain what George was saying. Colm didn't just accept it, or capitulate—he crumbled, dissolved into tears and said that he wished that there were non-disabled artists who could talk about their work so well. We completed the edit, added sub-titles, and peace broke out.

In fact, much more than peace. Colm's attitude to me changed and the balance of power changed but, more profoundly, his attitude to the series changed and his relationship with disability changed. I'd won my stripes but that wasn't important. Colm's understanding of the experience of people with disabilities had shifted to a whole new level. His interest in, and respect for, what people with disabilities were saying, for their lived experience and how they might express it, deepened exponentially and informed a lot of what he was to do over the next few years. He'd moved from committed collaborator to ally and advocate.

There was no turning back. The series was aired in early autumn 1992 and was a critical and popular success. In the *Sunday Tribune*, Nell McCafferty memorably wrote that the first programme, on education, was 'like watching blacks in America dismantle the argument for segregation'. Each programme was so watchable: the style was compelling, the contributors were electrifying, Donal was mesmeric. Disabled viewers celebrated their viewpoints getting respectful airspace for the first time; non-disabled viewers were stunned by the articulacy, depth of feeling and injustice on display. The visual style was seamless, with an unflinching gaze and camera angles that empowered. Even the theme music was composed by a significantly disabled young person. In what was then an innovation, each episode was accompanied by information sheets and lists of further contacts. 'In from the margins' became a popular concept for expressing desire for equality of all kinds ('And who made it fashionable? Since when has it become fashionable?', gloated Colm archly).

Without Colm, *In From the Margins* would have run a serious risk of being preachy and a turgid misery-fest. Because of him, it was a triumph: angry and direct, but shot through with wry humour and without a shred of whinge. When, in 1993, Donal accepted one of the last Jacob's Awards for Irish broadcasting, he was clear that it was Colm's prize, as much as his own. Now the award sits on my mantelpiece, and reminds me of Colm every day.

Two weeks after the Jacob's Awards ceremony, Mervyn Taylor TD, Minister for Equality and Law Reform, established the Commission on the Status of People with Disabilities, with the aim of advising Government 'on the practical measures necessary to ensure that people with disabilities can exercise their rights to participate, to the fullest extent of their potential, in economic, social and cultural life'. Working at the time for the National Rehabilitation Board I was intimately involved in the Commission's progress, supporting its secretariat by designing and delivering its innovative strategy of nationwide 'listening meetings', and finding and supporting technical rapporteurs for its working groups in particular.

This last responsibility involved also making sure that the 'cultural life' part of the Commission's remit didn't get crowded out by the weight of the economic and social aspects. With no other obvious technical rapporteur in sight, I took on the role for the Arts and Culture Working Group myself. It was going to be a tetchy and contentious group, so it needed a tough chair who was politically-minded, understood disability inclusion and was well-connected in the arts. It had to be someone who'd fight like a tiger for implementation once the Commission's report was published. Only one possible candidate, then . . .

The phone call was predictably tense. Colm was the special adviser to Michael D. Higgins, Minister for Arts, Culture and the Gaeltacht—could he do it? By now I knew how to soothe Colm's anxieties, and pointed out that, again, we'd balance each other: I'd navigate the disability landscape and do the writing if he'd contribute his peerless knowledge of the arts establishment and figure out how to make disability inclusion stick in the arts world. I valued his concern that stressing the importance of arts and culture in the lives of people with disabilities might result in an emphasis on 'marginalised activities for marginalised people'. I was also struck by how few disability organisations had any interest in the potential of the arts. We had to convince both sides and create commitment out of almost thin air.

At the start of the working group's deliberations Colm was predictably argumentative, brooking no opposition from any quarter. As his confidence grew, and he started to trust that I knew what I was doing, the group and its work progressed. The power balance shifted between Colm and myself and we became a team, prompting Colm's highest praise: that I was 'sure-footed'. His witheringly acid wit didn't flag, though: when a working group member said that they 'had a problem with the National Rehabilitation Board', Colm responded, 'I have a problem with the ESB but it exists, and I have to pay my bills.' Collapse of stout party, etc.

After a year of wrangling, I thought that the working group's report would be solid and workable, but it turned out to be far more than that. Completed in June 1996 and titled *A Mosaic of Life and Possibilities,* it drew inspiration from the assertion in the fifth programme of *In From the Margins,* 'Something to Celebrate', that, for people with disabilities, the arts were about 'realising ourselves and our possibilities; all we need is the opportunity to participate'.

Mosaic was assertive (imagine!) and broke new ground. Its many recommendations went way beyond the predictable physical accessibility demands to consider innovations such as inclusive and supportive arts education and training, inclusive performance, artists with disabilities on State boards, inclusivity as a key criterion for Arts Council funding, ring-fenced funding for artists with disabilities and the legal recognition of 'creative communication in sign language' as a specific artform. *Mosaic* also broke the mould of contemporary report-writing by including photographs and reflecting the creativity it promoted.

Most of the key recommendations in *Mosaic* were accepted by the Commission and appeared in its final report, *A Strategy for Equality,* published in October 1996. Colm's interventions and dogged insistence meant that the parts relating to statutory bodies, in particular, were politically astute and implementable. The Arts Council shifted from veiled hostility to being the first State agency to work meaningfully on any of the Commission's recommendations. Even in the 2020s, it's possible to see the influence of *A Mosaic of Life and Possibilities* in Arts Council policy and practice, and some recommendations are still to be implemented. Colm, the eternal, far-sighted, uncompromising visionary and *éminence grise,* continues to exert a spectral influence to this day.

The Arts and Culture Working Group also forged changes in Colm, copperfastening his commitment to disability inclusion in the arts and leading to his involvement in Arts & Disability Ireland. He and I collaborated on several diverse projects after the Commission, ever more harmoniously.

Working with Colm was always a challenging mosaic of life and possibilities, in which often huge effort was required to make the pieces fit together, but the beauty and rightness of the end result always justified the agony of running his pugnacious, determined, utterly committed gauntlet. Colm's unique and creative contribution to disability inclusion is an unsung but significant part of his vast legacy, and many people who have never heard his name owe him a real debt of gratitude. In the spirit of his driven and uncompromising character, the possibilities continue to multiply. It's a great outcome.

Arts & Disability Ireland

Pádraig Naughton

I find it very hard to think of Colm without remembering his very close friend and neighbour Séamus Ó Cinnéide. My relationship with both of them began when I took up the post of executive director of Arts & Disability Ireland (ADI). Colm, along with Freida Finlay, and Séamus, who was chair, made up ADI's long-suffering board. Colm and Séamus were the quintessential double act, on occasion assuming their respective roles as 'good cop, bad cop', a formidable pair in any situation. When I arrived at ADI in autumn 2005, the organisation was being project managed by Create (formerly CAFÉ Creative Art For Everyone). Both Create and ADI had their roots in the then closed City Arts Centre. The team at Create had spent the previous two years working with the ADI board to write a new organisational development plan. As the new and sole member of staff, I had the task of realising that vision.

In the years before, the ADI board had been through the wars politically so to speak, finding itself at the centre of an extremely polarised debate as to whether the organisation should be disabled-led, for and by artists, or should forge a role for itself as a development and resource organisation for the wider arts and disability sector in Ireland. Myself, Colm and the ADI board shared a belief that the arts do not just belong to artists with disabilities but to audiences with disabilities too; neither does it only belong to those who shout the loudest. Unfortunately, this debate had had many real casualties, with ADI losing its staff, home and the majority of its annual funding. At the very moment they could have walked away, Séamus, Colm, and Freida, to their eternal credit, put their shoulders to the wheel and committed to rebuilding ADI.

Consequently, my first meeting with the ADI board was a baptism of fire. Colm, at that time director of the National College of Art and Design (NCAD), had taken his battles with disabled artists over the organisations' annual funding extremely personally. What I remember most is Colm taking the first opportunity available to him at the meeting to

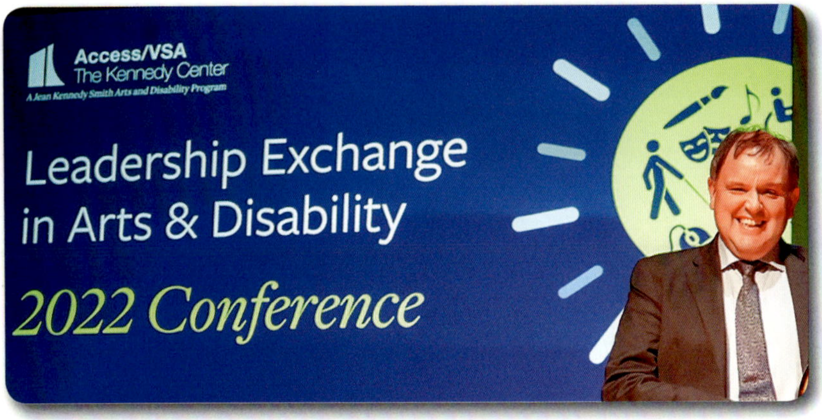

Arts & Disability Ireland Executive Director Padraig Naughton. (Courtesy of Arts and Disability Ireland)

launch into a monologue that progressed from rant to tirade. For myself, as incoming director, it was both scary and disconcerting. However, once I figured out that Colm was speaking his hurt and frustration, it was easier to spot the nuggets of wisdom and vision in these lengthy moments of grandstanding! At its simplest, Colm's thesis seemed to be that 'disabled artists were selfish'. While I might disagree, I could understand that to a board member of an organisation that had been brought to the point of being unviable, it might seem a reasonable assumption.

However, Colm's worldview is better interpreted as a deeply held conviction in a pluralist arts and disability environment. Here, Colm and I agreed and for the six years he remained an ADI board member, we never fell out or lost trust in each other, although we had many robust debates, with every proposal I brought to the board being tested and discussed in great detail. I came to realise that, in many respects, Colm's relentless testing and arguing about everything was his unique way of showing how interested he was and how seriously he took both the topic and his board responsibilities. The more engaged he was, the more he argued; if he was silent it generally meant that he considered the topic irrelevant or obvious. Colm appreciated that, while I had new ideas as the incoming director, I was committed to ADI's ongoing projects in drama and dance which the board had worked tirelessly to maintain despite shrinking resources.

Quick Bright Things was directed by dramaturg Declan Drohan and *Counterbalance* by choreographer Cathy O'Kennedy. Both were ground-breaking projects that sought to develop standalone companies of people with disabilities in performing arts. To this existing portfolio of projects I wanted to add Ireland's first regular calendar of audio-described performances (a live commentary of the visual elements of what was happening on stage). Colm never doubted the need for ADI to take on the challenge of meeting the access requirements of audiences with disabilities but always questioned the long-term sustainability of stretching resources to meet the needs of both artists and audiences with disabilities. This was ten years after the Commission on the Status of People with Disabilities report, *A Strategy for Equality*. While considerable progress had been made in the intervening years on the physical accessibility of a wave of newly-built arts centres, little if anything had changed for blind and visually impaired and deaf and hard of hearing audiences. Colm and his fellow board members were open to persuasion and so began ADI's new venture into access services with an audio-described performance of *The Importance of Being Earnest* at the Abbey Theatre in September 2006, with an all-male cast starring Alan Stanford. Since then, ADI has made performances accessible in at least 37 performing and visual arts venues throughout Ireland.

Colm's love for the arts was only equalled by the pleasure he took in ADI's successes. He revelled in the organisation's achievements and loved regaling an audience, any audience, with a good-news story. Very often the first recipient of these stories was Marian, Colm's secretary and personal assistant in his director's office at the NCAD. This was in the days before the ADI board were ready to embrace electronic payments, when I had a path worn to Colm's office to have cheques countersigned for yet another payment run. I remember on one such occasion imparting the news that ADI had just been awarded €38,120 in capital funding from the Arts Council to purchase audio description and captioning equipment, as well as a loop system.

Obviously, Colm was delighted about the fact that ADI now had the technical resources to deliver access for audiences with disabilities in live theatres across Ireland. However, what excited him most was that ADI had been awarded exactly the funding requested (never a given, and a rare occurrence). His initial comment to Marian was, 'this hasn't happened in years', after which he launched into one of his characteristic monologues, only this time he was extolling my achievements as the new director. In that moment Colm was so incredibly proud and from then on felt ADI was on the way back.

There were many subsequent occasions when Colm offered informal appraisals of my work; those that he shared with my parents at ADI's events over his years on the board were among my favourites. Since I was born in 1970 with a significant visual impairment, my parents' expectations for my future had been somewhat tempered by my disability. Although supportive and open in their approach, a career in the arts was not something they imagined for me. So, the fact that the director of my alma mater NCAD spoke so glowingly meant a great deal to them as well as providing the reassurance that perhaps I had chosen the correct career path after all.

Colm's first encounter with my parents was at the launch of the publication *Face On: Disability Arts for Ireland and Beyond.* Another one of my new projects, it was an anthology commissioned to explore disability arts (an arts practice reflecting a first-person lived experience of disability) in an Irish context. Colm was initially very reluctant to re-engage in the disability arts politics which he felt had almost destroyed ADI. However, we needed a mechanism by which all the key protagonists involved in past debates were afforded the opportunity to share their perspectives. The key was finding an editor for the anthology whom everyone respected and trusted with their contributions.

Into the breach stepped Irish-born, Welsh-based writer and dramaturg Kaite O'Reilly. Colm was totally won over by Kaite's extensive international track record. Steeped in the UK disability arts movement since the 1980s, Kaite combined this knowledge with her expertise in disabled-led theatre throughout the world, which meant she could engage in an individual dialogue with every contributor. What resulted was an anthology with 27 unique perspectives, the contributors describing themselves as artists, artists with disabilities, disabled artists and deaf/Deaf artists. Some identified as people with disabilities, others as disabled people, while yet more chose not to identify at all, with their arts practice reflecting a kaleidoscope of approaches from disabled-led to collaborative practice and every variation in between. For me, this very much vindicated Colm's world-view that arts and cultural life in Ireland belonged to us all regardless of our perspective on the intersection between disability and arts, and that ADI could and should hold that space for anyone and everyone to engage with on their own terms.

In my early years at ADI I loved nothing more than being directly involved in making projects such as these happen. Colm was acutely aware of this and I remember that at one particular board meeting, he gave the following advice: 'Pádraig, we pay you to direct, not to deliver'. It was a firm reminder that the role of directing any organisation is a delicate balance between getting your hands dirty and delegating to others. A piece of wise advice I have challenged myself to take forward to this day.

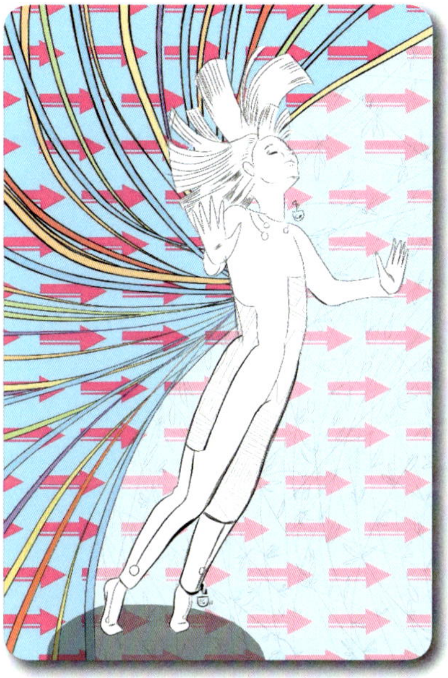

'The Spinal Stimulator' from *My Chronic Pain Diary*: a work by visual artist Ciara Chapman, who received an Art and Disability Connect Award in 2020.

As well as those ADI memories, there is an object in my kitchen by which I will always remember Colm. A heart-shaped Le Creuset casserole pot which he gave to my wife Avril and myself on the occasion of our wedding in 2011. While not big enough to fit a casserole for our now expanded family, it is ideal for a date-night dinner, while also serving as a reminder that in times past Colm and I debated much and worked hard to make a difference. Therefore, in conclusion I would say that Colm's legacy to me personally, and to ADI organisationally, was that the space we hold is entrusted to us for the benefit of everyone.

Passion and Commitment: Colm Ó Briain in the NCAD

Gary Granville

At a seminar in the NCAD School of Education in October 2002, launching a new, socially-engaged arts programme, Colm challenged us to 'explode' into the field, to lead and transform it rather than merely 'serve' it. It was one of his first public appearances as Director of the National College of Art and Design. He was making a statement of his own intent. Deep engagement with the wider public, rather than a restricted role with an artistic élite, was a core principle of his leadership.

When Colm came into NCAD, he brought with him the two passions that had dominated his public life to date—a passionate commitment to the arts and an equal commitment to social justice. I was hugely excited by his appointment, despite the fact that he had no prior experience in the management or politics of higher education. Indeed, I believed that was a decided advantage for him, coming without baggage and without expectations but with a clear track record of achievement in the arts.

At an early meeting with senior staff, Colm said that he had been told on many occasions that he was inclined to shout when engaged with issues: he was giving us a heads-up, he said, to ensure that we would take it in the proper spirit. He was indeed true to his word! I have never worked with anyone who raised his voice so frequently and caused me to do the same. I had known and worked with Colm in previous roles—on curriculum issues, when he was in the Arts Council, and later when working as adviser to Michael D. Higgins, Minister for the Arts. Most especially, I had worked with him in the Labour Party when he was General Secretary and I was Director of Elections for some (unsuccessful) local campaigns. But I had never had rows with him until his years in NCAD. I quickly learned, however, that he never held onto these exchanges; there were literally no hard feelings. Any such exchange only served to clarify issues and he would have no hesitation about changing his mind on a topic, if the arguments resonated with him. His animated manner was merely the expression of his passion and commitment.

He always had a relentless integrity. This applied not only to his perception of the role of public service, where he was scrupulous in delivering the highest quality of work practice, but also to his relationships and expectations of others. He was as impatient with the tardiness of civil servants as he was with the opportunism or greed of private enterprise when he encountered each of them. He could not tolerate closed shop practices and, despite—or rather, because of—his left-wing politics, he disliked intensely the excuse of 'custom and practice' when it came to resisting change. His sense of public service was such that he felt offended by the fact that the NCAD was closed at weekends and that part-time education was not treated with the respect it deserved within the academy. One of his happiest achievements was the opening of the college at weekends for such students and for research students.

The concept of 'community' was a constant point of reference for him. In the south inner-city home of NCAD, he sought and supported links with local groups and community organisations. This was manifested very early in his tenure in his support for our new postgraduate programme in socially engaged practice, and for related initiatives in the Schools of both Fine Art and Design. He also applied that sense of community to the internal processes of college and to the external environment of the art and design education sector in Ireland.

He valued the leading role of NCAD in art education in Ireland but he recognised that one of the inherent dangers of being the best is the tendency to be complacent, conservative and resistant to change. He wanted NCAD to be ahead of the curve—anticipating external developments, introducing internal reforms and fostering innovations in pedagogy and practices. For a small college, the separation of disciplines and practices within NCAD was very strongly defined and Colm sought to overcome these structural silos. He was a great admirer of the NCAD Core programme, the first-year integrated immersive experience that all undergraduates experienced before embarking on specialist art and design disciplinary tracks. He welcomed and actively supported our initiative in the School of Education to embed the hitherto separate education students within the common fold of studio practice in art and design. He took the heads of schools on a number of 'away days' in order to develop some kind of consensus and strategy to maximise cross-fertilisation; there were overnight sessions in Annaghmakerrig and other locations. Colm became understandably impatient with the lack of follow-through. When one such session ended with a strong and unresolved argument, I was concerned that the process had been set back. I phoned him the following morning to see how the damage might be repaired, but I was surprised to find that he was quite upbeat. To my comment that the meeting had ended badly, he was quite sanguine. 'If that's what it takes to get action, then fine' was his response.

An early change he introduced in college structures was to the composition of the Academic Council. He saw a role for that body as the engine of policy formulation within the college. The established composition of Academic Council had all heads of faculty and individual departments present on a large and unwieldy body. Meetings tended to be routine and frankly boring: heavy on reports, light on debate. His wish was for a lively forum where ideas could be aired and tested in the fire of passionate debate. He wanted it to be a forum of lively and informed academic discourse, where established practices could be questioned and new domains of academic endeavour could be explored. So he introduced a smaller compositional format, with about half the members elected by college staff rather than nominated by rank. That change was resisted by many. I remember bringing an item to the Academic Council, not long after its new format had been established. Whatever my proposal was, it was defeated after intense debate. I was appropriately disappointed, not to say bruised. Next morning, Colm rang me to thank me for bringing the item to AC: he said it had provoked the first decent debate he had heard in that forum. I put down the phone not knowing whether to feel pleased with his commendation or annoyed at the fact that my defeat didn't seem to bother him!

Perhaps the biggest external challenge that faced the college when Colm took over was the increasing importance of postgraduate research in higher education. He introduced a major strategic shift through the appointment of the first Head of Research in NCAD. This role extended across the full college, spanning all faculties and disciplines, thus realising another of his own priorities of overcoming the silo mentality. The result was a rapid growth in high-quality postgraduate research and the introduction of a suite of taught masters and structured doctoral programmes. NCAD became the national leader in art and design research and has maintained that position on the international stage.

In Ireland and internationally, art colleges lagged a long way behind other universities when it came to research funding, the major driver of financial support and growth for all higher education institutions. In the early years of this century, PRTLI—the awkward acronym for the government's Programme for Research in Third Level Institutions—was the major vehicle for higher education funding and advancement. In the first few rounds of PRTLI funding, no art college in the state had received any support whatsoever. There was a gulf in understanding between the arts community on the one hand, and the established hierarchy of academic disciplines on the other. There was no place for the arts in the evolving landscape of research, and the art and design sector itself had failed to articulate and promote a viable pathway for research.

Colm took a pro-active approach to the problem. He challenged the Higher Education Authority (HEA) to recognise different forms and concepts of research. He also challenged NCAD and the other colleges to clarify what research can mean in the context of art and design. His powers of persuasion and his strategic lobbying were successful. The criteria and terms of reference for future HEA funding were restructured to incorporate domains to which art colleges could relate. The result was that the first funding for arts-based research was secured in the next round of PRTLI funding, leading to the establishment of GradCAM, the Graduate School of Creative Arts and Media, a partnership between NCAD, DIT, IADT and Ulster University, housed in NCAD. This was a major breakthrough for the college and for the art and design sector in general. Colm's commitment both to the establishment of a strong research culture in the college and to the concept of inter-institution collaboration in the arts had achieved a remarkable success. It remains a landmark achievement which transformed the national eco-system of art and design education.

The transformation of the research agenda in the arts was a striking example of how Colm would engage with issues and challenges. He devoted considerable time and energy to educating himself on the topic. When he was confident of his grasp of the issues and of the merits of the case, he was relentless in his drive to achieve a desirable outcome. He took personal responsibility for leading the initiative and brought together key people with expertise to work with him. It was characteristic of him that he did not take easy options or hedge his bets: when he identified a goal, he committed fully to its achievement, knowing that failure was always a possibility but that the gain was worth the risk.

As well as academic challenges, the college was beset by other operational and practical problems. Chief amongst these was the size and state of the college's campus on Thomas Street. By the time of Colm's arrival, the campus had fallen into a state of shabbiness and disrepair due to lack of funding. He determined to address this and the formal acquisition of the old Fire Station next door to the college, facing onto Thomas Street, was a tangible outcome of this initiative. This brought to realisation a plan that had been in gestation for more than ten years and enabled the college to turn its face to the local community and to invite them in. The building incorporated a gallery, a long-cherished aspiration of the college community. The gallery featured a large window facing onto Thomas Street, a literal opening up of the long-hidden college.

The agreement reached with the City Council, owners of the premises, aimed to ensure that local community groups would have access to the facility on an annual basis. The Fire Station also provided the Harry Clarke lecture theatre, charmingly located within the tiled garage facility for the former fire brigades. Above the gallery, a bright new staff room was located, which was to become a favoured location where staff and colleagues from all areas of the college could meet and mix: an important contribution to fellowship across the college. Also provided was a suite of offices for staff of the School of Visual Culture as well as workshop and seminar spaces. The opening of the new building was a big morale boost for the college community.

But it was not nearly enough to meet the ongoing and future needs. When exchequer funding to develop college-owned property adjacent to the campus was denied, Colm looked to other possible solutions.

Despite his initial ideological reservations, he came around to the idea of a public-private partnership (PPP). Unfortunately, these plans too were unrealised as the necessary backing from the State was not forthcoming. So another strategy was required.

NCAD was already a recognised college of the National University of Ireland, where it had a special relationship with UCD as a 'mother ship'. Colm was alert to the possibilities that a partnership with UCD might bring and, with the active encouragement of the College Board, he explored these with vigour.

From these discussions emerged a scenario that would have seen NCAD move physically to a new state-of-the-art facility in Belfield, using funds from the sale of the high value city-centre property in Thomas Street. In one fell swoop, the plan would have resolved the great majority of the logistical problems facing NCAD—space, equipment, studio facilities, multi-disciplinary engagement, to mention but a few. It was a typical Colm move in its audacity and impact. Unfortunately, it did not chime with the social and cultural ethos of the college. It underestimated the resistance of staff and students to relocation so far from the city centre and their concerns about loss of identity within the larger campus. While the proposal was strongly supported by the Board, it failed to achieve traction with staff and students. After some attempts to negotiate a workable model, the proposal was withdrawn and Colm instead resumed the search for another solution to the space and resources problems.

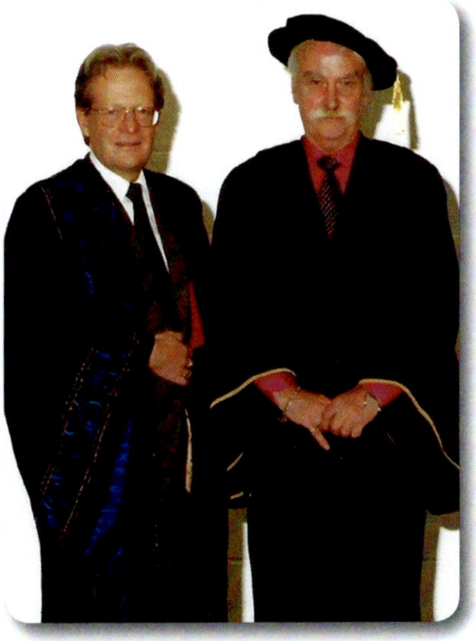

Colm Ó Briain, newly-appointed Director of the National College of Art and Design, 2002, with the outgoing Director, Noel Sheridan. (Courtesy NCAD)

Colm was upset, not so much about the abandonment of the plan but at the lack of other workable suggestions that he hoped might emerge from the experience. It was the one big item on which I could not support him. He was annoyed and disappointed at this and he did not hesitate to express it. But he never allowed it to breach our relationship at either a personal or professional level. It was a difficult time for all concerned. However, his positive legacy in NCAD has already outlasted that difficult episode. That positive legacy takes physical form in the new buildings on campus, in the growing culture of interdisciplinary collaboration in the college, and in the great advances he achieved in establishing the international reputation of NCAD as the premier research centre for art and design in this country.

In May 2008, close to the end of his time in NCAD, a conference hosted by GradCAM was held in the Project Arts Centre in Dublin. It was on the theme of arts-based research and was the first of its kind in Ireland. There is a photograph somewhere of the two of us at a coffee break in the conference. I sat with Colm and casually asked him if he had any plans for his post-retirement life in a couple of months. With characteristic passion and honesty he replied 'I have so many things on my desk that I haven't been able to think about it!'

Colm certainly wasn't in that zone of serene disengagement that most would hope to have at that career stage. He was still engaged in trying to solve some of the problems that the college faced, with no time either to reflect on the past or to ponder the future. But on reflection I thought that it was a most appropriate frame of mind for him.

It didn't occur to me at the time but that image of Colm in conversation brings to mind the memorial statement for the old English architect and scientist Christopher Wren: 'if you seek his monument, look around you'. There was Colm, sitting in the Project Arts Centre which he had done so much to establish, attending a GradCAM conference on arts research that he had also done so much to establish—but he had no sense of retrospective glory. Rather, he was still utterly focused on his immediate programme of reform. It was the commitment and passion of a born reformer, a revolutionary who saw what could and should be done and committed his unique creativity and enterprise to achieving it.

Fear ann féin dob ea Colm, agus ní bheidh a leithéid arís ann.

The Legacy of an Irish Cultural Leader

Ciarán Benson

It is hard to write about Colm Ó Briain without being prompted to be autobiographically reflective. Some reference to where I myself was coming from at the time of my first meeting with Colm in late 1977, and its leading to a lifelong friendship, is needed to describe the ignition of that first spark of admiration. There was a distinctive intensity about coming of age in the Ireland of the late 1960s and 1970s. What one was against, and what one was for, had much to do with where you had come from, and the excitement of where you might go.

One's own self was a theatre of volatility and insurgent change. Ideas swirled, the arts revelled in iconoclasm, conventions and boundaries were everywhere challenged, the Troubles flamed and horrified, and seriously powerful traditions—religious, class and political—whetted ideas and tested the destinations of our evolving values. What might previously have been thought of as isolated and contained emerged as interconnected and contested. Peter Sheridan (in this volume) recalls the artist Jonathan Wade telling him that 'all art is political', and that was a touchstone for Colm Ó Briain, and for those of us who came to be the animated beneficiaries of his refreshing leadership.

I was also one of the beneficiaries of Donogh O'Malley's free education scheme in 1967, to be followed by the grant scheme that enabled me to go to University College Dublin in 1968. The horizons of my world expanded and the fissile nature of intellectual life became clearer and ever more attractive. With hindsight I could see how significant policy decisions that transformed social structures helped transform my own life. In my case, the 'Gentle Revolution' in UCD in 1969 was another key occasion to witness youthful challenges to dominant orthodoxies of power, knowledge and education. The lure of 'Big Picture' descriptions and explanations of the world became permanently embedded.

Key to this was the realisation that a generous notion of 'education' (as against a narrow, inequitable, proselytising and transactional model of 'schooling') would have to be central to its connected ideal of informed and inclusive citizenship. After all, it was signal changes in educational 'policy' that had brought the likes of me to these fertile lands. Ideas about the powers of education associated with thinkers like Paolo Freire, John Dewey, Ivan Illich, amongst others, were invigorating, as were later sources like Neil Postman and Jerome Bruner.

I have no memory of having had a career plan. If there was a plan it was to seize opportunities as they presented themselves, while balancing the need to make a living for our young families by taking posts and contracts as they beckoned. This was not uncommon then. And if it was true of anyone, it was true of Colm. Apart from the lasting friendship, I had the experience of working with him all through 1978, then later when I voluntarily lectured on his arts administration course in UCD, later still in the mid-1990s when he was adviser to Minister Michael D. Higgins and I was chairman of the Arts Council, and yet later still when he was director of the National College of Art and Design in Dublin.

Nobody comes from nowhere. All the ideas and values that make us who we are have histories. At any point in time, but especially when we are young, our sense of those histories is at best vague. Now, in 2022, when we reflect on the work that preoccupied us many decades ago, we have the enormous benefit of the contextualising work of historians. In thinking of the achievements of Colm Ó Briain over a long productive life I am thinking of the work of Terence Browne (1981), Brian Kennedy (1990, 1998), Diarmaid Ferriter (2012), and, most recently, the detailed empirical and cultural historical analyses of Pat Cooke (2021).

Colm's long arc of contributions to the arts, and to society, spanned his membership of the National Association of Drama for Young People (NADYP) in the early 1960s, his role in establishing the pioneering Project Arts Centre, his work as a producer in RTÉ, his directorship of the Arts Council, his brief stint as general secretary of the Irish Labour Party, his role in founding the arts administration course in UCD, his role in advocating for and enabling business support for the arts through the establishment of Cothú, his contribution as adviser to Michael D. Higgins in establishing a vibrant new government department responsible for the arts and culture, and his directorship of the National College of Art and Design. Forty and more years of leadership and commitment.

What threads bound these phases of a life together? Certainly an early first-hand experience of the value of the arts, and particularly of theatre and acting; a strong sense of justice and of the struggle for equality which found an intellectual and collective home in his socialism and social democratic impulses; a clear recognition of the power of education and of the need for continuing educational reform; a quiet religious base; a family immersed in the arts,[1] a deep commonality of viewpoint and mutual support with and from his wife, Muireann; and his own combative, and sometimes fiery, style of engagement when trying to match actions to ideas.

His time as director of the Arts Council (1975–83) well illustrates his sense of how ideas about art, culture and politics in Ireland required a profound elaboration of civic and political structures if their neglected social value was to be realised and generalised. These ideas were part of the *zeitgeist* at the time. They are best illustrated by briefly contrasting the Arts Councils that preceded his tenure as director of the Arts Council, and what followed from it.

Both Brian Kennedy in his history of the Arts Council up to the late 1980s, and Pat Cooke in his recent encyclopaedic account of cultural policy in Ireland, are rich sources of detail and perspective on this. Here are just a few observations on vision, focus, leadership and social reach to sketch out the contrast, before and after Colm Ó Briain, in the standing and scope of the Arts Council.

Nearly a quarter of a century passed from the founding of the Irish Arts Council in 1951 and Colm Ó Briain's entry as its director in 1975. The contesting intellectual seeds of élitism and democratisation, of romantic individualism and social embeddedness, of political control and the 'arms-length' principle, of private patronage and State support, and the social class and generational rifts between 'fine' and 'high' art, and traditional and popular culture, can all be discerned in the record of those years.

Particularly in the fifteen years before 1975, it would be fair to say, the Arts Council was élite, male, socially homogeneous and aged in its membership, narrow in its conceptions of 'Art', focusing mostly on the visual arts, remote from the general public, extremely meagre in its resources, amateurish in its operations, uncommitted to any serious idea of 'policy', and politically docile in its demands for standing and resources. All of this has recently been well-documented (Cooke, 2021).

These tensions and tendencies in Irish cultural thinking had not gone unmentioned, and support for a much more complex and integrated understanding of the functions of the arts in Irish society had come from critics such as Mary Robinson in the Senate debate on the 1973 Arts Act, and Ruairí Quinn in a series of articles for *The Irish Times*. Quinn strongly advocated for the State to be the major patron of the arts (Cooke, 483).

This contrasted with the views of writers like Anthony Cronin who had little time for such views and was wedded more to the individualistic position of the 'romantic artist' in need of State support. Cooke puts it like this: 'Quinn's vision of the artist as a fully socialised being working to "expose the inequality, injustice and alienation within our society" existed at the opposite pole to Anthony Cronin's lonely romantic.' (Cooke 483). In 1972, it should be said, Fr O'Sullivan's Arts Council did set up a Central Survey Committee to address policy issues such as regionalisation, professionalisation, and so on. Many of its recommendations were promptly implemented by Ó Briain's Council in 1975 (Cooke 475).

The key to change was the 1973 Arts Act which ushered in a new and larger Arts Council and modernised its membership to include women and artists. And it enabled the employment of the first-ever full-time director, the thirty-one-year-old Colm Ó Briain. His referees, incidentally, were Seán MacBride,[2] and Christine, Countess of Longford, a playwright long associated with the Gate Theatre.

Policy creation, animated by ambition and energetic leadership, had arrived in No. 70 Merrion Square. Pat Cooke's recent assessment of the youthful new director is this: 'Along with his background as an actor, director and television producer, Ó Briain combined a capacity for strategic thinking with estimable administrative skills and an eye for organisational and financial detail' and 'Ó Briain's appointment marked the coming-of-age of a voluble, self-confident younger generation who felt their youth to be part of the promise they represented.' (Cooke 516).

As Ó Briain said himself: 'At the beginning, I realised that I had the choice of sitting back and waiting for things to happen, or of jumping in. So I jumped in.' A major addition, in both budgets and responsibility, came with the transfer of the Abbey Theatre to the Arts Council's portfolio, followed, in 1977, by the Gate Theatre, the Irish Theatre Company, the Irish Ballet Company and the Dublin Theatre Festival. These moves amplified the role of the Arts Council as a national body.

Regionalisation was also a priority as the Council reached out to local authorities. Festivals, for example, were encouraged to become richer and more diverse in the elements that composed them. The Arts Council had a largely unused role in issues of planning and conservation. Almost immediately upon taking office, in March 1975, Colm instigated a High Court action to prevent the demolition of five Georgian houses on Upper Pembroke Street on the grounds that property rights must be subject to the idea of a 'common good'.

The financial wellbeing of all artists, and not just already successful ones, was also a major priority. Bursary and grant schemes were developed.[3] The seeds for supporting artists through what would subsequently become Aosdána were identified and nourished, although the complex origins of this commonly supported structural solution to stabilising the precarious financial lives of most artists were later, in the early 1990s, to become an unseemly distraction over who was responsible for the original idea.[4]

The broader issues shadowing this controversy had to do with interpretations of the Council's autonomy, and what was known as the 'arms-length principle' which involved the Council's self-conception as a buffer between possible political preferences/demands and a defence of the ideal of equality of opportunity for artists and arts organisations when seeking State support. The chairman of the Council during this fraught time in the early 1980s was James White, and he was a staunch defender of the arms-length principle.

Another achievement of that time, long in its coming after Tyrone Guthrie left his property in Annaghmakerrig, County Monaghan, to the State was its establishment as an artists' residence supported by the Arts Councils in both parts of the island. This advanced yet another innovation of that time, active cooperation between the Irish Arts Council and the councils in Northern Ireland, Wales, Scotland (known as 'The Celtic Quartet') and, later, England. At a time of violence and dissension, this was a far-seeing and widely beneficial development.

Another innovative idea, championed by the sculptor John Behan who was a member of that Council, was the idea that a percentage of government building budgets should be dedicated to artists' contributions to the building and/or its place. This subsequently developed into what would come to be known as 'the per cent-for-art scheme' (Cooke 481).

The professionalisation of the Arts Council also improved exponentially with the early employment of specialist arts officers of very high calibre. Each brought their own distinctive interests and experience and, under Ó Briain's leadership, they quickly melded into a small but formidable team which worked very closely with similarly motivated Council members and with the artists and organisations they advocated for.

That leadership style contrasted sharply with what subsequently came to be known as 'managerialism', and inspired its own loyalties. Perhaps apocryphal, but one story in No. 70 concerned a loyal staff member bringing a tray of tea and biscuits to a meeting between her director and a senior person in theatre. On entering the room, and encountering a very high-octane atmosphere, she deliberately dropped the tray to defuse the situation and restore order. A creative intervention not to be found in a management handbook, but theatrically highly effective!

A particular innovation with long-term benefits was the commissioning of detailed policy research. The Richards Report of 1976 was the first expression of this new commitment to policy. Start with a map of the problem before attempting to navigate towards solutions. High on the list of problems identified was the lamentable state of the arts in Irish education. Amongst many lacunae in Irish cultural life at that time, the abject state of the arts in education was highlighted by the Richards Report.

Colm was a passionate advocate for educational reform in this area, as indeed were Michael D. and Sabina Higgins, amongst others. The Gulbenkian Foundation agreed to fund a two-year position to address this issue and I was employed to execute it. Colm and I discussed the timing of what we might produce and, because 1979 was designated as an International Year of the Child, and also because there was word of the Department of Education preparing a White Paper on education, we decided to try and complete two years' work in one. I started in January 1978 and the final draft was completed before the end of 1978.

The Place of the Arts in Irish Education was published in early 1979. The expected White Paper was published in late 1981 and, while having a chapter on the arts in education, it had little of significance to offer. But the terms of the work for subsequent decades had been benchmarked (Benson et al).

Subsequent valuable research on the living and working conditions of artists followed in 1980.

During Colm's eight years as director the budget of the Arts Council moved from £250,000 to £4.5 million. The Council's role in the formation of arts policy, and State support for the arts in Ireland, were consolidated. Ó Briain's own assessment of his achievements as director of the Arts Council was this: 'The main contribution which I made in Ireland was to move the arts agenda from the "sponsorship of success" to investment in artists themselves, and in facilities and outlets that encouraged creativity, and supported artistic endeavour.' (Private correspodence).

In retrospect, this was Colm Ó Briain's own account of his penultimate years as director of the Arts Council: 'By 1982 I was perceived as being too dominant in the whole matter of artistic policy in Ireland. That year it seemed that the Council would be reduced to having only an advisory role, and that its funding would be removed to the Taoiseach's office. The Council was probably only saved by the fact that the government fell, and Charlie Haughey became Taoiseach, and he had made the arts a concern of his election manifesto.' (Private correspondence). It should be remembered, however, that around 1970 Mr Haughey had himself toyed with the idea of breaking the Arts Council into three separate bodies.

Ó Briain resigned as director in 1983 and took up the position of general secretary of the Labour Party. This again was no easy prospect, and it is worth quoting Diarmaid Ferriter's recent synopsis of what such a position might entail: 'Committed members were sometimes wry in reflecting on the perpetual tribulations and navel gazing: for many on the left, it was the party, according to John Horgan in his 1986 book *Labour: The Price of Power*, "one would never dream of joining, the party one is thinking of leaving or the party one has just left." Horgan devoted a whole chapter to "Rebels and Outcasts" and noted the common perception of it as "a tattered remnant of something that might have been." He

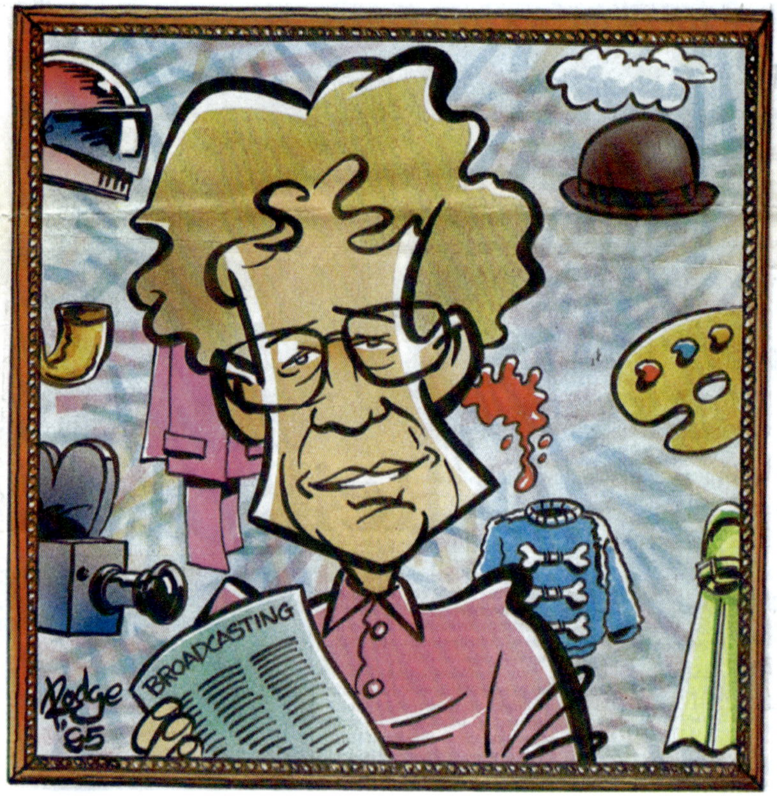

six children and grew up in a middle-class family in Drumcondra in north Dublin. His father, Peter O'Brien, ran a prosperous hardware business. Colm was educated by the Jesuits at Belvedere College. While he gave each sport on offer a try, Ó Briain preferred debating, drama and the school opera.

His first stage part was as a member of the chorus of the Belvedere College Opera, *Iolanthe* by Gilbert and Sullivan. The role of Queen of the Faeries in that production was played by John Bowman, while Terry Wogan was one of the Peers of the Realm.

Ó Briain, still a fluent Irish speaker, left Belvedere in 1962 and studied Law in UCD where classmates included former Attorney General Harry Whelehan and Ó Briain's wife Muireann, who has since become a senior counsel. Although Ó Briain graduated with a BCL, LLB from UCD, and a BL from the King's Inns, he never practised as a barrister. Instead, he joined the Gate Theatre in 1966, where he

'He would come into meetings of the administrative council wearing these colourful woolly cardigans with huge bones as buttons. That sort of caper might have been alright in the Arts Council but not in Labour'

the acquaintance of Michael D Higgins,

Dick Spring, whose position as party leader was under threat. Ó Briain's quest for consensus between left and right was in vain. At a time when Labour was imploding, he sought to innovate when he should have tried to consolidate. Many of the rank and file party activists found it difficult to relate to what they saw as the intellecutal and aloof Ó Briain.

"He would come into meetings of the administrative council wearing these colourful woolly cardigans with huge bones as buttons," said one source.

"He used always have this massive head of hair and sometimes he'd be in pink or yellow suits. That sort of caper might have been alright in the Arts Council but not in Labour."

Another person remarked on his love of tweed trousers and jackets. "I don't know where he used to put them all. He had more tweeds than Maeve Hillery."

Following his departure from Labour, Ó Briain produced the Beckett classic, *I'll Go On*, in the Gate Theatre starring Barry McGovern. He also designed and directed the new arts administration

A profile of Colm Ó Briain titled 'Socialist Dynamo wants to return to creative spirit of the 1960s' appeared in the *Sunday Business Post* on 30 April 1995 when the Green Paper on Broadcasting was published. (Cartoon by Rodge)

characterised it as "staggering from one vicissitude to the next, often down but never quite out" and there was to be another quarter century of the same.' (*Irish Times*, 1 March 2022, p. 10)

I recall having a drink with Colm in Kennedy's in Westland Row just before he was to take up his new position. 'I think I am the only rat about to join a sinking ship', was what I remember him saying!

But nothing in experience need go to waste, and during the 1980s Colm continued to amass his understanding of what needed to be done and of how to do it, all of which happily and productively came to pass when the first Department of Arts, Culture and the Gaeltacht was established in 1993. Indeed, he had a key role in conceiving of such a department and of its potential contribution to Irish life. His role as adviser to the inaugural minister, Michael D. Higgins, was to prove the start of a highly energetic, productive and complementary partnership.

There was a sense of urgency about not wasting this opportunity for advancing a cultural democracy, and a huge range of achievements were to mark those years from 1993 to 1997. The partnership of Michael D. Higgins as minister and Colm Ó Briain as adviser, together with the alliances they fostered with others, was founded on a shared understanding of what a generous notion of 'Culture' might entail, and a political commitment to the idea that full citizenship entailed full access to what 'The Arts' might enable.

If Michael D. Higgins started with a sense that he had 'inherited a bleak landscape', four years later that landscape was much more happily populated. Much of their work had to do with convincing civil servants, especially in the Department of Finance, of the need for proper funding. I saw this at first hand as then chairman of the Arts Council. On one occasion, I met the adviser to the then Minister for Finance, Ruairí Quinn, who said to me with a tone of exasperation, 'Your Minister didn't threaten to resign once', during the pre-budget wranglings. It turned out that Michael D. had threatened to resign twice!

Colm's experience with the civil service served him well, as did his common agreement with Michael D. and others as to what needed to be done. This was indeed a unique confluence of minds and opportunities, and one that they felt as a great responsibility. Hence the intense sense of urgency that often characterised those days.

Colm himself had this to say about those years: 'Within government we had the reputation of never being satisfied. There was so much to be done, and we were annoying our colleagues in other departments, principally Finance. "You can have Teilefís na Gaeilge or you can have the Arts Plan, but you can't have both" was being said at civil service level. The fact that we got both is testimony to the work done in those years, and to Michael D.'s adroitness in securing funding. He was totally passionate about the primacy of culture in State policy. We developed a relationship which had started in the mid-1980s in an extraordinarily cohesive way. Every issue that came before us was addressed in both intellectual and practical terms.' (Private correspondence)

The achievements of the period were many and some, alas,—notably Dúchas (1997–2002) with its integrative vision for heritage—proved short-lived as new political agendas took over. They included, as noted by Pat Cooke (2021), the first ever national, multi-annual arts plan which was requested from ourselves in the Arts Council; the establishment of an Irish-language television station, Teilifís na Gaeilge; the plan to develop Collins Barracks as a base for the National Museum, marking the first significant investment in the institution since Independence; legislation to place the national cultural institutions on a more autonomous footing under the National Cultural Institutions Act (1997); the re-establishment of the Irish Film Board, which had been abolished by Charles Haughey, along with changes to film legislation to ease investment in the industry; and the repeal of Section 31 of the Broadcasting Act, which lifted the prohibition on RTÉ from broadcasting interviews with representatives of proscribed political organisations; transferring the OPW's wildlife functions to the Department; transferring all of the heritage functions of the OPW to the Department of Arts, Culture and the Gaeltacht under Part III of the Heritage Act (1995); and, by 1998, re-branding these functions as Dúchas the Heritage Service. (Cooke, 599–60).

The budget for the Arts Council doubled in the period 1993–8. And, as Cooke observes, 'The projection of the Arts Council as the guarantor of artistic freedom in a democratic society reached a crescendo in the years following the foundation of a department for culture in 1993.' (Cooke, 742)

Many mistook Colm Ó Briain's intensity of engagement for abrasiveness. For his admirers, this very intensity, however, was simply the hallmark of his urgent ambition for the elements of 'culture' in all its multifariousness. And his admirers were many.

He himself was well aware of this: 'Of course we had disagreements; I had rows with Michael D. and I had rows with the civil servants, but by and large there was effective engagement between the political and administrative sectors. Also, because of our connections to the Labour Party, we could always rely on the support of other Labour ministers.

'I was described as a "touchstone for Michael D.". It is also true that we were both socialists, so we had similar political leanings. Importantly, we both realised that no government can legislate for talent, but that being in government we could create or support the frameworks in which talent can develop and flourish.' (Private communication)

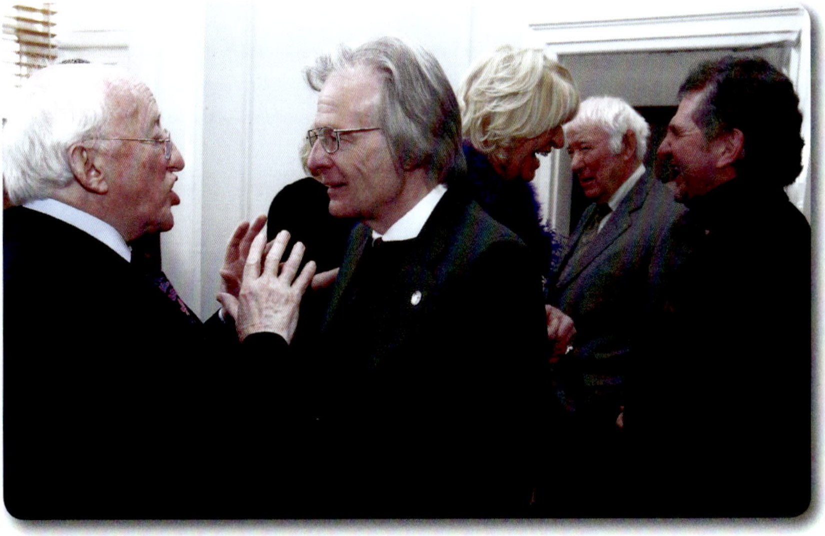

Still discussing the arts: Michael D. Higgins and Colm Ó Briain, with Sabina Higgins, Seamus Heaney and Ciarán Benson, c. 2006.

Colm Ó Briain ended his working career as director of the National College of Art and Design (2002–8). This was a challenging time, not least economically. As always, he had high ambitions for the NCAD, one of which echoed an earlier idea. Pat Cooke recently retrieved this far-seeing idea with which Colm, as director of the NCAD would well have concurred: 'At a 1968 symposium on art and design education in Ireland, Robin Walker, President of the Royal Institute of Architects in Ireland, proposed that architects, artists and designers should receive a common training in a single campus.' (Cooke 471) This possibility was tentatively explored by Colm Ó Briain with UCD, but met with opposition from some of his colleagues. (*Irish Times*, 5 May 2006, p 14) As it happens, that very possibility might soon be realised for the new Technological University Dublin on the Grangegorman Campus, if not for the NCAD.

Ó Briain was an outstanding cultural leader in Ireland in the second half of the 20th century. His quiet, often self-effacing, work behind the scenes will go on to shape and animate those same scenes for a long time to come.

Notes

1 His brother Art, for example was also a pioneer. 'The first organisation to operate explicitly under the banner of community arts was the Ballyfermot Community Arts Workshop, founded in 1974 under the direction of Art Ó Briain.' (Cooke, p. 574).

2 MacBride's reference described Ó Briain as 'a young man of energy and enthusiasm, with the ability and intelligence to channel this energy to positive achievement. He has a real commitment to Ireland and the Arts in Ireland, but unlike many people with a similar commitment, he is thoroughly practical in his ideas and aims.' (Private communication).

3 From an international perspective, Ireland was demonstrably slow in developing such forms of assistance to artists. Pat Cooke observes that 'the Norwegian parliament introduced travel grants for painters and sculptors for the first time in 1836. In Finland, modest levels of state support for the artist on an ad hoc basis dated back to the 1860s.' (p. 534).

4 Copies of Brian Kennedy's history of the Arts Council, *Dreams and Responsibilities,* were controversially shredded in the early 1990s following, reportedly, pressures from outside the Council. Pat Cooke notes that 'In 1990 Haughey took credit for Aosdána and highlighted the distinction that it conferred on those elected to it by giving them a status redolent of the old Gaelic chieftaincies. The image combined the romantic with the neo-feudal: the artist takes his place in a courtly caste of talented spirits, positioned just below the Chief.' (p. 536). When I became chairman of the Arts Council in 1993, I authorised the reprinting of the book which was reissued in 1998 before we left office. For a

final comment on this matter see the letter from Anthony Cronin to the *Irish Times* on the occasion of its reprinting, and the response of the then arts editor, Victoria White (*Irish Times*, Thurs, Jul. 30, 1998, 01:00).

Sources

Benson, Ciarán et al. *Time, Vocabulary and Art's Thoughtful Uses of Feeling? A reflection on forty years of arts and education in Ireland*, The Arts Council, 2021.
Browne, Terence *Ireland: A Social and Cultural History*, 1922–79, Fontana, 1981.
Cooke, Pat *The Politics and Polemics of Culture in Ireland, 1800–2010*, Routledge, 2021.
Ferriter, Diarmaid *Ambiguous Republic: Ireland in the 1970s*, Profile Books, 2012.
—*The Irish Times*, 1 March 2022, p 10.
Horgan, John *Labour: The Price of Power* Dublin, 1986.
Kennedy, Brian P. *Dreams and Responsibilities: The State and the Arts in Independent Ireland*, Dublin, The Arts Council, 1990/1998.
Ó Briain, Colm 'Art College Needs Its Own Grand Design', *The Irish Times*, Friday 5 May, 2006, p. 14.
Richards, Sir James *Provision for the Arts,* Dublin, The Arts Council 1996.

Glasnevin

Seóna Ní Bhriain

This is the place the brass band played
Where generous trees give up their shade
And where a spade is called a spade:
Where now my Dad's remains are laid.
In the gardens beyond the wall
I walked in the springtime and in the fall
Full-bellied, expectantly, in my wellies
In the hours before my girls were born.
I think my parents may have walked there too when I was due.
And I have been *here* with my Dad.
He showed the way.
We played at the edges and learned how to pray,
And how to live
Each beautiful day.
It is a kind place where his bones may rest,
On the side of the city that he knew best.

Colm Ó Briain: Friend, Colleague and Comrade

President Michael D. Higgins

Lir Academy, Dublin, 14 April, 2022

A cháirde,

It is a privilege to be here today for the launch of the Colm Ó Briain Endowment Fund. It is such an appropriate gesture, yet I find calling Colm to mind a source of personal sadness, at recalling the loss of somebody who was so aware, so alert to the dimensions of the renaissance life he lived, part of which I had the privilege of sharing.

Colm Ó Briain was a man I was fortunate to have been able to call a close friend, a colleague and a comrade. While his service to the arts and its practitioners was a defining characteristic of his life, and while that generous service was a greatly distinguished one, it was the courageous breaking of new ground for which Colm will be remembered, and, above all, of his being unafraid to push the boundaries. In so doing, he made many unique and exceptional contributions to Irish culture policy.

He was a remarkably inclusive director of the Arts Council, ensuring its remit would broaden to include younger artists and a wider range of artistic capacities. He was the source of the concept, and extended the original conception of Aosdána, recognising the need not only to support those courageous individuals who embark on life as an artist, but to be enabled to do so in a way that recognised their fundamental dignity and right to self-respect.

As my adviser during my time as Minister for the Arts, Culture and the Gaeltacht, he was involved in our building of a new Department of State. He was involved in all of the legislation I brought forward, involved in preparation for Cabinet, in everything we did and sought to do. His input to many important reports and pieces of legislation contributed profoundly to the cultural life of our nation. His contributions drew on not only his vast cultural experience and sensitivity but on a legal drafting competence.

His commitment to cultural policy which included the arts was innovative, timeless and steadfast. Colm's involvement in the preparation of Ireland's first ever arts plan, our attempt to implement the Benson Report, was key to the strengthening of support for the arts in our country and that, along with so many other special reports he prepared during my time as Minister, has left a legacy of which his family can be very proud indeed.

Colm believed in access to arts and culture as a fundamental tenet of democratic participation and citizen engagement. I recall campaigns such as those of Sandy Fitzgerald and others in CAFÉ Creative Art for Everyone—which he and I participated in. He and I worked together on an initiative that would have provided every child with access to a musical instrument or a book of choice. It is something I still believe should be adopted in policy.

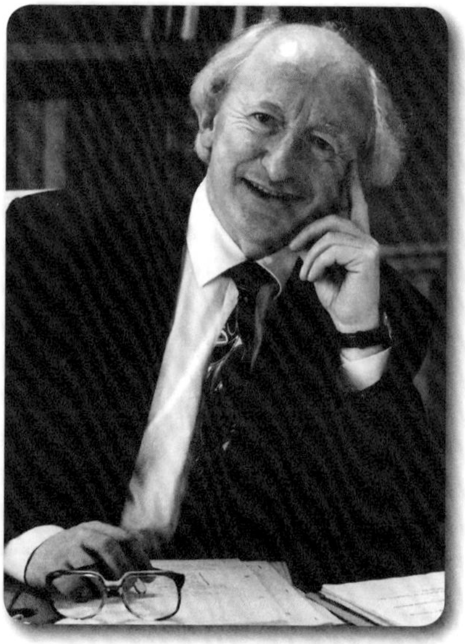

President Michael D. Higgins

Colm never made the error of viewing the arts as residual or as a tangential luxury to be indulged only when all the other 'necessities' had been met, but recognised them as an integral part of a functioning society. He understood art as an important, indeed vital, resource in enabling us to discover and interpret our world, to aspire to reach our potential, to participate fully in our society and in our world. For that we owe Colm much gratitude.

Our actors, together with our musicians, our writers, our artists and all those who contribute to the cultural dimension of our society, provide such liberating potential, such enriching vision, such daring challenging of the status quo; and, in doing so, are an essential and cohesive force in society, never failing to speak of new possibilities and a better world that we dare to dream. Colm Ó Briain was a champion of performance and performers of which he himself was a unique expression—life made possible through the arts.

Colm aimed to construct an Ireland that would be shaped to accommodate artistic expression in all its capacities and its diversity, and also the livelihoods that make it possible. Today his work and initiatives continue to impact on the world of arts and culture, through this greatly generous endowment gift offered to the Lir Academy by Colm's family.

May I, at this point, thank Muireann, and his family for this most generous act, which will so well reflect Colm's own generosity of spirit and his altruistic support of young people in the arts.

That you have chosen the Lir Academy, whose opening was an important landmark in Ireland's cultural life, and the culmination of an ambitious vision brought to fruition by the Cathal Ryan Trust and the Royal Academy of Dramatic Arts, for this valuable gesture in memory of Colm is greatly appropriate. Colm as director, producer, performer would be pleased.

Today the Lir Academy can claim an impressive list of talented alumni, and is renowned for its conservatory training for theatre, film and television.

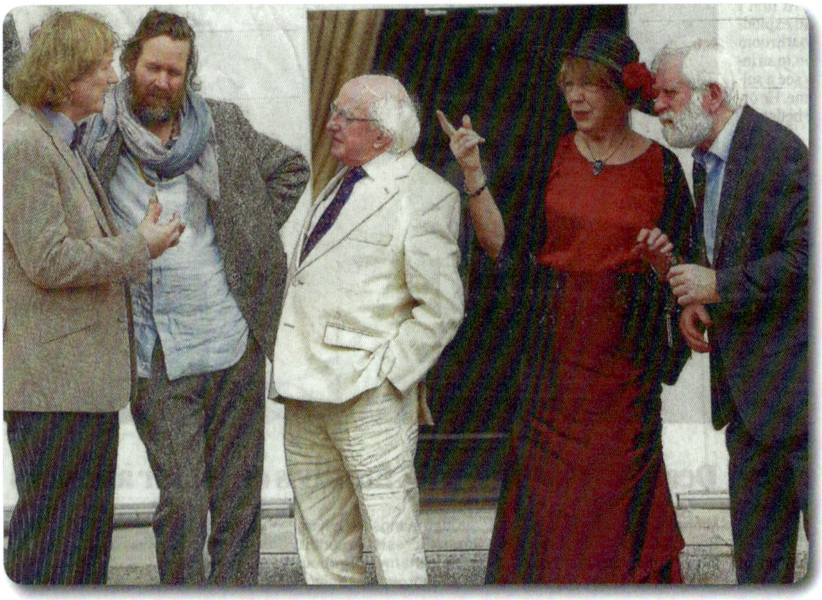

At the President's Garden Party, Bloomsday June 2015. (Left to right) Musicians Noel Grady, Liam Ó Maonlaí and John Sheahan with President and Mrs Higgins. (John Behal/Maxwells)

It is greatly apposite that Colm's memory will live on in a space where actors can hone their craft and are encouraged, as part of their training, to think and sense and feel in ways that are creative and emancipatory.

Endowments are a greatly important tool for the sustainment of arts and culture, ensuring that this critical element of our society can remain strong and vibrant. The supporting and funding of new generations of performers is essential for the generation of new and exciting work.

Talented aspiring artists are deprived of the opportunity to receive the training, the formations and experience that will develop their talent and allow them to realise their full artistic possibilities.

Endowments such as this one play a critical role in facilitating the cultural life of our nation. We must, however, also recognise the duty of a democratic state to extend the right to dignity to our artists; to acknowledge that they must be supported financially if they are to be allowed to develop the talents and produce the works which contribute so much to our society. Cultural expenditure is vital to citizenship and participation in the public space, and is fundamental for the structure of society and the imaginative possibilities of its people.

In this regard may I say how pleased I was by the launch, earlier this month, of the new Basic Income for the Arts Scheme which ensures that payments of €325 per week will be made to 2,000 artists and creative arts workers.

This is a greatly welcomed, albeit belated, recognition of the significant role of culture in our society, and of the value of investing in artists and in the work that they produce, and in the cultural space they make possible.

When we support artists and the development and retention of the cultural space, we support viable democracy. We also support all sectors of society, recognising that artistic work and a good and democratically structured cultural policy is an essential part of being human, a critical factor of citizenship and a crucial agent of citizen participation.

Today we are gathered to acknowledge and celebrate Colm's ongoing support for the cultural space through this endowment and scholarship fund, which recognises Colm's own work as an actor and director and, most importantly, his commitment to the dignity of artists and to the provision of the vital supports and recognition they need.

Colm's name is already deeply woven into the cultural fabric of our society. His courageous and pioneering spirit and his unfailing acknowledgement of our reciprocal obligation to, and solidarity with, our artists has left its profound impact on Ireland's artistic life. Today, in his name, we launch this endowment gift which will ensure that the values and priorities that so strongly guided Colm's life will continue to guide talented actors towards a future of possibility and full potential.

What an appropriate way to remember the generous, creative and visionary man that was Colm Ó Briain.

Ach mar focal scoir—For me at a personal level may I say *airím Colm uaim.* I miss the colour in which he manifested himself, the prospects for hope and change he represented, the generous, radical, emancipatory person I proposed for General Secretary of The Labour Party. Our arguments too, his care for me as I strove to deal with issues of censorship or the establishment of TnaG, but always there was the assurance of his unqualified commitment. What a privilege it was to share the genius and generosity of his life.

We Would Have Had a Lot to Talk About

Aoife Browne

First winner of the Colm Ó Briain Endowment Fund

I think Colm and I would have had a lot to talk about.

As a Donegal native, I'd probably begin by thanking him for the work he put into developing facilities in regional areas. I've reaped the rewards of this work for as long as I can remember, starting as a child in youth drama classes in the Balor Theatre, Stranorlar and the An Grianán Theatre, Letterkenny and indeed, continuing to work with them through my adolescence and into my early career—even as recently as last October.

Then we'd speak about our shared passion: making space for young people in the arts.

He'd speak about Project '67 and the importance of allowing artists to take risks; about the National Association of Drama for Young People. I'd speak about my work as a board member of Bruiser Theatre Company, Northern Ireland's foremost physical theatre company, where I represent and protect the interests of the next generation of theatre makers and audiences. I'd tell him about the Bruiser Development Ambassadors—a programme of workshops I devised where young people of all backgrounds were welcomed to discuss what changes they wanted to see in the theatre sector, and how we took these ideas and implemented a series of new projects dedicated to inspiring young artists.

He'd tell me about his time leading the Arts Council and I'd tell him about my time leading my university drama society while I studied for my first degree in English with Creative Writing at Queen's University Belfast. We'd compare stories of how we both strived to push the boundaries and diversify the work of our respective organisations.

He'd speak about his time as Head of Training at the Abbey Theatre and the years he served as Director of the National College of Art and Design. I'd tell him about the initiative I took to develop infrastructure within my university drama society to ensure that its members were

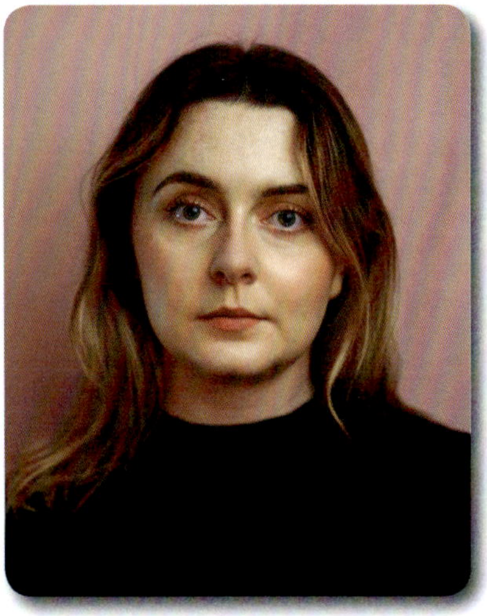

Aoife Browne, the first recipient of a bursary to attend the Lir Academy awarded by the Colm Ó Briain Endowment Fund. (Courtesy Lir Academy)

trained across various departments of theatre to make them the most rounded theatre makers they could be.

Yes, just like Colm I have devoted much time and energy into trying to develop the arts scene around me. To leave things better than I found them because I know they can be more; do more; say more.

Being accepted into The Lir has been the single most validating moment in my personal artistic development. I feel for the first time that my ambition is looking back at me and saying 'I see you'. I am beyond-words-excited to begin my training in September, and to finally give that time and energy that I have long spent giving to others to myself and to becoming the caliber of actor I was meant to be.

Colm's legacy is long and vibrant and generous and far reaching. His commitment to supporting and nurturing the Irish theatre sector is a hopeful reminder that change is possible. All of my past experience in the arts would not have been possible without him

The Contributors

Ciarán Benson is Emeritus Professor of Psychology, UCD, and author of *The Place of the Arts in Irish Education* (1979). He has chaired The Irish Film Institute, The City Arts Centre, The Irish Museums Trust, The Grangegorman Public Art Working Group and, currently, Poetry Ireland and the Interdepartmental Percent for Art Committee. From 1993 to 1998 he was Chair of an Chomhairle Éalaíon/The Arts Council, working closely with then Minister for the Arts, Culture and the Gaeltacht, Michael D. Higgins, and his adviser, Colm Ó Briain. He has also published as an art critic and contributed as a curator.

Marie-Thérèse Boissé née Brennan developed a life-long interest in theatre in education from her initial engagement with DramSoc in UCD where she acted in several productions in the 1960s. Subsequently she taught in Germany at the Rudolf Steiner School before being persuaded to return to Ireland where she taught German under Anton Trant at the Ballyfermot Vocational School in Dublin. Having spent her youth hoping to be 'discovered', the remainder of her life, until recently, has been spent in fear and trepidation of being discovered'!

Tony Boland was a senior television producer in RTÉ. In 1986 he founded the company Planet Pictures Ltd which produced *The Big Breakfast Show* on Channel 4 for several years. He now lives in Ireland and works as a psychotherapist and counsellor.

Aoife Browne is the first winner of the Colm Ó Briain bursary at the Lir Academy. She has a degree from Queen's University in Belfast in English with Creative Writing. She led the university drama society during her years at Queen's, and is currently a board member of Bruiser Theatre Company in Northern Ireland.

Pat Cooke was director of the MA in Cultural Policy and Arts Management at UCD from 2006 to 2020. Prior to that, he worked for Ireland's State heritage service for over twenty years, where he was director of two major historic sites, Kilmainham Gaol and the Pearse Museum.

He recently published *The Politics and Polemics of Culture in Ireland, 1800–2010* (Routledge, 2021).

Ita Daly was born in Co. Leitrim, and has lived most of her life in Dublin. She has published a collection of short stories, four novels and a memoir. She was married to the writer and editor David Marcus (1924–2009).

Ted Dolan joined RTÉ as a Studio Trainee in 1965 working successively as sound engineer, floor manager, producer/director, department head and programme controller. In 1989 he formed his own production company. He married Tish Barry in 2001.

Tish Dolan (Barry, née McAuley) worked in the theatre for four years, always behind the scenes. She married the television director Tony Barry in 1963 and later joined RTÉ as a production assistant, working her way up to senior producer. She married Ted Dolan in 2001.

Lelia Doolan worked as actor, director, producer in the Globe Theatre, RTÉ, and the Abbey Theatre, and for Bord Scannán na hÉireann. She studied social mores and anthropology in Belfast in the 1970s.;worked for Combat Poverty in Erris, Co. Mayo, and taught film and video in the College of Commerce, Rathmines in the early 1980s and later in Galway. Co-author with Jack Dowling of *Sit Down and Be Counted* (1969) about RTÉ's early years.

Gerry Dukes spent most of his career lecturing on literature in Limerick. His adaptation of aspects of Joyce's *Ulysses* for musicians, singers and actors, *Songs at Twilight,* premiered in Limerick to mark Joyce's centenary year in 1982 and played also at the Museum of Modern Art in Dublin. *I'll Go On*, an adaptation (with the actor Barry McGovern) for the stage of Samuel Beckett's trilogy of novels played first at the Gate Theatre in Dublin (directed by Colm Ó Briain) and has since toured extensively. He has edited and published an annotated edition of Beckett's post-war novellas and also published a brief but copiously illustrated biography of the writer.

Eithne FitzGerald was elected Labour TD for Dublin South in 1992. As Minister of State, she introduced the Ethics in Public Office Act and the Freedom of Information Act. Since leaving politics, she has worked mainly on disability policy, serving with the National Disability Authority, the Department of Health, and on a number of expert working groups and State boards relating to disability.

Dr Christopher Fitz-Simon was born in Belfast, raised in Monaghan and went to school and university in Dublin. In TCD he was Chair of Players and Editor of *Icarus*; Moderatorship in Modern Languages and Literature, 1957. After two years in the theatre and television in Canada and the US he joined RTÉ-TV in its first year, directing plays, drama series and arts documentaries. Later he was Artistic Director of the Irish Theatre Company, and later still Literary Manager of the Abbey Theatre for two periods. He is the author of almost 100 broadcast plays, adaptations and translations. Among his books are *The Irish Theatre* (Thames and Hudson), *The Boys* (Gill; also Heinemann), *Eleven Houses* (Penguin), *Buffoonery and Easy Sentiment* (Carysfort), *Rise Above!* (Lilliput); editor *New Plays from the Abbey Theatre and Players*, and *Painted Stage* (New Island), etc. Lectured on Irish theatrical topics in thirteen countries on four continents.

Maureen Gilbert worked for various disability-related NGOs and then became head of independent living services at the National Rehabilitation Board, while also being half of Celebrate Productions, the short-lived TV production company which made *In From the Margins*. Following a period as a senior policy and public affairs adviser at the National Disability Authority she left the Irish public sector and became a disability, intercultural, diversity and equality consultant working in Africa, Asia, Europe and US for the UN, statutory bodies, multi-national companies, NGOs and arts organisations.

Anne Gill joined RTÉ as one of its first production assistants. Some years later she was appointed personal secretary to Princess Shams Pahlavi, elder sister of the Shah, of Iran and travelled widely in the course of her work. On return to Ireland, she qualified as a teacher and guidance counsellor working in schools in Dublin and Drogheda. Subsequently she trained and qualified as a psychotherapist and practised privately.

Michael Gill worked with book publishers in London, Paris and New York before returning to Dublin to join his family's business. In 1968 he was appointed managing director of the newly formed Gill & Macmillan and led the amicable ending of the partnership 45 years later when the company returned to Gill family control. He served as President of Publishing Ireland on three occasions; was a founding member of the Irish Copyright Licencing Agency; a board member of the Ireland Literature Exchange; the Irish representative to the Federation of European Publishers and its President between 2000 and 2002. He has also served voluntarily as a board member on several other organisations.

Gary Granville is Emeritus Professor of Education at the National College of Art and Design (NCAD). He served as interim director of NCAD before retiring in 2016. He was Assistant Chief Executive of the National Council for Curriculum and Assessment (NCCA), a project leader in the Curriculum Development Unit, a member of the Higher Education Authority and of specialist committees of the Department of Education, Teaching Council, NCCA, Creative Ireland and other national and international bodies. Subjects of his research and publications include curriculum policy, arts education, education for global citizenship, educational evaluation and labour history. Through the 1970s and 80s, he directed election campaigns for the Labour Party in Dublin constituencies.

Nuala Hayes is an actor, storyteller and author, sometime broadcaster and independent radio producer. She trained at the Abbey Theatre and was a member of the company for five years. She set up the Young Abbey with Joe Dowling and Kathleen Barrington and was the founder member of Team Theatre in Education, which toured across Ireland for 30 years. She also worked with Field Day Theatre Company in Derry and played in the first production of *Translations* by Brian Friel. Her interest in the ancient art of storytelling led her to set up Scéalta Shamhna, the first International Storytelling and Music Festival in Dublin, which ran from 1991 to 2001. She is the author of *Laois Folk Tales*, published by The History Press, Ireland, and has collected stories on Cape Clear Island and in the Midlands. She was married to Colm's brother Art for 48 years. Art died just five weeks after Colm.

Michael D. Higgins is a politician, poet, sociologist and broadcaster, who has served as the ninth President of Ireland since November

2011. Entering national politics through the Labour Party, he served as a Senator from 1973 to 1977, nominated by the Taoiseach. Elected to the Dáil in 1981, he represented Galway West from 1981 to 1982 and from 1987 to 2011. Between these terms, from 1983 to 1987 he served as a Senator for the National University of Ireland. From 1993 to 1997 Michael D. served as the first Irish Minister for Arts, Culture and the Gaeltacht. He has been the Mayor of Galway on two occasions, and the President of the Labour Party from 2003 until 2011 when he became President of Ireland.

Garry Hynes was a co-founder of the Druid Theatre Company with Mick Lally and Marie Mullen in 1975, after they met through the UCG Drama Society. She was Druid's Artistic Director from 1975 to 1991, and from 1995 to date. She was a director for the Abbey Theatre from 1984 and was its Artistic Director from 1991 to 1994. She has also directed at the Royal Shakespeare Company, the Royal Exchange in Manchester, the Kennedy Center, and the Royal Court Theatre in London.

Brian P. Kennedy, author of *Dreams and Responsibilities: The State and the Arts in Independent Ireland* (1990), was Assistant Director of the National Gallery, Dublin (1989–97); Director of the National Gallery of Australia, Canberra (1997–2004); the Hood Museum of Art, Dartmouth College, New Hampshire; Director of the Toledo Museum of Art, Ohio (2010–19) and Director of the Peabody Essex Museum, Salem. Author of *Alfred Chester Beatty and Ireland* (1988), *Irish Painting* (1993), *Sean Scully: The Art of the Stripe* (2006), *Frank Stella: Irregular Polygons* (2008) and other books on art and cultural history. He has had a particular interest in Australian Aboriginal art and in Visual Literacy (receiving the Creative Achievement Award of the International Visual Literacy Association in 2021). He is currently President of Brian P. Kennedy Arts Consulting LLC in Salem, Massachusetts.

Bairbre McCann (née O'Brien) was educated in Loreto on Stephen's Green and in St Mary's College, Arklow. Now retired, she married in 1975, and embarked on an eclectic career in commerce and, latterly, as an artist whose paintings have sold to the UK, Australia and New Zealand, among other countries.

Derek McCann started his career in Williams & Woods of Dublin, then moved into the O'Brien business, remaining there until his retirement. He is currently employed by the State as caretaker in his local national school, proving that the cream always rises to the top!

Fiona McHugh Sankey is a writer based in Toronto. Her work includes TV scripts and dramas, radio plays and documentaries and books, including a children's version of L. M. Montgomery's *Anne of Green Gables*. She has also worked as a producer on CBC's series *Canada, A People's History*. With Kevin Sullivan she co-wrote the script for the film, *Lantern Hill*, based on Montgomery's novel. It was CBC's top-rated movie of 1990.

Hayden Murphy was born in Dublin in 1945. A poet and Arts journalist, he edited from Dublin *Broadsheet: Poetry, Prose and Graphics* (1967–78). He is now living in central Edinburgh with his wife Frances Corcoran. His latest publication is *In the Ear of the Owl* (Roncadora Press, 2018).

Pádraig Naughton was appointed Executive Director of Arts & Disability Ireland in 2005. He was Artists Manager and then Artistic Director with Equata: Disability Arts Development Agency for South West England (2003) and was nominated by Arts Council England to participate in the first Creative Cultural Leadership Programme established by Exeter University and Dartington College of Art (2004–6). He served on the boards of the Arts & Disability Forum 2002–3 and 2007–9 and Kildare Arts in Context 2010–12. As chair of VSA Affiliate Council in 2015 he guided this global network of affiliates from 37 US states and 50 countries to an open international membership of arts and disability organisations, managed since 2019 by the Kennedy Center.

Aisling Ní Bhriain is a daughter of Colm Ó Briain. She studied History and Politics at UCD and completed a Master's in International Relations at the University of Amsterdam. Aisling is currently the Vice-President Talent, for Shell, a global group of energy and petrochemical companies. A significant part of her role is leading the company's global Diversity, Equity and Inclusion agenda. She lives in London with her husband and two children.

Doireann Ní Bhriain has worked as an arts consultant, an independent radio producer and as a presenter and producer with RTÉ radio and television. She was Irish Commissioner of the *l'Imaginaire Irlandais* festival in Paris (1993–96) and was chair of the Strategy Committee of the C*entre Culturel irlandais* in Paris. She was named a *Chevalier de l'Ordre National du Mérite* by the President of France in 2016. Recently retired as a voice and presentation trainer, she now concentrates on voiceover and narration work, specialising in bi-lingual (Irish/English) narration of TV documentaries. (Hers is the voice used on the Luas public transport system in Dublin.) She is chair of Fishamble: the New Play Company.

Máirín Ní Bhriain did a BA in UCD and enjoyed the camaraderie and fun of Dramsoc. Her working life included youth and community work and teaching, interspersed with backpacking adventures abroad. She later returned to education and continues to work as a clinical psychotherapist.

Seóna Ní Bhriain is the youngest of Colm Ó Briain's daughters. Every path she took, which she thought was her own, turns out to have been paved by her father. She is currently head of Young People, Children and Education at the Arts Council.

Art Ó Briain (1947–2020) worked as a television, theatre and film director and producer and as an independent film-maker based in Connemara. He taught English and Drama in Ballyfermot Vocational School, set up the first community arts workshop in Ballyfermot and worked with the Irish Foundation for Human Development with Professor Ivor Browne. He produced a number of RTÉ programmes including *Pajo's Junkbox* and *Glenroe* and set up *Ros na Rún* for TG4. His last film, *Natural Grace: Irish Music and Martin Hayes,* was awarded Best Irish Feature Documentary at the Galway Film Fleadh 2012.

Muireann Ó Briain (née McHugh) studied law at UCD, where she met Colm Ó Briain; she married him in 1970. She started her working life as Assistant to Sean MacBride at the International Commission of Jurists in Geneva. For 28 years she practised law at the Irish Bar, and for ten of those years was also the Registrar at the Labour Court, providing legal advice to the industrial relations tribunal. During the years 1995 to 2008 she was a consultant to an international organisation combating the sexual exploitation of children; being for three of those years the CEO of the organisation. From 2004 to 2017 she was the Legal Manager at St. James's Hospital. She is a member of the National Research Ethics Committee.

Ruaidhrí Ó Briain attended the all-Irish primary school in Marlborough Street in Dublin and then Belvedere College. He took a primary degree in Philosophy and Logic in UCD. Feeling the need to do something useful, he advised CRH Computer Services that the Logic part of his education would be of advantage to them. He gratefully accepted a job there and then with Irish Cement, staying for 33 challenging and largely enjoyable years. He strongly feels that heroic things are done daily in the ordinary course of life.

Sean O'Faolain (1900–91): writer and activist; fought on the Republican side during the Civil War, became disillusioned and moved to the USA where he graduated MA from Harvard in 1928. Taught in Boston College and Strawberry Hill in Twickenham; returned to Ireland and became a full-time writer. Published ten volumes of short stories, four novels, five biographies and several prose works including his autobiography *Vive Moi!* Founded *The Bell* literary magazine in 1940 and edited it until 1946. Director of the Arts Council from 1956 to 1959.

Seán Ó Mordha is a television producer and member of the Broadcasting Authority of Ireland.

Peter Sheridan is author of the plays *Entry* (1976), *Emigrants* (1978), *Bust* (1982), *Diary of a Hunger Strike* (1982), and *Finders Keepers* (2005) and a series of memoirs based around his family, including *44: A Dublin Memoir, Forty-Seven Roses* and *Break A Leg*. Film direction includes *The Breakfast* and the feature *Borstal Boy*, based on the book by Brendan Behan. He was the Abbey Theatre's Writer in Residence in 1980, and with his brother Jim was joint Artistic Director of the Project Arts Centre, 1975–81. He was elected to Aosdána in 2014.

Constance Short is from Crossmaglen, Co. Armagh. She trained as a Graphic Artist in the Graphic Studio in Mount Street in Dublin. She has exhibited in the Soho 20 Gallery, New York, the Poetry Society Gallery in London, the Project Gallery in Dublin, as well as in France, Germany and the Czech Republic. Her works are included in the collections of the Arts Council, Athlone I.T. and Dundalk I.T., and in numerous private collections. As well as her art work, Constance has had a long and varied career as an advocate for the arts. She was heavily involved in campaigning for the renewed Arts Act of 1973. She was a founder member of the Project Arts Centre, Dublin. She set up the Arts Office for Dundalk UDC, and was Cultural Advisor to Co-Operation North, assisting in the implementation of its cultural arts exchange and cultural diversity programmes. She has been a shareholder of the Abbey Theatre and has worked on projects for Poetry Ireland, the Irish Film Board and the Northern Ireland Film Board. She lives in Dundalk, Co. Louth.

Paul Shovlin is a business adviser, currently Chairperson of Barclays Multi-Manager Funds plc. He was the Chairperson of the National Library of Ireland from 2015 to 2020, and has also served on the boards of the Royal Dublin Society and Oxfam Ireland.

Gerry Watson Having qualified as a chartered accountant, Gerry worked in corporate banking in Dublin and London for nearly twenty-five years. At that point, a lifelong interest in the arts brought him to Cothú—The Business Council for the Arts, where he served for eight years as its first chief executive. After leaving Cothú, he divided his time between working in the business sector as an independent strategic advisor, and in the visual arts sector, providing advisory and curatorial services for corporate and private art collections. He served for many years as a board member of the Irish Chamber Orchestra, and more recently on the board of Graphic Studio Dublin.

Index